PENGUIN BOOKS

LANGUAGE AND LEARNING

·

Born in Scarborough in 1908, James Britton graduated from University College London with a degree in English. He taught for eight years in State secondary schools, became education editor for the publishers John Murray, served overseas in the R.A.F.V.R. in the Second World War, and became head of the English Department at the University of London Institute of Education and later Goldsmiths Professor of Education. He has been visiting scholar in South Africa, Canada, USA and Australia; was awarded an Honorary Doctorate of Laws by the University of Calgary, and the David H. Russell award for Distinguished Research in the Teaching of English by the US National Council of Teachers of English. His publications include *The Oxford Books of Verse for Juniors* (1957), *The Development of Writing Abilities, 11–18* (editor and joint author, 1975), *Prospect and Retrospect* (1982), *English Teaching: An International Exchange* (1984). *The Word for Teaching is Learning* was published in 1988 in honour of his eightieth birthday.

LANGUAGE AND LEARNING

JAMES BRITTON

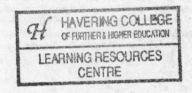

PENGUIN BOOKS

PENGUIN BOOKS

Published by the Penguin Group
Penguin Books Ltd, 27 Wrights Lane, London w8 5tz, England
Penguin Books USA Inc., 375 Hudson Street, New York, New York 10014, USA
Penguin Books Australia Ltd, Ringwood, Victoria, Australia
Penguin Books Canada Ltd, 10 Alcorn Avenue, Toronto, Ontario, Canada m4v 3b2
Penguin Books (NZ) Ltd, 182–190 Wairau Road, Auckland 10, New Zealand

Penguin Books Ltd, Registered Offices: Harmondsworth, Middlesex, England

First published by Allen Lane The Penguin Press 1970
Published in Pelican Books 1972
Second edition published in Penguin Books 1992

Printed in England by Clays Ltd, St Ives plc

Contents

Foreword

THE principal things I have learned and taught in the past fifteen years form the substance of this book. Ordinarily, we learn as we teach, and perhaps this is why I have found the writing rather a solitary task. To colleagues and students who have taught and learned in concert with me I offer my respects and a share of the responsibility for what has been written. To other colleagues, in the dens of their disciplines, I offer my apologies, for in applying what I have learned from them I have certainly taken risks they will find it difficult to excuse. Expertise is dangerous, used in the open, and the choice is between taking risks with it or leaving it alone – which, as I judge it, is no choice at all. After all, if I must confess, I am not a philosopher, a psychologist, a sociologist, a linguist *and* a literary critic: for the sake of the confessional I could have said '*or*', but not for the purpose of my argument.

Wherever possible I have referred to sources to which readers may go to follow the complexities of what I have simplified.

The reader I have had in mind is, in fact, anybody who for any reason wants to listen with more understanding to children and adolescents and who has for any reason a concern for what becomes of them. I could assume in such a reader an interest in their language and their learning. My own concern for teaching is, of course, clearly in evidence, but I have tried not to let it become exclusive: it is true to say that I have learned as much about children's language by being a parent as I have done by being a teacher.

Chapter 1 presents the theory upon which this whole book is based: the theory that we use language as a means of organizing a representation of the world – each for himself – and that the representation so created constitutes the world we operate in, the basis of all the predictions by which we set the course of our lives. Chapter 3 – another short chapter – presents a theory which grows out of the main one: it stresses the differences between two kinds of language-using behaviour. As participants, we use language to interact with people and things and make the wheels of the world, for good or ill, go round. As spectators, we use language to contemplate what has happened to us or to other people, or what might conceivably happen; in other words, we improvise upon our world representation – and we may do so either to enrich it, to embroider it, to fill its gaps and extend its frontiers, or to iron out its inconsistencies.

Chapter 5, a difficult and still unsatisfactory chapter, has two axes to grind: first to trace the development of cognitive processes, and then to attempt to right the balance by looking at the cognitive-cum-affective organization to be found in the arts, and applying the principles found here to more commonplace uses of language. Both these topics are of the utmost educational importance, but our ignorance regarding the second of them is positively dangerous.

Chapters 2, 4 and 6 – the long chapters – are differently organized: they are, so to speak, cut off into lengths of life. Chapter 2 tries to say whatever is relevant to language in the home from a child's birth to the time he goes to school. Chapter 4 is the most teacherly chapter in the book, its theme being the child in the primary school and its sections taking up each of the principal school activities related to language development. Chapter 6 has things to say about work in secondary schools, but its focus is wider – the adolescent wherever he may be. There are a number of good recent books about the teaching of English (see in the bibliography Creber, Dixon, Druce, Holbrook, Walsh and Whitehead), and to tackle language across the whole curriculum of the secondary school would have required a book in itself.

Preface to the Second Edition

THE educational landscape of the 1990s is a very different one from that of the 1970s when *Language and Learning* made its first appearance. This is to some degree true whether we have in mind the British scene or the wider landscape of Europe and the Western world. But in England and Wales, statutory demands have changed the face of state education more sharply than in any other familiar part of the world.

Teachers and administrators in the state system have hitherto enjoyed to a considerable degree the freedom to adjust educational provision to educational needs as they were perceived within individual schools and, in secondary schools, within the various subject departments. It was widely accepted that teaching and learning consist in teacher/pupil interaction as it takes place in and around the individual classroom: interaction that responds to the changing needs and potentials of successive populations of school children. This freedom was our proud boast when we compared our system with conditions as we saw them in other countries.

There were limits to that freedom, of course: when a delegation from the United States led by James Squire and Roger Applebee visited a sample of our schools in 1967 they remarked on the freedom to fit actual needs, but saw also that there came a time in the child's education when the demands made by external examinations exerted considerable pressure on the subject curricula a school had to adopt. Good teachers, in our experience, found ways of meeting the pressures while sacrificing as little as possible of that wider freedom. And we continued to boast: after all, external exams were subject to scrutiny and to the introduction of revised procedures – the inclusion of course work, for example, in place of written unseen papers or mindless forms of multiple-choice tests.

In June 1988, setting out what seemed to me the opinions of experienced English teachers, and in opposition to the prevailing tendencies of Government policies, I included the following claim:

PREFACE TO THE SECOND EDITION

Studies of language acquisition and development have indicated that the routes by which individual children acquire competence vary considerably. Indeed, it is *the child's intention* that above all releases the tacit powers that lead to mastery: freedom on the part of teachers to provide suitable activities adapted to particular children's needs, and allowing for individual choice, therefore becomes crucial. We believe that the considerable degree of freedom that teachers in the United Kingdom have hitherto enjoyed has enabled language programs in our schools to play a leading role as models in the international community.

But as things stand at the moment, the specification of teaching objectives and the attendant methods of assessing the degree of success in achieving them have been made statutory – laid down by law at the behest of the Department of Education and Science. Teachers in our schools no longer possess the freedom to suit educational provision to particular needs; and there is nothing to boast about in international debate on that score.

However, there is a strong tradition that takes in the findings of the Bullock Committee on the uses of language in schools (H.M.S.O., 1975), preserves many of the ideas that stemmed from professional organizations dismantled by the present government (as for example the Schools Council) and will include among its adherents many former and more recent readers of *Language and Learning*. There have been a number of people of this persuasion who, in spite of efforts to exclude them, have found ways of influencing, at various levels, the implementation of the National Curriculum.

It is to the promise afforded by this lasting tradition that I dedicate this new edition of *Language and Learning*: in the hope too that in the course of time the National Curriculum in English may offer attractive possibilities of a take-it-or-leave it kind, along with a professional framework within which to debate its merits and its shortcomings, and so at the same time will cease to rob teachers of their right to teach.

And, finally, I am grateful to Penguin Books for supporting this renewed endeavour.

April 1991

Acknowledgements

I am grateful to the following for permission to reproduce copyright material:

To the Estate of the late T. S. Eliot and Faber and Faber Ltd for the extract from 'Animula' from *Collected Poems: 1909–1962*; for 'Blue Umbrellas' from *Bread Rather than Blossoms* by D. J. Enright to Martin Secker and Warburg Ltd; for the children's writing on pages 179, 215, 250, 251 and 260 to the authors and the *Daily Mirror*; for the extract on page 262 from *The School that I'd Like*, edited by Edward Blishen to Penguin Books Ltd; for the transcripts on pages 240 and 244 to the pupils of Norwood Comprehensive School and the British Broadcasting Corporation; for the transcript on page 147 to Mr Tom Stabler and Mr J. P. Reid.

I am grateful also to Dr Muriel Kay, Mr John Naylor, Mr Bernard Newsome, Miss Janet Rée and Miss Margaret Tucker for supplying material I have incorporated.

CHAPTER ONE

Language and Experience

I

FROM a childhood in city suburbs, I went at the age of fourteen to live on the outskirts of a town. I could walk into the country. On Saturdays we did, my brother and I. As we explored the area we drew a map of this precious bit of countryside, and I can recall one name on it – there was a long winding lane called Hobbleythick Lane. With the name comes a picture of a tall, ragged hawthorn hedge: one only, though I suppose there may have been a hedge on the other side also.

The map was a record of our wanderings, and each time we returned we added to it or corrected it. It was, though a crude one, a representation of the area; we valued it as a cumulative record of our activities there. Furthermore, looking forward instead of back, the map set forth our *expectations* concerning this area as we approached it afresh each time. By means of it we might hope to move around more purposefully, more intelligently: and this would be particularly true if we had returned to the place after a long absence, or if a stranger had gone to it and used our expectations to guide his movements.

There were other representations made of the area, too – not I think on my part, but my brother certainly used to stop occasionally and make a drawing of something he had seen. Neither the drawing nor the map *was* Hobbleythick Lane: each was a representation, and each representation was differently related to the thing itself. Each was in a different way a record of experience and each was capable, in a different way, of setting up or reviving expectations about the area. The map, we might say, was a more general representation, the drawing more particular.

II

In the summer, when we went there often, we carried, of course, our own expectations, 'in our heads'. The place was 'familiar' to us – which is another way of saying that the general outline of our expectations regarding it was appropriate. Indeed, the picture I can still see of a tall ragged hedge is 'an expectation' that has survived in me from that time.

I have arrived at this general point, then (*via* Hobbleythick Lane, which may have seemed to you as circuitous a route as I remember it to have been): that we construct a representation of the world as we experience it, and from this representation, this cumulative record of our own past, we generate expectations concerning the future; expectations which, as moment by moment the future becomes the present, enable us to interpret the present.

If I suddenly catch sight of a familiar face in a crowd, what I have just seen must somehow chime with something I already 'possess', something I carry with me: that something is an example of one kind of representation, a visual image. We shall see later that there are many kinds, many ways of representing the world to ourselves. The matter is complicated enough if for the moment we limit ourselves to visual images. As I sit here I can visualize with greater or less distinctness the faces of scores of my friends and acquaintances. But my storehouse, my representation of the world, in terms of the visual images of faces alone, is far, far richer than that, since faces I cannot recall would be familiar to me if I saw them again. Further, from past looking I would find a great deal that was familiar about faces I had *never* seen before – that they were human faces, that they were male or female (though not always), that they were old or young, perhaps, or Red Indian or Eskimo or Chinese.

In suggesting that a visual image of this sort *represents* a face I know, or a kind of face I know; that the drawing *represented* something in the landscape, and that the map *represented* an area of the countryside; further, that we habitually create representations of one kind or another of the things we meet in the actual world in order to use them in making sense of fresh encounters – in suggesting all this I am putting forward a view of human behaviour, or *one way of representing* what goes on in man's transactions with his environment. The view or the theory is, in fact, an example of itself. When the theory is put forward in its most general terms, and avoiding what are no doubt over-simplifications in the way I have put it, the word 'symbol' is usually used where I have used 'representation', and 'symbolizes' for 'represents'. It is a theory that attempts to explain what is characteristically human about human behaviour, what essentially distinguishes man from the other animals.

There have been other ways of explaining this distinction. Man has been called 'the talking animal' and that might have seemed an appropriate starting point for this book on language. But language, as we shall see, is only one way of symbolizing what is in the universe, and we cannot explain the particular workings of language unless we see their relations with other ways of symbolizing and with the nature of the symbolizing process itself (or with what is common to all ways). Philosophers have frequently taken *reason* to be the essentially human characteristic. Ernst Cassirer, the German philosopher, disposes of that claim:

Reason is a very inadequate term with which to comprehend the forms of man's cultural life in all their richness and variety. But all these forms are symbolic forms. Hence, instead of defining man as an *animal rationale*, we should define him as an *animal symbolicum*. By so doing we can designate his specific difference, and we can understand the new way open to man – the way to civilisation. . . . That symbolic thought and symbolic behaviour are among the most characteristic features of human life, and that the whole progress of human culture is based on these conditions, is undeniable. (Cassirer, 1944, pp. 26 and 27)

The ability to speak and to reason are, of course, highly

characteristic features of human life, distinguishing man from the other animals, but the point is that we have to dig beneath them to get to the root of the matter since both are dependent upon the ability to generate and use symbols, the ability to create representations of actuality. The world we respond to, in fact, the world towards which our behaviour is directed, is the world as we symbolize it, or represent it to ourselves. Changes in the actual world must be followed by changes in our representation of it if they are to affect our expectations and, hence, our subsequent behaviour.

Your representation of the world differs from mine, and this is not only in so far as the world has used us differently – that is to say we have had differing experiences of it. It is also because your *way of representing* is not the same as mine. We are neither of us cameras. A part of what we do at any moment can in fact be explained in terms of the camera, for just as the screen of the camera bears a picture of what is there outside, so our representation of the world is a partial likeness. It is a partial likeness because, at any moment, at the same time as we are drawing in from the outside world (to put it very crudely) we are also projecting our own wishes, our hopes and fears and expectations about the world. Our representation of that situation is the resultant of the two processes, that of *internalizing* and that of *externalizing*: and because what you project is a function of your personality (your mood of the moment as well as your habitual ways of feeling and thinking about things), and what I project is a function of my personality, our representations of the shared situation will be different. Moreover, the way I represent similar situations on different occasions will be different. Thor Heyerdahl, in the story of Kon Tiki, records how the party had a frightening experience with snakes one afternoon in the garden of a place they were visiting. Later that evening, we are told, they were sitting indoors by the light of oil lamps and they mistook the giant shadow of a perfectly ordinary scorpion for the shadow of a *giant scorpion*. Their representation, in other words, was strongly influenced by the feelings set up by the previous experience.

My representation of the present moment, then, reflects both the mood I happen to be in and also more enduring features of my personality. My way of representing encounters with the actual builds up, over a period of time, to produce my 'world representation': which, as we said at the beginning, is different from yours.

I look at the world in the light of what I have learned to expect from past experience of the world. That is to say, there is on the one hand my world representation – the accumulated record of my past experience – and there is on the other hand the process of representing to myself whatever of the world confronts me at any given moment. It is as though, in confrontation, my world representation were a body of expectations from which I select and match: the selecting and matching being in response to whatever cues the situation offers (but influenced also by my mood of the moment). What takes place in the confrontation may contradict or modify or confirm my expectations. My expectations are hypotheses which I submit to the test of encounter with the actual. The outcome affects not only my representation of the present moment, but, if necessary, my whole accumulated representation of the world. *Every encounter with the actual is an experimental committal of all I have learned from experience.* If what takes place lies entirely outside my expectations, so that nothing in my past experience provides the basis-for-modification, then I shall be able to make nothing of it: it might constitute 'an experience' for somebody else, but for me it cannot. (What does the infant who gazes in fascination at the bright light of the screen make of the television drama that his mother will call 'a gripping experience'? It is the flickering light that fascinates him and constitutes this 'experience' for him: the 'experience' for his mother – a slice of life in photo-images – is one the infant can 'make nothing of'.)

George Kelly, an American psychologist who died recently, has put forward a general theory of human behaviour which is consistent with what I have been saying, and with much that is yet to be said about the workings of language. Kelly suggests that all men behave in what is essentially the way a scientist behaves. He tells us how he arrived at this view:

One of my tasks in the 1930s was to direct graduate studies leading to the Master's Degree. A typical afternoon might find me talking to a graduate student, doing all those familiar things that thesis directors have to do – encouraging the student to pinpoint the issues, to observe, to become intimate with the problem, to form hypotheses either inductively or deductively, to make some preliminary test runs, to relate his data to his predictions, to control his experiments so that he will know what led to what, to generalize cautiously and to revise his thinking in the light of experience.

At two o'clock I might have an appointment with a client. During this interview I would not be taking the role of scientist but rather helping the distressed person work out some solutions to his life's problems. So what would I do? Why, I would try to get him to pinpoint the issues, to observe, to become intimate with the problem, to form hypotheses, to make test runs, to relate outcomes to anticipations, to control his ventures so that he will know what led to what, to generalize cautiously and to revise his dogma in the light of experience. (Kelly, 1969, pp. 60–61)

The scientist's method of inquiry is to formulate hypotheses, or make predictions about the way things are, and then to put these to the test of what actually happens, and reframe his hypotheses in the light of what does happen. Kelly suggests that we look upon this as typical of human behaviour in general. This is a very different view from that of the popular legend about Newton – that truth hit him on the head with the apple. It stresses the *active* nature of man's approach to experience. To enlarge on it in Kelly's own words:

Man looks at his world through transparent patterns or templates which he creates and then attempts to fit over the realities of which the world is composed. The fit is not always very good. Yet without such patterns the world appears to be such an undifferentiated homogeneity that man is unable to make any sense out of it. Even a poor fit is more helpful to him than nothing at all. (Kelly, 1963, pp. 8-9)

Thus, the television drama that was a notable experience for the mother I referred to above, remained for the infant 'an undifferentiated homogeneity' of flickering lights and persistent noises. The template Kelly refers to is the equivalent of the 'representation' of the present moment actively produced by selecting and matching and modifying expectations drawn from the 'body of expectations' that constitutes an individual's representation of the world.

The 'template' and the 'representation' are crude analogies, crutches on which to lean until we can do without them. What Kelly first calls 'fitting a template' he goes on to describe as 'construing' or 'placing a construction upon' experience. And he has this to say about the cumulative nature of the process:

Experience is made up of the successive construing of events. It is not constituted merely by the succession of events themselves. ... It is not what happens around him that makes a man's experiences; it is the successive construing and reconstruing of what happens, as it happens, that enriches the experience of life.

The outcome of this process, and the equivalent in Kelly's theory of what we have called the 'world representation', is a person's 'construction system'.

The constructions one places upon events are working hypotheses which are about to be put to the test of experience. As one's anticipations or hypotheses are successively revised in the light of the unfolding sequence of events, a construction system undergoes a progressive evolution.* (Kelly, 1963, pp. 72 and 73)

Kelly's conception of man as essentially concerned to anticipate events and to extend and improve his predictive apparatus is important to the purposes of this book. It is a view of human behaviour that makes living very like learning; that equates learning with learning from experience; and that underlines therefore the importance of our present inquiry into the means by which a man brings his past to bear upon his present.

Events take place and are gone: it is the representation that lasts and accumulates and undergoes successive modification. It is from the representation we make that we gain a sense of a continuing existence in a world that has a past and a future, a world that remains in existence whether we are there to prove it or not. Cassirer calls the world of space and time a human world. 'Only symbolic expression', he says, 'can yield the possibility of prospect and retrospect, because it is only by symbols that distinctions are not merely *made*, but *fixed* in consciousness.' (Cassirer, 1946, p. 38)

What is fixed in consciousness is there to go back to: a prediction, an expectation, is formulated by reference back. Our representation of past experience constitutes a frame of reference by means of which we recognize familiar aspects of the present (the face of a friend in the crowd or the strange face recognizably a child's or an old man's or Chinese). Moreover what remains in consciousness is there to go back to and *modify* in the light of the fresh encounter: it is a continuing sense of the world that is continually brought up to date.

*We have suggested that there are many ways of representing experience, varying in the relationship between the representation and what is represented. It seems appropriate to suggest that Kelly's 'construction system' does not cover all forms of representation, but is in fact more like the map than the drawing or the visual image.

We can discuss representation no further without making specific reference to language. Language is one way of representing experience, but it is, as we shall find when we examine the matter more fully, a key way. It is for most of us the means by which all ways of representing combine to work efficiently together.

The modification, the 'bringing up to date', of our representations of experience is something that we habitually accomplish by means of talk. We have spoken so far as though the 'successive reconstruing', the modification of our representation, took place only as our expectations were put to the test in moment-by-moment encounters with the actual. But we habitually use talk to go back over events and interpret them, make sense of them in a way that we were unable to while they were taking place. This is to work upon our representation of the particular experience and our world representation in order to incorporate the one into the other more fully. We may of course achieve a similar end without talking: we may simply meditate in silence upon past events. In doing so we should, in my view, be using processes which we had acquired as a direct result of our past uses of language.

We habitually use talk also as a means of modifying each other's representations of experience. Martin Buber, the Jewish philosopher, came to London many years ago and gave a series of lectures that I have never forgotten. One of the things he said was, 'Experience comes to man "as I" but it is by experience "as we" that he builds the common world in which he lives.' We each build our own representation of the world, but we greatly affect each other's representation, so that much of what we build is built in common. We must suppose that primitive man's struggle to represent the world to himself with the help of language went on side by side with his attempts to bring his experiences of it into the area of communication with others. At no stage, therefore, could his representation be unaffected by the representations made by other men. This human characteristic is central to the distinction between man's social nature and the gregariousness of animals.

What has been said so far about language as a symbolic system, one of the means of representing the world, may be summed up in the words of Edward Sapir, the great American linguist. Sapir notes that 'the primary function of language is generally said to be communication' but goes on to offer an alternative view:

It is best to admit that language is primarily a vocal actualisation of the tendency to see realities symbolically . . . an actualisation in terms of vocal expression of the tendency to master reality not by direct and *ad hoc* handling of this element but by the reduction of experience to familiar form. (Sapir, 1961, pp. 14–15)

The primary task for speech is to symbolize reality: we symbolize reality in order to handle it.

We have been considering how man represents the actual world to himself in order to operate in it. It would be a mistake, however, to limit our idea of man's symbol-making to such activities. Indeed, it is clear that once we see man as creating a representation of his world so that he may operate in it, another order of activity is also open to him: he may operate *directly upon the representation itself*. He may opt out of the handling of reality for a time and improvise to his own satisfaction upon his represented world. In gossip, in our dreams and our day-dreams, and in much of our reading, we improvise freely, wildly, light-heartedly upon our representation of past experiences with little concern for what those experiences have shown the world to be really like. Perhaps even the wildest fantasies may be found in the long run to be related to our need to extend and enrich our predictive capacity, to build up so vast a store of hypotheses that no conceivable possibility of experience could find us unprepared; but certainly our improvisations vary very widely in the degree to which we regard them as hypothetically related to actuality, the degree to which we regard them as of practical use.

Susanne Langer sees man as a proliferator of symbols, and speaks of 'the stream of symbols which constitutes the human mind'. Our participation in the world's affairs does not account for the whole of this activity.

The material furnished by the senses [to quote Susanne Langer], is constantly wrought into symbols, which are our elementary ideas. Some of these ideas can be combined and manipulated in the manner we call 'reasoning', others do not lend themselves to this use, but are naturally telescoped into dreams, or vapour off in conscious fantasy; and a vast number of them build the most typical and fundamental edifice of the human mind – religion.

She goes on to suggest that the expression of these elementary ideas, these symbolizations, is 'the typically human form of overt activity'. 'How else shall we account for man's love of talk? From the first dawning recognition that words *express* something, talk is a dominant interest, an irresistible desire.' (Langer, 1960(a), pp. 42–3).

II

In what ways does language differ from other means of representing the world to ourselves, what claim has it to be called a 'key system', and in what ways is it related to the other systems or means of representation? What has to be explained may be put briefly: language is a highly organized, systematic means of representing experience, and as such it assists us to organize all other ways of representing.

We can most of us recall having had experiences in which so much was happening at the same time around us that we were in utter confusion. We could make nothing of it all. (A backwoodsman coming to a cinema for the first time and seeing Fellini's $8\frac{1}{2}$ or some such film might be similarly at a loss.) Robert Graves in 'Welsh Incident' makes his eye-witness describe the strange creatures he saw on the beach in these words:

> But at last
> The most odd, indescribable thing of all
> Which hardly one man there could see for wonder
> Did something recognizably a something.

In a struggle to convey what he saw, he seems to have a method of working but not much to work it on!

But to speak of 'an experience', 'an event', 'an incident' is already to have moved some distance out from confusion. What the senses encounter moment by moment is a stream, an un-broken continuum: 'an incident' – thinking of the smallest item that might refer to – is a segment of that continuum. Before we can make something of what the senses deliver us we have therefore to extract from the stream some segment that is, from some aspect, a repetition of previous segments. (Or rather, of what may now be recognized as segments of the past con-tinuum, for the recognition must be made on the basis of the similarity.) George Kelly refers to the process as 'construing the replications of events' and describes it thus:

> The substance that a person construes is itself a process. . . . It presents itself from the beginning as an unending and undifferen-tiated process. Only when man attunes his ear to recurrent themes in the monotonous flow does his universe begin to make sense to him. Like a musician, he must phrase his experience in order to make sense of it. The phrases are distinguished events. The separation of events is what man produces for himself when he decides to chop time up into manageable lengths. Within these limited segments, which are based on recurrent themes, man begins to discover the bases for likenesses and differences. (Kelly, 1963, p. 52)

Bruner (Bruner, Goodnow and Austin, 1956) has pointed out that it is of no value to a man to know that in a sequence of his past experiences Event A was followed by Event B. It is of no value, because Event A will never happen again. But it is a different matter altogether to recognize that an event of *Type A* was followed by an event of *Type B*: that is to learn from experience, for when next an event of Type A occurs we shall be in a position to anticipate an event of Type B. To recognize segments of experience that are, from certain aspects, repetitions of previous segments is to begin grouping or classifying events, to begin labelling events as Type A, Type B, Type C and so on.

It is clear from their behaviour that animals are able to link together similar events and form what are, operationally speaking, categories. Most dogs – in surburban homes at all events – get excited when somebody in the family picks up the lead. They have learnt from past experience to expect that an event of type A – reaching for the lead – tends to be followed by an event of type B – going for a walk. The training of animals relies upon the setting up of linked categories of behaviour and experience: the creature must connect categories of its own actions with categories of subsequent reward or punishment. But because man uses language he is able to handle an infinitely greater number of categories than any other creature can. Language is our principal means of classifying, and it is this classifying function that goes furthest towards accounting for the role of language as an organizer of our representations of experience.

The objects of the world do not present themselves to us ready classified. The categories into which they are divided are categories into which *we divide them*. And the fact that we use language as a means of doing so may be inferred in a number of ways. From a child's own experiences of the world he comes to divide objects in very much the same way as his parents do, though the way he labels things shows that this is not true of his early experiences. The fact that as an infant he may call a whole variety of creatures 'ba' indicates that he is grouping together many objects that his parents would distinguish. It is as he learns to use language that he takes over, for the most part, the class divisions embodied in the language. But another child, growing up in another part of the world will divide experiences in a somewhat different way: he too is taking over, in general, the divisions embodied in his language, but it is a different language. Languages differ from each other in the way they divide objects into categories.

Malinowski, the British anthropologist (Malinowski, 1923, p. 331) suggested that societies classify their surroundings in accordance with their own particular needs and purposes. Thus, in one island community, he found there was a name for the kind of tree from which the natives made their canoes, a name for the kind of tree whose fruit they ate, and one general term (equivalent to 'the green thing', perhaps) for all other trees irrespective of any differences between them. And the same was true of fish: the fish they ate and the fish that if they were not watching out would eat them – these each had a name: all other fish were lumped together so that any one of them would be called 'the swimming thing'. An observer who did not know their language could have produced a simple classification of trees and fish (and so on) in terms of the islanders' behaviour with regard to them: and the trees and fish with which there were no particular dealings would have been left in the mass, unclassified. Going on to study their language he would have then found that it was by means of language that the behaviourally required categories had been set up and maintained. The categories into which the world is divided are the categories into which we have divided it to suit our particular purposes, and language is the means by which we mark the distinctions and pass them on.

One of the first things that anybody does who discovers a new feature on the earth's surface, or produces a new kind of rose, or invents a new game, or even a new system of analysis, is to give it a name. He may also plot it, register it, give it a serial number, or patent it – but it is the name that marks its existence in his society or in the world of human affairs. We take over in childhood the classification of experience embodied in our mother tongue: but we find no difficulty when the need arises in re-classifying by adding new items to the language.

The way we classify colours is one of the best (and most widely used) examples of the fact that categories are *made* and not *given*, the fact that different languages make them differently, and the fact, above all, that we could not handle experience at all if we did not first divide sense data into categories. The colour spectrum is a continuum: any colour we perceive must lie at some point on the infinity of points of that continuum. Bruner (Bruner *et al.*, 1956) records the fact that according to the estimates of physicists the human eye can distinguish one shade of colour from another seven million times over throughout the spectrum. That is to say, using the word colour in a rather special sense, there are seven million distinguishable 'colours'. But this is a statement about the discriminating power of the human eye rather than a statement about human purposes. For most of our ordinary human purposes we use a word that refers not to a 'colour' in this refined sense, but to a whole area or band of the spectrum. The point to be made is that we have to use broad categories if we are ever to get through the business of the day in terms of colour alone. If any one of the minimally distinguishable colours – the seven million – be regarded as a unique colour experience, then we usually handle this experience by referring to it with a word which represents a grouping of thousands of such unique experiences: the word 'red', for example. I say 'usually' because if our purpose requires us to be more specific we can be: we may say 'a particularly vivid scarlet', or 'a dull cherry'. But it would be *un*usual for us to say, 'Pass me the particularly vivid scarlet ink, please'.

Anthropologists have found languages in existence which do not divide the spectrum into the same bands as are found in the languages familiar to us. Bruner quotes two examples, one a language in which blue and green form a single group, and another in which brown and grey do so. Other examples could be used to show that languages divide phenomena differently. (The Eskimo language is said to have seven words for our one word 'snow'. Snow, which they see more of and which enters more into their purposes, for good or ill, has been divided into seven classes where we make one of it.) Our interest in such examples is the evidence they offer that classifying relies upon language.

The point to underline, however, is the degree to which we rely upon the process of classification. Experience is kaleidoscopic: the experience of every moment is unique and unrepeatable. Until we can group items in it on the basis of their similarity we can set up no expectations, make no predictions: lacking these we can make nothing of the present moment. Without categories of experience, therefore, we should remain imprisoned in the uniqueness of the here and now. What Piaget has called 'the manifold and irreducible present' is in fact conquered by what Sapir described as 'the reduction of experience to familiar form'.

The cutting into segments of the stream of sense experience and the recognition of similarities between segments enables us to build up a representation, let us say, of an object such as a cup. From the overlap of many experiences, focused upon as the word 'cup' is used by other people or ourselves, the basis of similarity and dissimilarity becomes more clearly defined and more objects, different from the original cup in what does not matter but alike in what does – what defines the category – are admitted to the category. The word, then, unlike the visual image I have of a cup I have seen and can recall, is a generalized representation, classifying as it represents.

Taking a leap from there, it is difficult to imagine how some experiences could be classified at all were it not for the agency of language. Four-year-old children will cheerfully and confidently talk about their *holidays* – about who is on holiday and where they have gone, and about what they are going to do on their own holidays. The definition of the category, criteria by which to decide what is properly called 'a holiday' and what is not, would be a complicated task for us and certainly the four-year-old could not attempt it. And there is nothing to point to, as he might point to a cup to show he knew the meaning. The ability to operate the category has grown from the overlap of experiences of the *word in use* as applied to his own familiar experiences.

It is not simply in the number of categories they possess that men are superior to dogs, but also in the inter-relatedness of the categories. Language, because of its own highly complex internal organization, provides us with systematically related categories of many kinds. There are categories of meaning, one of which, 'synonymity', is essentially the relationship we have been considering in speaking of the process by which the word 'cup' or the word 'holiday' comes to apply to a class of items instead of a single item of our experience. *Oppositeness* is another relationship that is built into language. In referring to the 'width' of a thing, for example we have a set of three words at our disposal – 'wide', 'narrow' and 'width'. A child may discover that what seems wide to him on one occasion, in one context, seems narrow to him on another, and then he comes to learn that even the narrowest thing is said to have 'width'; and similarly even the lightest thing is said to have 'weight'. He can ask 'How heavy is your bag?' when obviously it is not heavy at all and 'How old is the kitten?' when it is obviously very young. In other words there is built into the English language a way of helping him to deal with the complicated nature of bi-polar oppositeness. Perhaps the most powerfully useful relationship in language is that of *hierarchy*. We have seen that all words are generalized representations; there are among them, however, different *levels of generality*. Since all buttercups are flowers but all flowers are not buttercups, it is clear that 'buttercup' represents a class of objects that is a sub-class of that represented by 'flower'; and that in turn is a sub-class of the class of objects represented by 'plant'. It is the existence of classes at different levels of generality that finally makes possible the higher forms of thought process, including what we call 'reasoning'. To be able to group objects in accordance with words existing in the language at different levels of generality is a mere beginning, but it is the essential foundation for the higher thought processes, as we shall see later when we come to look at the development of language and of learning in children. There is no need to add here that man's representation of the world owes more to the mental processes achieved in this way than to any other agency.

Grammatical relationships constitute another kind of organization to be found in language, and as such affect the way we represent experience in speech and thought. Aspects of our experience are habitually represented as nouns while others are represented as verbs: their further relations are governed by rules of syntax. But we shall postpone to a later chapter (Chapter 5) a fuller consideration of some of the complicated ways in which these factors affect what we make of our experiences.

Our world representation is a storehouse of the data of our experience: it is of predictive value to us in so far as the data are retrievable. And this calls for complex and efficient organization. Language, we are told, is 'rule-governed behaviour': as we represent experience in words we submit it to the rules, we bring to bear upon it the highly complex relationships systematically embodied in language itself. The process begins – though, as we shall see, it does not end – in talk.

III

What I have loosely referred to as 'a world representation' has been more elaborately christened 'a verbally organized world schema'. *Verbally organized*: what is organized is far more than words. Woven into its fabric are representations of many kinds: images directly presented by the senses, images that are interiorized experiences of sight, sound, movement, touch, smell and taste: pre-verbal patterns reflecting feeling responses and elementary value judgements:* post-verbal patterns, our ideas and reasoned beliefs about the world: images derived from myth, religion and the arts.

(I am well aware that hierarchies of psychological angels have feared to tread where that brief paragraph has trod, and that any attempt to refine its crudities would lead to endless argument. The work of Piaget on sensori-motor experiences gives ground for accepting the first item in my list. He shows how, for example, a movement, once successfully accomplished, becomes interiorized to form what he calls 'a schema', and he relates this to 'imitative representation' (which in the young child is a stage on the way to 'verbal representation'). (Piaget, 1951, pp. 277–90) It can hardly be doubted that ways of construing experience exist in children before they have learned to use language, and persist in adult life, where they may be modified and probably added to. Kelly's 'construction system' resembles what has here been called 'a representation' and among the ways of construing that result in the system he includes pre-verbal patterns and is opposed to any attempt to distinguish cognitive from affective constructs. Hence, in rough compromise, my second item.)

My looking and listening is not normally purposeless and undirected. In any situation, therefore, I organize my representation of it to some extent in the act of perceiving. I am able to do this, to perceive selectively, to focus, because I enter the situation with expectations; these expectations, as we have seen, are the fruits of my past 'representing' *of all kinds*, and of whatever organization verbalizing has given to them.

---

* 'A person's behaviour may be based upon many interlocking equivalence-difference patterns which are never communicated in symbolic speech.' (Kelly, 1963, p. 51)

What is organized is far more than words: as we recall some past experience, even a remote one, we may find that things in it come back to us with much of the vividness of sense experience – the colour, the movement, the sound – and that strong feeling may be 'reawakened'. We cannot prove that the effects of verbalizing these experiences at some time has made these recollections accessible to us, but there are suggestive indications that this is the case. Most of us will at some time have been vividly reminded – perhaps without knowing what has reminded us – of some past experience. And as we struggle to recover the details we find that we are searching after *a word*, the name of a place or a person, perhaps, and that when we have found the word, the circumstances, the sense impressions, come flooding back to complete the recollection. It was as though a word was the Ariadne's thread that could lead us through the maze. Again, nothing so encourages recollection of the remote past as talk: it will often happen that people will recover in talk about a shared experience far more of the detail than either of them could have supposed before they started. The converse of the process is too familiar to need illustrating: a chance word may at any time start a train of vivid recollections (and sensations, emotions and ideas, in clusters that differ widely from each other, may be called up by a succession of words that show minimal phonetic differences: *far*, *fire*, *foe*, *fay*, for example, or *liver*, *lover* and *loofah*!)

Be all that as it may, we habitually use talk as a means of coming to grips with current or recent experience. The newspaper accounts of important events will be talked about in every train and office and on every street corner. As people talk, each is relating the event to his own experience, his own world: creating his own personal context for it. In doing so he is using talk to add the new event to a body of experience that exists very largely as the outcome of similar talk on past occasions. Joseph Church, an American psychologist, has this to say about the process we are considering:

It is obvious that for many people the verbalisation of experience must take place retrospectively and that it requires the help of another person. The morning after the big dance the telephone system is taxed while the matrons and adolescents exchange impressions until the event has been given verbal shape and so can enter the corpus of their experience. (Church, 1961, p. 113)

The main purpose of this chapter has been to suggest that, by various means of representation, and with the aid of language as an organizing principle, we construct each for himself a world representation: that we modify this representation in the light of further experience in order that our predictions may be better: and that we improvise upon it for a variety of reasons. A final word or two must be added on the whole idea of a 'world representation'.

In describing how very young children form sensori-motor schemas by imitating movements they observe, Piaget points out that it is not any and every movement that they will tackle: what they tend to work on will be a movement which has some features in common with movements they have already mastered, and some novel features. Referring to children under the age of one, he says:

It is true that as yet it is only models which have some analogy with the child's schemas which give rise to imitation. Those which are too remote from the child's experience leave him indifferent, as for instance unfamiliar movements which would have to be made without being seen. But sounds and movements which are new to the child, and yet comparable to those he has already made, give rise to an immediate effort at reproduction. The interest thus appears to come from a kind of conflict between the partial resemblance which makes the child want to assimilate, and the partial difference which attracts his attention the more because it is an obstacle to immediate reproduction. It is therefore this two-fold character of resemblance and opposition which seems to be the incentive for imitation. (Piaget, 1951, pp. 50–51)

Other psychologists, in more general terms, have suggested that what engages our attention and interest is likely in a similar way to straddle the familiar and the unfamiliar.*

Such evidence encourages us to accept the notion of a 'world representation' as a single whole. For Piaget's observations imply growth from a centre; the new being incorporated only at points where it relates to what is already there. Psychotic behaviour may not conform to this pattern, recollection under hypnosis may be an exception, but I think most normal people would reasonably and rightly regard their constructions of experience as constituting *a view of the world*. I believe in fact that many of the things we do most earnestly are directed towards preserving or restoring the unity, coherence and harmony of this view. But that is a story for a later chapter.

*See, for example, D. O. Hebb, *The Organisation of Behaviour*, pp. 229 *et seq.*

CHAPTER TWO

Learning to Speak

I

THE homes into which most babies are born are places where people talk. They will talk about the baby and a great many other things as well, and before long – long before they expect any response – they will talk to the baby. Among the other noises that reach his ears are likely to be television programmes, singing, greetings across the wall to neighbours, and the talk that goes on when someone comes to the door. Most of this of course goes unheeded, but it is surprising how early in his life he begins to make some discrimination, some selection from the background of noise. It has been observed that by the time a child is one month old the sound of his mother's voice when she is out of sight will be enough to soothe him – not when he is yelling blue murder, but in the kind of whimpering that indicates minor distress. Other forms of language exist around him, from words on the baby-powder tin to words on street hoardings, from newspaper headlines to books on baby-care. In fact there exist in some form or other verbal counterparts of almost everything that goes on in his environment.

It is small wonder, then, that (after a great deal of listening) the first words he uses are more by way of comment than by way of command. He begins to supply, as it were, his own verbal accompaniment to what is going on. Being hungry, or thirsty, or bored, or wedged under a chair, or out of reach of something important – these are a part of what goes on, and commands or requests will be the appropriate verbal accompaniments of such states of affairs, but they will bulk far less large than what might generally be called comment in a child's early speech. Yet the view is still put forward that the satisfaction of

33

physical needs provides the main incentive for a child to learn to speak, and the reason why he makes such rapid progress in doing so. This, it seems to me, is to ignore several factors in the situation: first the child's evident *pleasure*, long before he can speak, in suiting his actions to other people's words ('Pat-a-cake, pat-a-cake', 'hands up high!', 'Fetch Teddy' and so on); his evident pleasure in pretending to speak – imitating intonation patterns and the like; similarly at a later stage, when he does speak, his pleasure in the process itself, which seems far more evident than any concern for speech as an instrument; the fact that he continues, some while after he can speak, to demonstrate his needs less by speaking than by other forms of behaviour – crying or giggling or running towards or running away and so on; and finally the fact that the dramatic extension of his powers of speech comes at the point when he seems to gain some realization of (or begins to operate in the light of) the general truth that *everything has a name* – a truth far more relevant to representing experience in words than to getting what you want by asking for it.

Here is a list – highly selective certainly, but selected at the time, not to support or refute any thesis, but to be *representative* (in particular of peaks of achievement) of the utterances that marked the first twelve months of one girl's speaking life.

REPERTOIRE OF NOISES AT TWELVE MONTHS
A ba ba (repeated and punctuated with squeals of delight)
Mumumum (peevish, distressed)
A wa wa wa (her most chatty sound)
A continuous excited 'war cry' as she crawls for something
Dadad
Ung (for the little brush she likes to hold)
Something near to 'Hello' and 'Bye-bye', in imitation

SPEECH AT EIGHTEEN MONTHS
Playing with toys: *black bow-wow; eyes; push pram; wow-wow sit there.*

At meals: *backie* (biscuit)*; more backie;* (offering it) *mama backie, dada backie; jam; samidge; more bun; hung(r)y girl; please mummy; fi(n)ished;* (on being given something) *mummy, there you are.*

At breakfast one morning: *bun, butty, jelly, cakie, jam, cup of tea, milkie.*

Hearing the radio: *man: more moosic, more moosic.*

Seeing the washing on the line: *dada pajama!*

In response to 'Mary, Mary how does your garden grow': *dada did mower.*

About things, and so on (Cee refers to herself):
   mummy c(h)air, daddy chair, Cee chair;
   shoe, nother shoe, two shoes;
   mummy have a cup of tea, daddy have a cup of tea, nan-nan have a cup of tea, Cee have a cup of tea, all peoples have a cup of tea.

SPEECH ON ONE OCCASION AT TWENTY-TWO MONTHS (about a friend and her six-year-old twin daughters who had been coming to visit, but could not because one of them had a sore ear):

Auntie B's little girls come see Cee today. Auntie B got two little girls – other one all right – other one come and see Cee today on her bicycalt. (No, because it was raining) *Where's the pram gone – Auntie B pop her in the pram and put hood up and put mackintosh on and keep her all nice and dry and bring her to see Cee today – and other little girl come and Cee tuck her up in Mummy's bed all nice and comfy and put Johnson's baby cream on sore ear.*

Susanne Langer, in the face of evidence of this and other kinds, propounded what she called her 'heresy':

I believe there is a primary need in man, which other creatures probably do not have, and which actuates all his apparently unzoological aims, his wistful fancies, his consciousness of value, his utterly unpractical enthusiasms, ... This basic need, which certainly is obvious only in man, is the *need of symbolisation.* (Langer, 1960, a, p. 41)

She refers, in support of this idea, to the case of Helen Keller who lost the powers of sight and hearing in early infancy. All attempts to teach her to communicate her wants by means of language – in the form of finger spelling – had failed: one day by chance Helen became aware of another use for language, another need it could satisfy. Here is her description of what happened:

She [her teacher] brought me my hat and I knew I was going out into the warm sunshine. This thought, if a wordless sensation may be called a thought, made me hop and skip with pleasure.

We walked down the path to the well house, attracted by the fragrance of the honeysuckle with which it is covered. Someone was drawing water and my teacher placed my hand under the spout. As the cool stream gushed over my hand she spelled into the other the word *water*, first slowly, then rapidly. I stood still, my whole attention fixed upon the motion of her fingers. Suddenly I felt a misty consciousness as of something forgotten . . . and somehow the mystery of language was revealed to me. I knew then that w-a-t-e-r meant the wonderful cool something that was flowing over my hand. That living word awakened my soul, gave it light, hope, joy, set it free! There were barriers still, it it is true, but barriers that in time could be swept away.

I left the well house eager to learn. Everything had a name, and each name gave birth to a new thought. As we returned to the house every object which I touched seemed to quiver with life. That was because I saw everything with the strange new sight that had come to me. (Keller, 1936, pp. 23–4)

The discovery that 'everything has a name' represents the discovery as to 'what language is all about' – and clearly for Helen Keller this had a good deal to do with the need to think, and little to do with the need to drink.

It is, everyone agrees, a colossal task that the child accomplishes when he learns to speak, and the fact that he does so in so short a period of time challenges explanation. We can imagine ourselves cast up on a remote island and living with people whose language we did not know, whose alphabet we could not read: in the course of time, in the course of a great deal of activity where action and speech have gone together, we might succeed in resolving the stream of spoken sound into segments with meaning – given of course that we have infinite curiosity and patience and that the people around us have infinite patience and goodwill! But the endless streams of undifferentiated sound represent only one of two problems that face an infant learning his mother tongue. There is for him also the endless stream of undifferentiated *experience*. This is something we can imagine only very imperfectly, for once in any language we have organized experience to form an objectified world we can never reverse the process.

Perhaps it is here that the secret of the mystery lies – perhaps it is *the way these two tasks enmesh* that explains how a child is able to perform his astonishing feat of learning. 'Eagerness and enthusiasm to talk,' writes Cassirer, 'do not originate in a mere desire for learning or using names; they mark the desire for the detection and conquest of an objective world.' (Cassirer, 1944, pp. 132–3) I dare say no other learning can ever hope to pay such dividends – no other understanding so abundantly prove its value in *making sense* to its user: immediate, since it can give point to anything he does: cumulative in a way that must strike anyone who has ever watched a small child daily advancing his frontiers, striking out on fresh explorations based on yesterday's discoveries. (It is an *operational* success to the child, of course, and nothing he could reflect upon in the way we have been doing.)

Language learning begins, as we have suggested, with listening. Individual children vary very much in the amount of listening they do before they start speaking, and late starters are often long listeners as their first utterances will show. (It is said of Thomas Carlyle that his first words were, 'What ails thee, Jock?', addressed to a play-fellow in difficulties. A colleague of mine was told by her mother that the first words she ever spoke were, 'Please, Mummy, may I have a drink out of my Miss Muffet cup?') Most children will 'obey' spoken instructions some time before they can speak, instructions of the kind I have already quoted in 'Hands up high', 'Pat-a-cake', 'Fetch Teddy'. The word 'obey' requires its inverted commas above because it is hardly apt as a description of the eager and delighted cooperation usually shown by the child. Before they can speak many children will also ask questions by gesture, by pointing and making questioning noises: the demand may be principally one for action or demonstration but the accompanying speech will at some stage also be a part of what is demanded and a part of what is learned from.

Any attempt to trace the development from the noises babies make to their first spoken words is fraught with difficulty and differences of interpretation. It is agreed that they enjoy making noises, and that in the course of the first few months one or two noises sort themselves out as particularly indicative of delight, distress, sociability and so on. (Some examples were given on p. 34.) But since these cannot be said to indicate the baby's *intention* to communicate such states of feeling, they can hardly be regarded as early forms of language usage. It is agreed that from about three months they play with sounds in a way that appears to be deliberate and certainly enjoyable; that by the time they are about six months old they play with and 'practise' sounds that are new to their repertoire; and that this self-imitation leads on to deliberate imitation of sounds made or words spoken to them by other people – or of words overheard from other people's conversations. The problem then arises as to the point at which it can be claimed that these imitations, by saying what the child wants to say, conveying his meaning, amount to 'speaking'.

It is a problem we need not get our teeth into. The meaning of a word is something that can best be handled in terms of what a particular person means by it in a particular situation: and it is clear that what a child means by a word will change as he gains more experience of the world and that this change will in general be in the direction of what an adult speaker would mean. Thus the use, at say seven months, of 'mama' or some such sound as a greeting for his mother cannot be dismissed as non-speech, meaningless sound, simply on the grounds that he also applies the term at other times to his father, his toy dog, and anything else that he feels warm and comfortable towards. Again, much early speech consists in repeating familiar 'formulas' in the situations in which grown-ups have used them to the child – 'Pat-a-cake', 'Hello', 'Bye-bye', and so on. When the child provides the formula which completes the 'meaning' of the situation as he responds to it, he is, it seems to me, using words to convey his meaning: we convey no more and no less when we say 'Good morning', 'How are you?' and 'What'll you have?'. There is on p. 35 an obvious example of this process of saying-what-has-been-said-to-you in a given situation – obvious because, though the word of address has been changed, the rest of the expression has not and is the wrong way round: 'Mummy, there you are', said when something was given to the speaker. The child paralleled this a couple of months later by asking for some cake in these words: 'You have some of that over there'!

Playful and apparently meaningless imitation of what other people say continues after the child has begun to speak for himself and must certainly have the effect of increasing his powers of articulation. I doubt, however, whether anything is gained when parents cash in on this process in an attempt to 'teach' new sounds. The following record by Valentine, the English psychologist, indicates that a child's own play may not be so meaningless, left to itself, as it becomes when we interfere. The note refers to his daughter aged twenty-one months:

Tried to get her to say 'coffee'. Several times she responded with 'foffee', the third time with signs of some annoyance. Then to my next reply of 'No! Coffee' she suddenly and emphatically cried 'Tea!'.

In support of my comment let me quote the case of a girl who at first had difficulty with initial *l*. At nineteen months she was saying *yook* and *yovely* and *yucky girl:* in her twenty-third month she said *look* and *lovely* and *lucky girl* – and *les* for 'yes', *lies and lears* for 'eyes and ears' and *lawn* for 'yawn' and so on: but less than two months later she had the two sounds in their conventional places.

The one-word utterances that characterize the beginnings of speech in most children are frequently one-word sentences. In the situation in which they are spoken listeners have no difficulty in understanding what is meant by such 'sentences' as *gone*, *finished*, *man*, *shoe*, *up*, *more* and so on. In replying, they are likely often to provide a fuller version ('Yes, Mummy's gone shopping', 'You've finished, have you?'), an important point that we shall return to later.

An influx of words used rather differently, the names of things, usually finds its way into a child's speech at some time between the ages of one-and-a-half and two. Most children, whether or not they can be said to have made any general discovery about the nature of the world (the discovery Helen Keller made so dramatically that 'everything has a name'), do seem to take up naming and the pursuit of names with some concentration. An early manifestation of the touching and naming game is given in the breakfast-table catalogue on p. 35. A child will increase his repertoire both by asking questions and by drawing inferences from what he hears – these inferences being tested out, of course, as the naming game is played. To understand the full significance of the game we must conceive of it being played in the middle of a great sea of the un-named and hence (with some exceptions) the unfamiliar, the as-yet-undifferentiated. After the speaking of names has conferred a new status upon what was already familiar by use, the learning of new names adds fresh conquests – fresh objects are 'possessed' as they are differentiated. It is a process of 'bringing into existence' the objects of the immediate environment, the here and now. As new instances crop up of what has once been named, the word becomes the means of building up a category, a filing-pin upon which successive experiences may be filed.

A word does not possess this classifying role from the start. A name may at an earlier stage refer only to a particular object, and appear to function as an inherent attribute of that object. A child who hears the word 'cup' used by his mother whenever she gives him his drinks is likely to create links between the sound of the word and the object, but the sound may well be linked to the object in very much the same way as its shape, its colour, its hardness to the touch. Before the word can function as a generalized name (refer to a class of objects), and as a word related to other words, links of this kind with a particular object must be loosened. A Russian psychologist reports the following concerning a child of twelve to fourteen months:

The familiar word 'cup' was the 'name' of one cup only – a small, pink cup with white spots. When a large white cup, to which the child did not yet relate the word, was placed before him, and he was asked, 'Where is the cup?', the child waved his hands about and looked at his mother with a puzzled air; his perceptual knowledge did not yet have a generalized character. (Liublinskaya, 'Development of Children's Speech and Thought', in Simon, 1957, p. 201)

Vygotsky, another Russian psychologist whose work we shall refer to often, shows that after a name has ceased to act as though it were an attribute, a property, of a particular object, it may still have the relationship of attribute to a *class* of objects.

The word, to the child, is an integral part of the object it denotes. Such a conception seems to be characteristic of primitive linguistic consciousness. We all know the old story about the rustic who said he wasn't surprised that savants with all their instruments could figure out the size of stars and their courses – what baffled him was how they found out their names. Simple experiments show that pre-school children 'explain' the names of objects by their attributes. According to them, an animal is called 'cow' because it has horns, 'calf' because its horns are still small. ... When asked whether one could interchange the names of objects, for instance call a cow 'ink', and ink 'cow', children will answer no, 'because ink is used for writing, and the cow gives milk'. (Vygotsky, 1962, pp. 128–9)

As we have seen, what a child means by a word will change as his experience, both of the world and of language, increases: the point made by Vygotsky represents one kind of change. We shall refer to it again when we come to consider other kinds of change.

Three of the remarks made by the eighteen-month-old girl and quoted on p. 35 seem to illustrate a stage in the process by which a word becomes the name of a class. 'Mummy chair, Daddy chair, Cee chair', 'shoe, nother shoe, two shoes' and 'mummy have a cup of tea, daddy have a cup of tea, nan-nan have a cup of tea, Cee have a cup of tea, all peoples have a cup of tea' – objects and actions that have been, so to speak, separately labelled with a common label are paraded together, and perhaps this may be seen as a verbalizing of the process by which what is common to the separate manifestations will be abstracted and result in a name that truly stands for a class – a 'chair', somebody's, anybody's, here, there, anywhere – and a 'shoe' and 'having a cup of tea'.

II

What is meant by the statement that children learn language by imitation? It would seem to be nearer the truth to say that they imitate people's *method of going about saying things* than to say that they imitate the things said. This is most evident when we look at the grammatical forms children use. They appear to be engaged in deriving some kind of system from what they hear and applying it in what they say. Such improvisation results in utterances that they could not have heard other people make. Thus one child of two years and seven months:

'I'm spoonfulling it in.'

Trying to button up her coat: 'I'm seefing it will go in' (from hearing, 'See if it will go in'); and later, when she was successful: 'I'm a button-up-er.'

Skipping ahead down the road: 'I'm jumper than you are.' 'Daddy fews some out for me.'

I once overheard a child of about three, or perhaps four, say to her mother, 'We better cross here, bettern't we?'

There is a similar freedom in using language in the following examples, and the term improvisation still seems appropriate, though we cannot conceive of a system being induced and tried out in the same way as we can with the grammatical examples. They are taken from records of two-and-a-half- to three-year-olds (the child's remarks are italicized):

1. *a strokey cat*
2. (Watching her father comb his hair) *I don't think that looks nice.* Don't you? How do you like it?
   I like it smuttered in your eyes.
3. What are you doing?
   I'm just zzz-ing about.
   And what's Teddy doing? Is he zzz-ing too?
   No. He's waiting for me to stop zzz-ing.
4. *Don't go away where I am.*

What Piaget found to be true of earlier forms of imitation still holds in general for linguistic improvisation: what is newly observed is used to modify behaviour patterns already acquired, and the child's fresh product is the outcome of that interaction.

Roger Brown and Ursula Bellugi, psychologists working at Harvard University, have made a special study of the grammatical characteristics of young children's utterances. They found that not only do children imitate adults, but that in speaking to children adults imitate their forms of speech, and that the two processes dovetail. They made frequent recordings of two children, a girl of eighteen months and a boy of twenty-seven months, each in conversation with his or her mother. (Brown and Bellugi, 1964)

Here are some examples of utterances in which the child copied the mother:

Mother's utterance	*Child's imitation*
Daddy's brief case	Daddy brief case
Fraser will be unhappy	Fraser unhappy
He's going out	He going out
It's not the same dog as Pepper	Dog Pepper
No, you can't write on Mr Cromer's shoe	Write Cromer shoe

It will be clear why they call the child's imitation a *reduction*. He seems to be able only to go to a certain length – a length which may compass most of the mother's shorter utterances, but cuts the longer ones down. They found that the children's spontaneous utterances kept at this stage to roughly this same length: the limitation seems to be, they suggest, on the amount that a child can plan or program in speech. They comment on the kinds of words retained and the kinds of words omitted in reducing: it is the words that carry most information that are retained, as they would be in a telegram. These are the nouns, verbs and adjectives, roughly speaking – the 'open-class' words: moreover (and this they suggest may explain how the child operates), these are the words that carry the main stresses in speaking. The words omitted are the function words, or the grammatical signals – the words that tend to relate the informative words rather than be themselves informative; and these are the unstressed words. (Clearly what is omitted is sometimes not a word but a part of a word, a grammatical inflexion.)

When mothers imitate children their utterances are not reductions but expansions: they offer back to the child their version of what they think he intended to say. This may often be a way of checking what it was he did intend, though it may also arise from an adult's more or less unconscious desire to have things said properly. In any case, the authors believe, the

44

process is likely to be a valuable one since it puts before the child specially-tailored models of sentences. Here are examples taken from their recordings:

Child's utterance	Mother's expansion
Baby high-chair	Baby is in the high-chair
Eve lunch	Eve is having lunch
Mommy sandwich	Mommy'll have a sandwich
Sat wall	He sat on the wall
Throw Daddy	Throw it to Daddy

The mother's utterance is an imitation of the child's in the obvious sense – what she says is based closely on what the child said. But it is imitation also in a less direct sense: she consistently uses short and simple sentences, unlike the conversational style of adults – language in fact rather like the speech of a child, but a child a little more grown up (in his speech) than the one it is addressed to. Anyone who has talked to young children will know that we tend to behave in this way automatically. I need not point out that what the mother supplies in her version are precisely words (or parts of words) of the kind that the child omitted in his imitations with reduction. The wider implications of what she is doing we shall return to in a moment.

The authors go on to show that a number of the children's spontaneous utterances could not have been directly imitated from anything they had heard (for example, 'Cowboy did fighting me') and they suggest that these are 'mistakes which externalize the child's search for the regularities of English syntax'.

The facts to be explained are these. That from almost their first words children produce utterances they have never heard anyone else say: that the majority of these are in general accordance with the rules of English syntax: that by the time a child is six years old he is likely to be able to produce 'well-formed', that is grammatically acceptable, sentences covering all the basic sentence types in the English language. (Hockett, 1953, p. 860) Imitating what he hears other people say would not take a child any distance along this road.

Somehow, then [to quote Brown and Bellugi], every child processes the speech to which he is exposed so as to induce from it a latent structure. This latent structure is so general that a child can spin out its implications all his life long. It is both semantic and syntactic. The discovery of latent structure is the greatest of the processes involved in language acquisition and the most difficult to understand.

To make explicit, to describe, the system that the child operates would be to write a grammar of the English language, something that taxes, as we know well enough, even the most learned of adults. What a child knows as a result of the processes we are considering is *how to do things* with words – he does not know (any more than most of us do) *what it is he is doing*.

As he listens to people talking he must be taking in more than they say: he must be perceiving the general *forms* utterances take: 'forms' in terms of what words may occur before and after what other words, that is to say in terms of the arrangement of classes of words. The classes have, ultimately, no other criterion than this 'arrangeability'. The forms make up what Brown and Bellugi call 'latent structure', and these authors suggest that children generate their own spontaneous utterances in accordance with it and even extend their knowledge of it by trying out variations on it. It may be that the listening is not so different from the speaking as would at first appear: George Miller, another American psychologist who is very much concerned with the way language works, once suggested* the possibility, as a speculation not yet supported by any evidence, that when we listen to somebody speaking, or read a book, we are able to take in the syntax of the sentences spoken or read because we

* In a lecture given in London in 1964.

are ourselves generating alternative possible sentence structures and matching with what we are given.

Other evidence suggests that the immediate imitation of adult speech, as in Brown and Bellugi's 'reductions', does not lead to grammatical progress. Susan Ervin, of the University of California, is impressed with the observation that children produce sentences which have *regular patterns* that are different from those of adult language; that it is sensible to think, therefore, in terms of a grammar peculiar to a child's language at a given stage of immaturity. She suggests that children may employ successive grammars – a series of changing systems that leads them finally to the system of adult speech. Approximation to the adult system she sees as largely brought about under the influence of listening to (and comprehending) adults: but the existence of the earlier systems reflects a *creative* tendency in children and a tendency to work by *analogy*. She sums up an account of some experiments thus:

The pattern of development, and the rules that might describe usage at a particular point in time, differed for these different sentence types and differed for different children. Yet there were rules; errors were not random.

In all these cases, we find that children seem to be disposed to create linguistic systems. . . . It is hard to conceive that children could, by the age of four, produce the extraordinarily complex and original sentences we hear from them if they were not actively, by analogic extension, forming classes and rules. (Ervin, 1964, p. 186)

All three authors referred to in this paragraph have contributed points of detail to what might be called 'the grammar of young children's two-word utterances'.

Similar work has been done by another American author, Ruth Weir (whose book is described more fully on pp. 79 ff). She suggests that, in the particular monologues of her two-and-a-half-year-old son that she analyses, three kinds of sequence occur that would not be part of the grammar of normal English.

47

They indicate, rather, transitional stages on the way to that grammar. The first kind she called 'build-ups', as in:

> *Donkey*
> *Fix the donkey*

or in:

> *Block*
> *Yellow block*
> *Look at all the yellow block*
>
> (Weir, 1962, pp. 80 and 82)

The second – which she called 'break-downs' – work in the opposite direction:

> *Anthony jump out again*
> *Anthony jump*

And the third are 'completions'; they are sentences delivered, as it were, in two or more stages, but without the repetition (as in the build-up) of the whole put together:

> *Look at those pineapple*
> *In a pretty box*

And:

> *Bobo's goes*
> *To the bathroom*
> *Clean off*
>
> (Weir, 1962, pp. 82 and 83)

Dr Weir explains these transitional sequences as follows:

The production of a sentence at first try often overtaxes the child's linguistic capacity, and speech measures from the intended sentence may appear, preceding or following it; unauthorised pauses sometimes also intrude and separate phrases intended to be a single sentence . . .

These three cases give us build-ups, break-downs and completions respectively. (Weir, 1962, p. 144)

Work on the grammar of young children's utterances opens

up fascinating possibilities, most of them as yet to be explored.

Leaving the matter of syntax, I want to go back to the examples from Brown and Bellugi of the mothers' extensions and see what else was afoot, over and above the grammatical. When the child said 'Mommy sandwich' and the mother 'Mommy'll have a sandwich', she did so in the light of the situation. (In another situation the same remark from the child might have been turned into, 'Mommy didn't eat her sandwich' or in another, 'Yes, Mommy will make you a sandwich'.) What she is doing is to verbalize more of the situation than the child has done, make more of the situation explicit. Often she will do so experimentally because the child's utterance could be taken to imply different formulations and in order to enter into the conversation she needs to know which he intended. Where her utterance is simply and truly a more explicit version of his (that is to say there has been no change in what is being formulated) the mother will be demonstrating the process of 'making more explicit'. As she does so repeatedly over a variety of situations she presents the dimensions along which in our society we represent experience: how we place it in time and in space. To quote from Brown and Bellugi's original account, 'It seems to us that a mother, in expanding speech, may be teaching more than grammar; she may be teaching something like a world view.' (Brown and Bellugi 1964, p. 148)

To present the situation as still less like 'the language lab of the nursery', I should like to take one more look at it, with the idea of imitation kept well in the background. The point to be made is similar in orientation to one that arose in connexion with the twenty-one-month-old girl who practised how to say 'coffee'. The way a small child construes experience differs from the way his mother does: these two different ways come into contact on occasions of the kind we are considering: the situation is shared, and the language of each is focused upon it. The mother's experimental expansions are attempts to *learn* how the infant is construing the situation, and they are matched by utterances on the part of the child, for he also formulates experimentally and tries again.

In most ordinary relaxed conversations we are interested both in the topic and in the other person. The question, 'What is he like?' presents itself, in relation to such occasions, in the form of, 'What does he make of things? How does he see the world?'. (It may at times go under in favour of a concern for the topic and 'Why can't he see it straight?' – i.e. the way I see it – but it is unlikely to be entirely absent.) With the mother and child the relationship will not be a straightforwardly reciprocal one. The overwhelming question for the infant might be formulated, 'What is it like to be *me*, here, at this moment?' Of course, no such formulation is possible to him: 'me, here, at this moment' probably represents for him an undissociated whole, one that makes no clear distinction between the self, the mother's self, and the surrounding here and now. As Piaget has put it, 'his ego is mingled with his picture of both people and material things'. (Piaget, 1959, p. 272) Thus, 'What does she make of the world?', 'What is the world like?' and 'What am I like?' are all questions that are conflated into the one.

Clearly (and this is the point I am making) the *onus lies on the mother*. If in such situations 'experience *as we*' is to be used to build the common world in which they live, she must succeed in her efforts to enter into his way of construing experience. (Children have to face disappointments, it is true. 'He has to learn' is a statement that in general cannot be denied. But its application in a particular situation will be just or unjust in accordance with *our* ability to appreciate the nature of the re-construing of the *child's* world it demands of him.)

III

Exploration of the here and now begins from birth, becomes a more evident activity once a baby can crawl, continues on a new level when names give an additional dimension to objects, and goes on to make full use of talk as a further instrument of inquiry and a means of facilitating activities. From about two years of age most children are prolific talkers. (Valentine notes that a transcript of one day's talk by a two-and-a-half-year-old occupied twenty-seven pages of a learned journal.) At this early stage, the talking mainly consists, where this is possible, of highly active, sociable and inquisitive exchanges with parents and other members of the household. It is from listening to conversation that children gain experience of language before they can talk, and conversation provides the framework for their first efforts in speech.

The verbal exchanges will normally accompany, or rather form a part of, a continuous chain of activity. A transcript of such talk is meaningless unless we are given some idea of what is going on. The two-and-a-half-year-old (Alison) in the following record has her four-and-a-half-year-old sister (Clare) and her father to talk to (though her father is rather occupied with what he is doing):

ALISON: Mummy give me some milk! I'm a baby. Hna-hna! Hna-hna! I'm a baby – listen to this baby! Hna-hna! Hna-hna!

CLARE: What's she say? 'Hna-hna: hna-hna'?

ALISON: . . . have my Teddy and tucker.

CLARE: Get on, get on! (*addressed to a stool with a belt around it for stirrups*).

ALISON: What are you going to do?

CLARE: Get on this. Dad, don't think these stirrups are very good 'cos your knees stick up over the horse's back. Dad. Just can't get my knees down. (*She starts to sing, gets off the stool and says to Alison who is by now playing with the doll's house*): Now get on my back. And I'll take you round and round.

ALISON: I want to sweep. Now all going to have a lovely sweep. Sweep the kitchen.

CLARE: That's not the kitchen. That's the bedroom. And that's the bathroom. (*Silence.*) I'll ask that ole Mum if dinner's ready. (*She goes out.*)

ALISON: I tripped with my shoe lace. . . . Open door! Open

door! Want to go shopping. (*At the door.*) Want to go shopping this way Dad! Open door! (*He does so. Alison goes out, comes back with a large shopping basket filled with odds and ends. Clare is with her.*)

CLARE (*sings*):

> I danced over water I skipped over sea
> All the birds in the air couldn't catch me
> I skipped as slow as I could over water
> I danced as slow as I could over sea
> All the silly birds in the air couldn't catch me.

ALISON: I've gone shopping. Could you have any spouts today?

CLARE: What?

ALISON: Could you have any spouts today?

CLARE: Spouts? You mean sprouts.

ALISON: No, spouts.

CLARE: Of teapots and things?

ALISON: Yes.

CLARE: Well, did you know that I have?

ALISON: No.

CLARE: Well I have.

ALISON: Where?

CLARE: In the kitchen.

ALISON: Dad, will you open the door – I want to find the teapots.

CLARE: No, spouts. Teapots and spouts's the same thing.

ALISON: Open the door, Daddy! (*But she is persuaded to stay.*) I'm just going shopping for a minute. I'm going to get Henry. (*Henry, a stuffed toy dog, is on the table.*)

CLARE: Well get him.

ALISON: Can't . . . heavy. You . . . (*Clare takes her basket for her.*)

CLARE: Surely you can!

ALISON: Can't.

CLARE: Put one foot on one, and one on . . . and get him. Only put one foot on.

ALISON: Can't.

CLARE: Well have your heavy things, then, and I'll get it. (*Does so.*) Didn't try hard enough, did you? If you want to fall down just put *both* feet on the doll's house. . . . Don't suppose you want to.

52

ALISON: I'm going to school. Going to leave my things. You have him (*gives Teddy to Father*). You have him (*gives Henry to Clare*). Good-bye.
CLARE: Good-bye.
ALISON: See you soon.
CLARE: See you soon.
ALISON: Good-bye. Just going to school. Good-bye.

The two-and-a-half-year-old uses talk to initiate activity, to carry the action in the make-believe scenes, to comment upon what she is doing, and to get cooperation from other people. Her talk at this stage with an adult tended to be rather more inquisitive, and rather less 'active' than is found here.*

There is at first not a great deal of difference between talk of the kind we have looked at and the talking aloud that accompanies solitary activity. In the following example, Clare at twenty months is sitting on the floor surrounded with things and talking to herself. While her language is quite obviously less advanced than Alison's at two and a half ('Buy shoes', 'Going shopping' as compared with Alison's 'I want to sweep', 'Want to go shopping' and 'I've gone shopping'), it shows a similarly close relationship between what is happening and what is said, and it is spoken in a similar conversational tone.

Oh, nice comfy comfy girl. Nice comfy comfy girl.
Put shoes on. Show Mummy.
  (*Her mother puts her head in the door for a moment and withdraws again.*)
Mummy come back. (*Not as a request but a flat statement.*)
Cee's bricks. Ballee. (*She gets it.*)
In there. And Cee's nappy. (*Putting things in a shopping basket.*)
Shoes. Shoes shoes. Shoes shoes.
Look Teddy. See-saw Margery Daw,
              Johnny ave a noo mas-sur. (*Sing-song, rocking to and fro.*)

*For an example of talk between a two- to three-year-old and an adult, see p. 91.

(*Puts shoe on her hand.*) Glove.
Buy shoes. Buy shoes for Cee. Going shopping. Nice.
Take-a your basket. Going shopping.

I quote this for its interest as a forerunner. Such fragmentary talk accompanying fragmentary activity leads to a highly characteristic and important kind of talk, the running commentary. This is a monologue that many children use frequently to accompany the sort of sustained activity they are capable of at three or four years old.

This is Fiona, aged four years and one month, drawing a picture. She spoke in rather soft tones except where she addressed a remark to her granny, and here she spoke in clear conversational tones. (The remarks of this kind are printed in italic.)

I'm going to draw a picture now.
Big park and another bit of it coming below. Two bits of it. Colour it in and make it all into one park. Draw St James's Park.
Look! Now I'm going to draw a person walking around.
A little round head. A little eye and another little eye. A little nose. A little mouth. And how big the body is and there's the feet. Hands.
I'm drawing a little girl in the park.
That's a little girl walking round.
What nice coloured clothes she's got on. What lovely coloured clothes. Clothes. Coloured clothes . . . (*she whispers to herself*).*

Clare at four years seven months is playing with a set of model farm animals and farm buildings. Again, the remarks made to her mother (italicized) were spoken in quite different tones from the rest of the talk:

Mummy look, the horses and cows in the same field – they're changing their field.

*With acknowledgement to Mrs E.W. Moore, formerly of the University of London Institute of Education, for permission to use this extract.

'N the farmer went and took his own cow and brought it in. Then the land-girl took her big horse back in and got Buttercup calf and brought it back and stayed and looked after it. 'N the chook-lady took its own mum and brought it beside. Then she went back and got the other calf and. – This one hadn't any. – She went back. – She went and took a horse into that field.

And then Mummy they all, all of them took the cowshed in the other field.

Last – when they could get. – Then sheep came through into the cows' field, and another one followed her. And she went and took the biggest horse carefully through the gate and put it down. And then the farmer came along and opened the gate and took the bull through. They couldn't let him stay there very long without a cage. And then they did it all up into one whole side 'cos the next thing they were going to – going to put the cowshed in so all the people, the land-girl and everything – the farmer – all the people went – all round the cowshed – the milk-lady and chook-lady and the bull-man, the milk-man and the land-girl. They all went at the front – then he went there and he went there. – Nobody holded the side they didn't need anybody. Then all of them lifted up and put it in the other field. Oh dear, some of the horses needed coming back so she went and took a donkey back. The land-girl and the milk-girl came in. – And one field was only for cows not for any other except cows. – One thing the cowshed – quite a lot were in the shed – two calves could go in one place in it. They put the bull in one corner – put his pen there – the bull in the pen. The cows and the milk – she went and – the milk – those people – and the land-girl stayed close beside her foal in an empty corner where there was quite enough room for her. And the sheep – they went in the horse field. The pig sty was put in. . . . (*The game goes on many minutes more, but there are no more comments.*)

So many features of the original speech are of course missing from the written version that it is perhaps difficult to draw satisfactory conclusions. I hope it may be clear nevertheless that in both extracts the differences between the remarks addressed to somebody and the running commentary did not lie only in the tone of voice used. At several points in the commentary there are gaps: sometimes what is unspoken can be supplied, but even when it cannot there is no breakdown in the stream of speech. ('Last – when they could get. – Then sheep came through . . .'; 'The cows and the milk – she went and – the milk – those people'.) It seems likely that satisfactory moving of the pieces was enough, left no sense of incompletion arising from the utterance. That is to say, joint action-and-speech remains continuous though the utterance is broken. The conversationally directed remarks, on the other hand, are pretty firm statements complete in themselves: usually they are statements of intention or recapitulations of the situation.

Both extracts illustrate the fact that the commentary has a tendency to 'go underground'. In particular, the second one suggests that with the end of a problem in sight the support of the commentary was no longer felt necessary, and the activity was satisfactorily concluded in silence.

This introduces an important new hypothesis: that the verbalizing does in fact provide support for the activity. Clare has her toy farm laid out in front of her – fields with fences and gates and full of people, animals, sheds: and she sets herself the problem of organizing by so to speak 'realistic' methods a general post. There are 'rules' obviously arising from previous play – whose job it is to look after what, which cow the calf belongs to, and so on. As she makes her successive moves, new aspects of the problem and further possible moves reveal themselves; and – to come to the point – I think we can perceive her verbalizing these as they arise. Thus, 'She went back' in line 7 seems to be amended, as the idea strikes her, to, 'She went and *took a horse*'; when the farmer arrives with the bull it becomes apparent to her, we presume, that being a dangerous animal he can't be left unpenned and untended; again, she seems to work, in speech, towards the problem of disposing the people who are to lift the cowshed – the first move by which they are all at the front has to be amended to put the two men at points elsewhere, and the problem of the un-manned side is then solved, aloud, by dismissing it: 'Nobody holded the side they didn't need anybody'. Finally, it is clearly indicated that when all that is successfully managed a new problem arises: 'Oh dear . . .'.

The running commentary is in fact a characteristic form of what Vygotsky called 'speech for oneself'. The child, he suggests, learns to speak in the to-and-fro of talk with those about him, that is to say in speech that has the form of *social speech*. But once he has learned to speak, he uses speech to serve his own development – or, roughly speaking, as an aid to his own exploratory activities. What Fiona was doing when she drew St James's Park and what Clare was doing in manipulating her models were, in this general sense, 'exploratory activities'. Such activity is not of course restricted to solitary occupations and running commentary: it was actively present in the social exchanges between Clare and Alison quoted above, and it characterizes talk with an adult. The point to be made is that when activity *is* solitary, the child at this stage may still need to use talk in support of his activity, whether or not anyone is listening. The speech is both *to* himself, in the sense that it seeks no response from a listener, and *for* himself in that it helps him do whatever it is he is doing.

Obviously, a child does not give up social forms of speech when he begins to use 'speech for himself'. The two forms are at first undifferentiated, being early social speech in substance, put to two uses. But as the two uses become established, modification of the form takes two directions: social speech becomes better communication, while speech for oneself becomes *less* communicative, more individualized, better able to serve the particular purposes and interests of a particular child. Thus, the early monologue at twenty months quoted on p. 53 is a form of speech that differs in some respects from the remarks addressed by Fiona and Clare to their listeners, and in other respects from the language of their running commentaries.

It has been shown, on the basis of a number of observations, that the running commentary grows in prominence in the speech of most children from the age of about three, is at a peak at four and five (incorporating some changes in its character which we shall describe shortly) and declines until at seven it is a comparatively rare occurrence. Alternative explanations have been given to account for its decline. Piaget believed that it disappeared as a child's speech became more effective *as communication*. He described monologue, including the running commentary, as 'egocentric speech' and in doing so made an important point which we must consider before going any further.

We have indicated that a child's first speaking takes the form of a conversational exchange: we could have added that a young child is a poor conversationalist. He speaks from his own point of view and is incapable of taking up any other. Effective communication, on the other hand, demands that a speaker take into account the view-point – and the knowledge and experience and interests – of his listener. It is common enough to find mothers and fathers acting as interpreters to other people of what their small child is trying to say. From intimate knowledge of the child and all his circumstances (including of course his speech habits), they are able to understand his speech in spite of the egocentric view-point he expresses.

Children [says Piaget] are perpetually surrounded by adults who not only know much more than they do, but who also do everything in their power to understand them, who even anticipate their thoughts and their desires. Children, therefore . . . are perpetually under the impression that people can read their thoughts, and in extreme cases, can steal their thoughts away.

When they talk to other children, therefore, they usually fail to understand each other for the very reason that 'they think that they do understand each other'. (Piaget, 1959, p. 101)

Perhaps the best illustration of a child's egocentrism of view-point is that given by Piaget when he says, 'a boy of six to seven years old is ready to declare that he had a brother but that that brother has himself no brother'. It is a matter of being unable to step outside himself in order to see the world from another person's point of view: thus it is equally a sign of egocentrism that a young child will often omit himself altogether when he tries to count how many people there are in the room. (Piaget, 1959, p. 275) This limitation of view-point will affect in some degree everything a child says: it is Piaget's point that attempts to converse run counter to this egocentrism, whereas the running commentary and other forms of monologue run with it. (He divides early speech into two categories: *egocentric speech* – the monologue; and *socialized speech* which includes questions and answers, requests, and information that has undergone some kind of adaptation to take into account the demands of a listener.) Piaget regards the gradual disappearance of the running commentary as a natural consequence of a child's improved ability to internalize his listener, to escape from the limitations of his own view-point: egocentric speech is, according to Piaget, gradually replaced by a more mature form, socialized speech.

It was Vygotsky who, in commenting upon Piaget's ideas, pointed out that a child's first speech derives from conversations he has listened to and takes the form of social interchange as we have seen: and that only later does the speech thus acquired come to be used in monologue. He stressed the function of monologue, that of assisting activity, organizing a child's experience.

This function, exhibited for all to hear in the running commentary, was one which Vygotsky felt continued to be necessary: and if the need continued it seemed unlikely that the speech process would merely wither away. Vygotsky did not therefore speak in terms of 'egocentric speech' developing into 'socialized speech', but of 'social speech' developing in two distinct directions under the influence of two distinct uses. In continuing to serve the purposes of social exchange it becomes, as we have already seen, more *communicative*, better able to take account of a listener's point of view, and increasing in range and complexity. As *speech for oneself*, or egocentric speech, it becomes individuated and abbreviated: individuated in order to suit, as we have seen, an individual child's own interests and purposes: abbreviated in the sense that parts of the utterance would be left unspoken – since the child is talking to himself he needs to verbalize only the changing elements in his theme and not those that stay constant. (For example, in Fiona's commentary on p. 54: '*Now I'm drawing* a little round head. *Now I'm drawing* a little eye and another little eye. *Now I'm drawing* a little nose. . . .') Thus social speech and speech for oneself in this respect develop in opposite directions: a listener's needs are more and more taken into account in social speech and less and less considered in speech for oneself – appropriately enough since in this case a listener is, so to speak 'vestigial'.

The drift of all this towards Vygotsky's final explanation will be clear enough. He believed that the monologue did not fall out of use or wither away, but became internalized, became what he called 'inner speech'. As such it continued its function of supporting a child's activities, but in accordance with the simple logic that if we talk to ourselves and not to a listener we do not need to talk aloud. Vygotsky saw the increasing individuation as indicating both the adaptation of speech to the purpose of serving individual needs and by the same token as a reason for its becoming silent: its vocalization became 'unnecessary and meaningless and, because of its growing structural peculiarities, also impossible'. (Vygotsky, 1962, p. 135) It is conceivable that some of the incomplete utterances in Clare's monologue (p. 55) are half spoken because they are too difficult to find words for. She seems, for example, to be concerned with some sort of calculation as to whether there will be room for all the animals when she says, 'And one field was only for cows not for any other except cows. – One thing the cowshed – quite a lot were in the shed – two calves could go in one place in it.'

There will presumably be times when the commentary raises problems which cannot be solved either with or without the help of speech: and other times when the commentary is used to raise a problem and a strategy is worked out for its solution with the help of egocentric speech at a level more advanced than that at which it can be uttered (in accordance with Vygotsky's thesis). Which of the two situations is represented in this example cannot be inferred from the record.

Here, at all events, is Vygotsky's explanation in his own words:

To explain this [i.e. the decrease in egocentric speech] let us start from an undeniable, experimentally established fact. The structural and functional qualities of egocentric speech become more marked as the child develops. At three, the difference between egocentric and social speech equals zero; at seven, we have speech that in structure and function is totally unlike social speech. A differentiation of the two speech functions has taken place. This is a fact – and facts are notoriously hard to refute.

Once we accept this, everything else falls into place. If the developing structural and functional peculiarities of egocentric speech progressively isolate it from external speech, then its vocal aspect must fade away; and this is exactly what happens between three and seven years. . . . To interpret the sinking coefficient of egocentric speech as a sign that this kind of speech is dying out is like saying that the child stops counting when he ceases to use his fingers and starts adding in his head. In reality, behind the symptoms of dissolution lies a progressive development, the birth of a new speech form. (Vygotsky, 1962, pp. 134–5)

The new speech form is 'inner speech', the child's 'new faculty to "think words" instead of pronouncing them'.

The respect, therefore, in which the speech of the twenty-month-old-child talking to herself differs from the monologues of the four-year-olds – a point we raised on p. 57 – is in the degree to which the utterance represents the total verbal activity. Both kinds of utterance are fragmentary, but in different ways.

With the younger child, what is spoken is all she is able to verbalize: the rest is unconquered territory; and the nature of her behaviour in general reflects this, for her interests and activities are also fragmentary. With the older children, the gaps represent (in general) a substitution of inner speech for talking aloud. We commented earlier on the sustained nature of their activity, and spoke of a continuity of action-with-speech (p. 56). We can now see it as a continuity both of action and of verbalization, using the word to embrace audible speech and inner speech.

It seemed plausible to interpret Clare's silence as she completed her game with the farm as indicating a decline in the difficulties of her undertaking: when the most complicated part of the manoeuvre was over she was able to dispense with words and complete it in silence. Vygotsky's experiments and observations would support this conclusion: he found that speech for oneself in older children changed from an inner to a spoken form when their difficulties rose above a certain level. It is probably true for most of us as adults that we speak our problems aloud in moments of unusual stress: I certainly remember checking off audibly what I had done to try and make the car start when still it wouldn't.

Vygotsky went to great pains to observe the changing characteristics of the monologue as children grow older, because he perceived here a unique opportunity, that of finding out what inner speech itself was like. The changes he perceived in 'speech for oneself' before it finally became silent might be presumed to indicate the direction in which further changes would take place: if we project them we might arrive therefore at some idea of the processes of thinking itself, first in the form of inner speech, and then, more remotely, in the form of verbal thought.

We have already referred to these changes as abbreviation and individuation. As a child accompanies verbally what he sees or hears or does at any moment, he will tend to omit reference to the constants in the situation and refer only to what happens to them or what additional characteristics he notices: in other words the subjects of sentences tend to be suppressed and only the predicates put into words. Other relationships usually expressed in ordinary conversation will often be omitted also, so that the speech becomes discontinuous, fragmented. Our tendency to create private associations for words – associations arising from our own particular experience and not *generally* recognized – is something we must keep a close control over when we speak to be understood: but when a child has no audience in mind and speaks to himself, such associations may be a very valuable part of his commentary. In a similar way, he may join words together to make compound words which are highly meaningful for him, but only for him. (In telling herself long stories about big girls, Clare at three years nine months, told about one who went to an 'eighteen-school' and another who had 'tall-up socks and mummy-long pants': not, I realize, that these are unintelligible to us, perhaps because they come at an early stage, but they may serve to illustrate the word-building process.)

Vygotsky distinguished between the 'meaning' of a word and its 'sense', the latter being all the private and peripheral associations of it ('the sum of all the psychological events aroused in our consciousness by the word'), and goes on to say that in inner speech 'a word is so saturated with sense that many words would be required to explain it in external speech'.

Beyond the plane of inner speech lies the further plane of thought itself. Vygotsky sees speech, inner speech and thought dynamically related in this way:

Inner speech is not the interior aspect of external speech – it is a function in itself. It still remains speech, i.e. thought connected with words. But while in external speech thought is embodied in words, in inner speech words die as they bring forth thought. Inner speech is to a large extent thinking in pure meanings. It is a dynamic, shifting, unstable thing, fluttering between word and thought, the two more or less stable, more or less firmly delineated components of verbal thought.

Speech consists of separate units in a temporal sequence: thought has no such divisions. 'Direct communication between minds is impossible, not only physically but psychologically. Communication can be achieved only in a roundabout way. Thought must pass first through meanings and then through words.' (Vygotsky, 1962, pp. 149–50) The journey is not always completed: Vygotsky quotes at the head of the chapter we have been considering this extract from a Russian poem: 'I have forgotten the word I intended to say, and my thought, unembodied, returns to the realm of shadows.'

The air may be too thin for some travellers when speculation reaches these heights. They may be comforted, however, to realize that the term 'post-language symbols' has been widely used to refer to some of the elements we deploy in our thinking. There can in my view be no reasonable doubt that talk in infancy is the beginning of a developmental process that finishes where we can no longer observe it, in the workings of a man's mind.

IV

The examples of speech we have considered so far have shown a general tendency to be intelligible only to someone who shared, or was told about, the situation in which they were spoken. We have suggested a function for much of the speech at this stage that would go some way towards explaining this tendency: that talk is used to support the speaker's activity within the situation. We shall now make the categorical observation that a child's talk during the first eighteen months or so of speaking shows a marked change in this particular respect; from being closely interlocked with the situation and his activities in it, it becomes, by the end of the period, capable of comparative independence. With one exception, the examples of speech at eighteeen months given on pp. 34–5 relate to things present in the situation and actions taking place. 'Dadda did mower' is an exception in that the remark was called forth by a word referring to something the child cannot see ('garden') and prompts her to refer to something she *had* seen (not many hours earlier) but cannot now see. Early speech shows a marked pre-occupation with the here and now, and the words comprising it will rarely refer outside the immediate surroundings; but there will be exceptions, words for example referring to things that were already familiar and important to the child before he spoke at all (e.g. 'Mummy') and words that have become associated with particularly striking and pleasurable experiences.

Thus, what happens somewhere around the age of three in most children does represent a milestone in their speech development. Their ability both to understand and to use words comes to rely less and less on the cues offered by the present situation: that is to say, words begin to stand *in place of* things. Perhaps we can best appreciate the importance of the change by looking at what it is that a child cannot do until he has achieved it. He cannot make much in speech of other times and other places: he cannot recount what he did on some previous occasion nor outline what he is going to do – except at short term and in direct relation with objects of the here and now (e.g. 'Put it there for after my supper'). This is a difficult point to be clear about: obviously a young child plays with many objects that are *familiar*: that is to say, past experience of them enters into his present activities with regard to them, and his talk while he does so may reflect that experience. But, at this earlier stage, it is *their presence* that enables him to revive his past experience: at a later stage he will be able to call them to mind in their absence, bring them into the conversation, or go and seek them out.

The support speech can offer to his activities is noticeably strengthened by this change. When instead of accompanying action, as in the running commentary pure and simple, he is able to *anticipate* action, the commentary becomes as it were a plan. The Russian psychologist Luria, following up the work of Vygotsky, made a special study of this aspect of speech. He showed that both 'narrative speech', recounting the past, and 'planning speech', anticipating action, arise from the running commentary once a child's language transcends the bounds of the immediate present. And in particular, that the act of formulating a plan in words has the effect of increasing a child's ability to resist the distractions of other cues in the environment and carry the plan to its conclusion. The verbalization has in fact a *regulatory function*.

Fiona's remark, 'Look! Now I'm going to draw a person walking around!' in the extract on p. 54 is a clear example of planning speech: in fact all the remarks that step out of the commentary and are addressed to the adult in the monologues of both Fiona and Clare (pp. 54–5) have something of this character. It is as though, at this comparatively early stage, the stock-taking and plan-making functions and the desire to bring the adult into the activity coincide and are mutually supportive.

Luria offers striking evidence of the importance of language as a regulator of behaviour when he describes work he did with a pair of five-year-old identical twin boys. When he found them, their speech was retarded, partly as a result of the fact that they were twins and did not need much skill as talkers to get on happily with each other, and partly for other reasons, social and physiological. He estimated that they were about two years behind the normal in speech development: not only this, they were similarly backward in many aspects of their behaviour.

The content of their play [he tells us] was always very primitive and monotonous and led to the manipulation of objects independently of any other aspect of the play materials provided. Not once was there observed any tendency to the simplest construction with building materials; cubes were only piled up or laid in a row on the ground. They liked large building materials but their play with these consisted only in transporting them from one corner to another without any attempt to use them for building. Play of a creative, meaningful character was rare and extremely monotonous, being repeated without variations. Such games as lotto did not attract their attention at all.

The twins seldom played with the other children [*in the kindergarten*] and only occasionally took part in mobile games with simple actions, such as chasing and catching and 'train' which do not require strict division of roles nor unification of the separate elements of play in a general imaginative whole; they never took part in complex meaningful play nor in such creative activities as modelling, drawing etc. Only after several months did they produce their first 'drawing', a few greasy marks with paint which obviously did not correspond to their age. (Luria and Yudovich, 1959, pp. 33–4)

In the course of ten months Luria was able to bring the speech level of the twins up to the level normal for their age: and in that time their behaviour changed from that of three-year-olds to that of six-year-olds.

All these improvements took place within a very short period, during which, of course, natural 'maturation' played only an insignificant role but which was marked by the introduction of an important new factor in the shape of a leap forward in speech development. This permits us to deduce that improvements in the productive activity of both twins took place in close connection with the acquisition of a language system which introduced new potentialities for the organisation of the child's mental life. (Luria and Yudovich, 1959, p. 102)

The experimental treatment that was so effective with the twins was simply a matter of placing them in different groups in the kindergarten in which Luria found them. As an additional experiment, one of them was given individual help in the form of regular 'conversation classes' and speech exercises: while this made him progress a little faster and go a little further,* the differences between them after ten months were minor compared with the major change from 'before' to 'after' that both had undergone.

It has been known for some time that a particular kind of damage to the speech area of the brain may leave a patient's powers of conversation superficially unaffected and yet rob him of the power of speech to control behaviour: he is unable to pursue any verbalized purpose. From such evidence, J. R. Firth, the English linguist, wrote in 1930: 'It appears probable that the physical basis of speech is part of the central machinery for the control and co-ordination of behaviour.' (Firth, 1930, p. 152) Experiments carried out more recently, by Luria and others associated with him, indicate several stages in the development of the regulatory function of speech. At the earliest, speech will have an impelling function but not an inhibiting one: children of twenty to twenty-four months were told to put a set of rings on to a bar and began to do so: while they were busy at it, they were given the instruction, 'Take them off' – and the effect was to intensify the putting on! With three-year-olds, performances in button-pressing experiments (e.g. 'When the green light comes on, press') were clearly improved when they used their own speech to accompany action. At this stage, however, it appears to be the *act of speaking* and not *what is spoken* that has the principal effect: when the instruction was to press twice, performance was improved when the child said, 'Go! Go!' (a double prod, so to speak), but not when he said, 'I shall press twice'. Similarly when the instruction was 'Press

*'Twin A who had undergone continuous systematic exercises in speech, developed a "*theoretical attitude*" *towards speech* proper to his age. In case of this twin, speech became an object of special perceptual activity, its structure was perceived, and precisely because of this elementary discursive operations became accessible to him while remaining inaccessible to the other twin.' (Luria and Yudovich, 1959, p. 119)

for every third signal', and the child said, 'Press – don't press – don't press' the effect was a devastating increase in wrong button pressing! Luria suggests that the final stage, the effective regulation of behaviour by their own speech in terms of what it means, is not reached by most children before they are four years old. By that time also 'speech for oneself' carrying the regulative function will be beginning to move from audible to inner speech. (Luria, 1961)

Perhaps the idea that we use language to regulate our own behaviour can more easily be made to seem feasible in other ways. We have already referred to the fact that a child of a month old is soothed by the sound of his mother's voice even when he cannot see her; and we have commented upon the eagerness with which a twelve-month-old child will 'obey' simple verbal instructions. Such confidence and such cooperation suggest that human speech – in the voices of those about him – comes to be associated from an early age with the possibility of satisfaction and achievement in a world which may otherwise seem threatening and confusing. If for him the 'grown-up world' stands for love and law and order – a powerful combination – and if he invests human speech with these properties – it may well be that when he takes over speech for his own use it retains such properties and is able to exercise a co-ordinating and regulating function over other forms of his behaviour.

To put it in this way may, however, be to claim too much for language. Before a child can 'make something' of experience, in the sense of turning it to his advantage, he must 'make something' of it in the sense of reducing the flux to order: and there can be no doubt whatever that language is a principal agent in achieving this in all normal cases. It is to the 'interpretative function' of language that we turn our attention now.

'Narrative speech', recounting what has happened, is of course speech that is not involved with action as it is in the running commentary. The running commentary *is* a kind of narrative, but action may well substitute for some of its links, whereas in recounting the past all that is relevant will be put into words. The first appearance of narrative speech may be an occasional reference to past events in talk mainly concerned with the present; as in this conversation between Stephen (aged two years ten months) and his mother while he plays with his trains:

That's going on – on – on the carriages. That's going to go next to the carriages – you see? And we shall put on the brake, you see? We shall put on the brake. We got the diesel trains haven't we? I play with that, then Jonathan played with that train and then I played with those two trains. And he played with Punch and Judy when Daddy was ready to go to work.

(Did he?)

Yes, he did. . . . Then fall down like this. Oh that's going to go on this, do you see? And then it's got a (. . . ?) like that. Mine's a black engine, isn't it? And that engine is going to be on that train you see. . . . There – I get up on my lap – your lap myself, didn't I? You didn't pick me up, did you? no –

(You're a big boy now.)

I put my feet down there – so they won't get out of the way – will it? When I was a little boy I used to (. . . ?) myself – like Daddy – Mm – I did.

(You used to *what*?)

A little boy – I used to be a little boy years ago, weren't I?

(Mm. Was it a very long time ago?)

Yes, it was – it was . . .

(How long?)

At six o'clock I was a tiny boy – yes – now I'm a big boy like Daddy, aren't I? and when I'm a big boy like Daddy I always to put that fire on – and know how to put it off . . .*

But at this age a talkative child will tell the story of his recent activities to anyone who is prepared to listen, and it is one of

* With acknowledgements to Mrs P. D'Arcy for permission to use this extract.

70

the most *sociable* forms of his behaviour. 'I went shopping with Mummy and we went to the butcher's and I told her where your car was. . . . My Daddy went horse riding and he got sore.' (Neville, a boy of two years three months.) As we listen to the chatter it is easy to underestimate the value of such everyday formulations as *interpretation*: the flux of events has undergone considerable change before it reaches the sequence and definition of a narrative, even a simple one. For some children narrative speech comes into its own only when they have left home and gone to school – and come back at the end of the day, full of adventures. What a child makes of his school experiences may rely a good deal on the interested, unanxious, helpfully informed responses of the members of his family. He builds his school world into his home world with their help.

Though we interpret experience in the course of undergoing it, and the orienting speech, sizing up the situation, that is one feature of running commentary has an interpretative function, nevertheless it is in narrative speech that the focus is upon interpretation, and most of our interpretation is in fact done retrospectively (as we have already noticed, p. 30).

'Speech for oneself' incorporates narrative – and this is particularly true of a kind of monologue we have yet to consider. As 'speech for oneself', narrative speech undergoes in the course of time those changes by which it turns into inner speech. Going over past events in our minds must occupy for many of us a good deal of our spare time, and might be called the typical form of mental activity for many old people. It has been pointed out that 'memory', as we usually think of it, takes a narrative form. It may well be that the stage at which narrative speech becomes possible to a child is the point at which memory in this sense begins: recollections from an earlier stage are both sparse and fragmentary.

I believe narrative speech develops principally, however, as a *social* activity: the possible relevance to other people's lives of events that happen to each of us gives those events a general interest that one person's particular *plans* would be unlikely to have. Thus, though both planning speech and narrative speech may take the form either of 'speech for oneself' or social interchange, the stress differentiates them: development of the planning speech and the regulatory function are likely to take place mainly in a child's speech for himself, while narrative speech and the interpretative function are likely to develop mainly through his social speech.

To recount an event is to place a construction upon experience, to interpret it: but of course we interpret also more directly, explaining experience, commenting, bringing generalizations to bear upon it.

To speak of the interpretative function of language is to bring into focus the most important aspects of what this book is all about. We do not learn from the higgledy-piggledy of events as they strike the senses, but from the representation we make of them.

Clare, at two years three months, met strawberries for the first time. 'They're like cherries,' she said. And when she had tasted them 'They're just like sweeties'. And a little later, 'They are like red ladybirds'. Successive experiences had made some things familiar to her, and she draws on these in order to 'place' the new experience. From the familiar she creates links, a context, for the new. We employ the converse of the same process when we stigmatize something as 'neither fish, flesh nor good red herring'.

At the age of four, she made more complex generalizations in an attempt to interpret a more difficult experience: a small dog snapped at her heels when she was out for a walk, and after a little while she said:

Lots of people get frightened easily, don't they? Specially children. 'Cos they haven't had lots of things explained to them, have they? – so they get frightened. . . . Dogs and things get a bit sort of wild when they've changed their country and want to go back. That dog's a Scottie.

The generalizations describe her world: the whole effort in her comment seems to be directed towards reconciling an unfriendly act with her conception of the world as a friendly place. Interpretation implies making something of the new experience in the light of what is already familiar: but it implies in addition modifying the total picture towards being consistent with the new. If the world is a friendly place, children have no need to feel frightened and we must explain therefore why they sometimes do: and in a friendly world dogs should not snap at their friends – we must look for a reason why they sometimes do.

Alison, at the age of six and a half, took to watching her father go down the road in the mornings until he was right out of sight. One morning, after doing this faithfully for a couple of weeks, she left the window and went into the kitchen and explained to her mother, 'You see, I hate seeing things going away – even the bath-water!' Well, certainly the bath-water does go away, and some infants sometimes are distressed that it does. But Alison at six was dredging a long way back in her experience to bring this to light. Perhaps from infancy it had stood for 'things that go away and don't come back': like most young children she had not been easily comforted when lost or broken things were replaced by others even when they were so like the originals that she could not have told the difference. No doubt children have to learn from experience what are the possibilities, the limits of experience (and even, in due course, the *probabilities*, the odds for and against); they have to learn from experience what things go away and come back and what things go away and don't come back. There is no doubt that at the level of conscious expectations Alison knew her father would come back. But the uncertainty of her infancy, still alive, must have found expression in this situation – hence the need for a long, last look every morning. What her comment that morning attempted, then, may have been a deep-seated adjustment, the laying of a doubt about the world, rather than the interpretation of a daily occurrence. At all events, the morning ritual was no longer necessary and was soon given up and forgotten.

Nothing so momentous is afoot in most everyday talk. We will conclude this section with a record of one Saturday morning when Clare was four years eight months, and Alison was two and a half – Alison at the stage when speech remains pretty well tied to the here and now, the stage Luria's twins were at when he found them; Clare more like the twins were when he had completed his 'treatment'. Clare is sitting on the sofa with a drawing block on her knee and Alison is everywhere, pretending at first that she is a goat: and their father is sitting at the table, writing.

CLARE: I'll have to put you in the yard soon – with the horses and chickens and cows. Special department for you – you'll be the only goat. Oh no you won't – 'cos I bought the whole family – I think (*Alison is butting her, kicking up her legs.*) Eh! – stop it – what are you doing? Nanny! Nanny! (*Alison stops.*) Nice old fellow, Nanny, aren't you? (*More kicking.*) Oh – no – no – no! No, you funny old goat. 'Spect you'd like to go out with your friends – *if* you'll go. Will you, old goat? – old Nanny?

ALISON (*kicking*): The legs go up – let it down.

CLARE: Silly old thing, aren't you? (*To herself, at her drawing of a horse.*) Want to make your tail a bit shorter – that's what you're wanting. I wonder how we'll get you home – if it's dark? 'Spect we'll get you home all right.

ALISON: Two legs are going up!

CLARE: Nanny! You're a bad old goat. Nanny! What did I say – you're a bad old goat.

ALISON: No, I'm not!

CLARE: Yes you are – Goaty. Go over there to your fire. Get down! Go on! Go on you silly thing (*pushing her*) – go on! Now, there, there, can't come up. (*Alison starts to climb back on to the sofa.*) Eh! I said can't come up – naughty old goat.

ALISON: Good old goat. (*She goes over to Father.*) Daddy, I'm a *good* old goat.

74

CLARE: No you're not – you're a bad old goat.

ALISON (*indicating the pencil*): Daddy that's mine! What are you writing?

FATHER: I'm working.

CLARE: Eh, come and sit in your place – Goaty, come here! Come here, I said! . . . You bad old goat.

ALISON: I'm not a bad old goat, Daddy.

CLARE: Yes you are.

ALISON: I'm not a bad old goat, Daddy. Daddy, what's this! What's this – what's this, Daddy?

FATHER: It's a ruler.

CLARE: Are you a *parrot*?

ALISON: No, I'm a Nanny goat.

CLARE: Well you sound like a parrot anyway.
(*Clare goes on drawing, muttering over it: Alison is examining the ruler on the table.*)

ALISON: Mm – mm . . . Father! Hello, Father!

FATHER: Hello, Alison.

ALISON: Hello, Father – I want to ? ? ? (*Crawls under the table.*) Like this . . . (*Comes out again.*) This house is all – What are you doing, my Father?

FATHER: I'm writing.

ALISON: Oh, I don't want you to.

FATHER: Don't you, why?

ALISON: No. (*Climbs on the chair behind him.*) Daddy, I hurt two hands. (*She climbs down, goes to the window, climbs on a chair and makes continuous 'ff' noises: Clare is drawing, the fire is crackling.*)

ALISON: Daddy! (*She gets a shoe and starts taking the laces out.*)

CLARE (*to herself*): Inks – different colour inks . . .
(*Silence for several minutes.*)

ALISON: Daddy, want those shoes. They're my sweety shoes. Want those. (*Putting one on.*) This (*offering foot to Father.*) This shoe first – this shoe, Daddy. Are you ready? This shoe! This shoe, Daddy!

FATHER: But that's the wrong foot.

ALISON (*offering the right one*): This one. This foot. This little foot. (*Shoe is put on, she brings the other.*) This shoe on – I

don't want the door. Daddy, will you . . . (*she goes over to Clare*).
I'm a Nanny goat!

CLARE: Come on now – come on silly old thing. See what you
can do up here. That's the thing to do. (*Helps her on to sofa.*)
Now you're not drawing any more, I want your blue.

ALISON: No! *I* want it!

CLARE: But you weren't drawing, were you? Were you? I'm
drawing and I want the blue – you can't have the whole box.

ALISON: *I* want it! *I* want it!

CLARE: You can have a grey and a red and. . . . The grey's
instead of the blue, 'cos I need it.

ALISON: What are you drawing?

CLARE: A swimming pool – and there's a little girl swimming.
(*The door opens.*) Mummy – Ali's a little goat still, Mummy!

While all this was taking place, Clare completed two drawings, one of a horse and one of a girl diving into a pool – both
matters relating back to her particular interests on holiday
three months earlier – interests that she had talked about a good
deal at other times. Alison's 'here, there and everywhere'
behaviour has a thread of continuity only in 'acting the goat',
and we might infer from the dialogue that Clare did more than
Alison to keep that game going: probably (as mothers do) with
the idea of occupying the child and keeping herself free from
interruption. In her speech and in her activities Alison is still
very strongly influenced by what is there – and what is going
on – round her, shifting her attention from one thing to another
as they 'come her way'. The only clear reference she makes to
anything outside the situation is when she speaks of her
'sweetie shoes' – shoes for her mean shopping, and shopping
means buying sweets! And this, of course, is provoked by the
shoe itself. Clare's speech includes planning speech – and part
of that is 'muttered' and no doubt a good deal more was
already inner speech: the planning refers to drawings which
are based on previous experience, called to mind. And, for the
rest, her talk might be seen as an attempt to regulate in speech
not her own but Alison's behaviour!

V

This account of young children's speech cannot be completed without pointing out – and perhaps it should have been done before – that speech is noises. No doubt this is what Clare meant when someone asked her what a word is and she answered, 'Words are voices'. There is a substance to language, and for the non-reader, non-writer no choice as to what that substance is – sound. Moreover, children will respond to this substance as they do to every other, by playing with it. The story is told of a small boy, brought to collect his father from some psychological conference, dancing through the hall to the chant of 'Maximum capacity! Maximum capacity!' Enjoyment of the sounds of words is obvious in much of their talk, and overflows easily into the importation of word-like noises. Here for example is Clare at two years two months, with chalks and paper:

Big eye. There's a eye – there's a eye – there's a eye
    there's a little eye.
More big ones.
Draw a coat down.
Draw a ling-a-ling-a-ling.
Draw a little thing – little ear squeer
    big eye – little ear here – *eye!*
A little girl called Sinky and she's *walking*.
And there's Humpty Dumpty – pull him down!
Is that too tight? No it isn't!
There's papa – there's his hat – and there's a man called Simon
    looking after him. . . .
My big brother is called – don't remember what he's called.
P'raps my big brother is called Babbu.
And he goes crawly-crawly and he slides about - like this!
And my big sister's called Hunky. I'm writing to my sister.
I'm writing to my sister – I'm writing to my sister – and my big
    sister's called Hunkron, isn't she?

And Daddy's sister's called Grandma and my sister's called
Kronkilánma.
My sister's called Mac – aunty Mac – not uncle Mac – aunty
Mac – not uncle, aunty Mac. And aunty Clare and aunty Mac
– aunty Nance – aunty – (*Turning to her father*.) What are you
doing, Mrs Jimmy?

In most of our traffic with words we look *through* the substance to the meaning: the corporeal quality of a spoken word
is paid very scant attention in bare, ordinary discourse, and
properly so. Understanding such speech is a matter of reading
off vocal signals in their correct relation to each other within
the system. The actual sound of 'file' as I speak the word on a
given occasion has an absolute and not a relative value and does
not concern you as you listen to me: what concerns you is how
that sound in my speech relates to others – 'fail', 'foil' for
example – and only when, with the help of many contextual
clues, you have my sound placed in the system as I speak it will
the word be unambiguous to you. Of course we make rules for
ourselves that supersede these rules when it is more than bare,
ordinary discourse we are after: speakers care how they sound
for many reasons over and above intelligibility; lovers make
wooing noises with their words; and poetry is the supreme
example of a kind of utterance that employs the corporeal
qualities of speech (and of writing).

Experiments show that young children are not free to choose:
words are predominantly physical stimuli for them and only
gradually does the instrumental value, the meaning, come to
dominate. Luria found that children under three tended to
associate together words that *sounded* alike (e.g. 'drum' and
'dram'), but children over three tended to group together
words of similar *meaning* ('drum' and 'flute') (Luria and
Vinogradova, 1959). Their response to sound does not, however, disappear with this change of dominance. We could
perfectly well skip around to the sound of 'Maximum capacity' if we wanted to, but in fact the five-year-old is more likely
to choose to do so!

Play with words and other sounds is particularly marked in certain kinds of monologue. When we looked at monologue in the form of running commentary we saw that it seemed to serve the purpose of supporting the child's activities, and that this might be quite taxing: when a child is pursuing his curiosity in talk with an adult, that may, of course, be taxing too. But when he is talking to himself, and not engaged in any other activity – and particularly perhaps when he is sleepy – play with language seems naturally to take over: he talks then for the pleasure of using words. It has often been observed that children will talk to themselves in bed before they go to sleep, but no detailed study of it was available until Ruth Weir published, in America, in 1962, her *Language in the Crib*. Here she records and analyses the pre-sleep monologues of her two-and-a-half-year-old son Anthony over a period of about two months.

She provides us with some fascinating material. Anthony's play, she points out, often takes the form of 'playing upon' certain sounds: as for example the 'l' and 'k' sounds in (Weir, 1962, p. 104):

> blanket
> like a
> lipstick

And there seems to be no reason for bringing the following words together that would outweigh that of composing in terms of the labial sounds 'p' and 'b' and the velar sounds 'g' and 'k' and 'ng' (Weir, 1962, p. 104):

> Like a piggy bank
> Like a piggy bank
> Had a pink sheet on
> The grey pig out

The play aspect is evident when meaningless sounds enter into the designs, as in (Weir, 1962, p. 105):

bink
let Bobo bink
bink ben bink
blue kink

The most surprising finding Dr Weir reports is the fact that in nonsense sequences the boy reproduces what appear to be 'substitution exercises' of a kind linguists prepare for people learning a foreign language. In the following sequences, for example, he seems to be practising his use of pronouns:

I go up there
I go up there
I go
She go up there

and (Weir, 1962, p. 110):

Stop it
Stop the ball
Stop it

Commenting on the following sequence (Weir, 1962, p. 109):

What colour
What colour blanket
What colour mop
What colour glass

Dr Weir points out that 'blanket', 'mop' and 'glass' use related sounds – that they are brought together on the principle we noticed earlier in the case of 'drum' and 'dram' – but she concludes: 'However, the primary function of this paragraph is pattern practice, sound play being relegated only to the selection of items within the form class to be substituted.'

Play and practice: the observation that young children practise language before going to sleep was made by Valentine in 1942: a boy of about two 'was frequently heard, when settling down to sleep to be systematically "revising" his vocabulary;

repeating to himself in succession all the nouns he had learned so far.' (Valentine, 1942, p. 444)

Anthony on occasion reinforces the idea of 'practice' by commenting on his own attempts (Weir, 1962, p. 112):

> One two three four
> One two
> One two three four
> One two three
> Anthony counting
> Good boy you
> One two three

and even on one occasion corrects his own pronunciation (Weir 1962, p. 108):

> berries
> not barries
> barries
> barries
> not barries
> berries

Dr Weir sums up: 'Sound is what is played with, and it is done within the framework of paradigmatic and syntagmatic exercises.' Play and practice: nevertheless, I find the distinction difficult to accept. In the absence of a communicative and inquisitive or a regulatory purpose, sounds are freely associated into satisfying patterns: and so, it seems to me, are syntactical forms. We might at any stage make an obvious distinction between play and imposed practice: we can in the case of adults make a distinction between play and self-imposed or voluntary practice: when applied to three-year-old children that distinction seems to me to have no meaning at all.

Anthony's pre-sleep monologues employed a much more restricted vocabulary than his day speech: and one of the methods of selection certainly seems to have been that of choosing the things he felt most deeply about. By far the most frequent among the nouns are 'blanket' and 'Bobo' with 'Anthony', 'Daddy' and 'Mommy' coming next. (And we are told that he showed particular attachment to his blankets – 'takes careful count of them, identifying them by colour and by wearing one of them after the fashion of a toga'. Bobo was a favourite toy to whom much of the talk was ostensibly addressed.) One long sequence is all about 'daddy', and about who belongs to whom, or, as Dr Weir puts it, 'belonging and hence love are one of the underlying themes of the paragraph'. It is important to notice that what we might call 'ideas' are being freely associated in this play, as well as sounds and syntactical forms.

I have a small group of pre-sleep monologues spoken by a girl of two years eight months, called Karen, during a week when she was staying away with relations because her mother was in hospital. She had more on her mind than Anthony had because she had this situation to cope with. Though nobody was there for Anthony to talk to, his speech took the form of a dialogue, sometimes with Bobo, sometimes more straight-forwardly with himself; though someone was with Karen, her talk makes no demand for a response and she frequently answers her own questions. Both forms of speech are in fact examples of 'speech for oneself'.

Karen had a nylon rabbit which she took to bed with her, wrapped up in a scarf. Here she is making herself at home in a strange bed:*

> Nice and soft in my bed
> Nice and soft in bed.
> I'm like a bunny-rabbit now
> Wrapped up like a bunny-rabbit now –
> I'm getting soft like a bunny-rabbit –
> Yes, like a bunny-rabbit.
> Bunnies are soft like feathers.

*With acknowledgements to Mrs Beryl Spence, who gave me the transcripts.

> Dogs are soft too, and lambs are soft.
> I like things soft, don't you?
> Yes, I like things soft.

There are signs of the 'substitution exercise' in Karen's monologues: they seem to occur most frequently where she is least concerned with her mother's absence:

> I've been sick every day in the car.
> That's why I've got a cold.
> But I don't be sick like this;
> But I don't be sick in bed,
> But I don't be sick on the beach.

And again:

> When I'm little bit older,
> When I'm little bit older,
> I'll have a cup of tea,
> I'll have a cup of tea,
> When I'm little bit older,
> When Mummy comes back again.

But it is the preoccupation with Mummy and home – the 'theme of belonging and hence love' – that stands out most clearly.

> My home is at Belstone.
> I don't know where it is, Belstone.
> We can't see Belstone from here.
> We couldn't go down there, could we?
> No, we couldn't.

One other form of monologue that gives full rein to these play features we have been concerned with is what we might call 'the spiel'. It is in contrast to the pre-sleep talk because the speaker demands an audience and remains highly aware of it. On the other hand, it contrasts sharply with both running commentary and social interchange, first because, as we have said, it seeks no practical or communicative or inquisitive ends, and secondly because it constitutes an individual performance which an audience should attend to but not interrupt. The fact that it is a performance is indicated in several ways: it may be said in a sing-song voice, intoned or even sung: it is often accompanied by rhythmical movements – from pacing to and fro, to and fro, to something near to a dance. Since children are unlikely to have heard their elders using language in this fashion – the strong rhythmic beat, the sing-song – we may well ask why they do it: and perhaps we can best explain it as one more example of the 'play principle': the tendency children have of investing any achievement with *value for its own sake*, a worth-doingness, and thus to carry it out in a way that capitalizes intrinsic elements in its substance while ignoring its instrumental qualities.

Here is a short piece of a long spiel from Clare, rising three:

There was a little girl called May
and she had some dollies –
and the weeds were growing in the ground –
and they made a little nest out of sticks
for another little birdie up in the trees
and they climbed up the tree –
and the weeds were growing in the ground
   (*I can do it much better if there's some food in my tum!*)
The weeds were growing in the ground –
the ghee (?) was in the sun and it was a Sunday –
Now we all gather at the seaside
and the ghee was in London having dinner in a dinner-shop
and the weeds were growing in the ground –
and we shall go there again – we shall go there again –
we shall go there again
'cos it's a nice Sunday morning and a fine day
and we had a pony
and the weeds were growing in the ground.

The performance is a kind of celebration, and fragments of past experience are caught up into it. 'I can do it much better . . .' (in which the sing-song tones changed to brisk conversational manner) indicates that there is an 'it', a performance, a some-thing, in the child's mind. Quoted language plays a larger part in the spiel than in other kinds of speech at this stage; and repetition seems an intended part of what is afoot. Concern for sounds runs more to rhythms than – as in Anthony's talk – to individual sounds, and the practice-play of structures is hardly a feature at all.

What the spiel and the pre-sleep monologue have above all in common is freedom for a word (and the experiences connected with it) to call to mind the next words by a process of free association – association of sound or structure or meaning. And for this reason – word summoning word without the inter-vention of things (or things being done to things) – most children use speech *not* tied to the here-and-now first in these kinds of monologue and only later in communicative or regulatory speech.* For Anthony, alone in the dark, there was nothing *but* language to play with: Clare, by choice, constructs her 'it' out of language alone.

The fundamental process by which language is used to con-struct a representation of reality offers by its very nature an invitation to play. We can easily forget that fact – either in our preoccupation with the practical uses of language for com-munication, or in the subtle complexities of our philosophical speculations on this very matter, the relation between reality and the formulation. Children are free of both these kinds of sophistication and stand face to face with the newly acquired language on the one hand and the material it works upon on the other. Any verbal representation is a kind of template, and, as Kelly showed, we try the template for fit. Discrepancies are both matters of serious concern and, looked at with some detachment, opportunities for laughter. Moreover, we may take the joke a stage further and deliberately create a misfit.

*Piaget, though he does not comment on it, records that the first evidence, in the case of one child, of a word used to *recall* something came in pre-sleep talk at the age of one year seven months. (Piaget, 1951, p. 222)

We have already seen some evidence of play of this kind. Clare improvises a misfit when she first quotes two lines of a song and then amends them:

> I danced over water I skipped over sea
> All the birds in the air couldn't catch me
> I skipped as slow as I could over water
> I danced as slow as I could over sea
> All the silly birds in the air couldn't catch me.

(See p. 52.) And again, when, having played around with the sexes in terms of 'Not Uncle Mac, Aunty Mac...', she attacks her father with, 'What are you doing, Mrs Jimmy?'

This is a kind of teasing, of course; and something I value highly as an element in the pattern of family relationships. It is the kind of teasing that *envisages something over and above the obvious*: and since most of our stereotypes are primarily linguistic products, it seems particularly valuable that this sort of thing should be one of the ingredients of talk. It helps to drive a wedge between words and things: to encourage openness to alternative formulations of experience. In the egocentric years it will be only the thin end of the wedge that penetrates. *His* way of formulating, *his* construction, has a strong hold for the child, of course: but in areas of experience where he is confident or can afford to entertain doubts, teasing and joking may have considerable scope.

Chukovsky is a Russian writer who has made a special study of young children's language, and produced a book translated under the title of *From Two to Five*. Here he quotes a number of examples in which children exploit the gap between reality and verbal formulation and goes on to make the obvious connexion between this feature of their talk and their passionate delight in the nonsense of nursery rhymes – the wonderful Derby ram, for example, whose horns reached the sky, or the four-and-twenty blackbirds that sang in a pie. He coins the name, 'Topsy-turvies', for such rhymes, and makes out an excellent case for their educational value.

One can cite [he says], any number of such [absurdities] which testify to the inexhaustible need of every healthy child of every era and of every nation to introduce nonsense into his small but ordered world, with which he has only recently become acquainted. Hardly has the child comprehended with certainty which objects go together and which do not, when he begins to listen happily to verses of absurdity. For some mysterious reason the child is attracted to that topsy-turvy world where legless men run, water burns, horses gallop astride their riders, and cows nibble on peas on top of birch trees. (Chukovsky, 1963, p. 96)

But the reason grows less mysterious as the author proceeds:

The child plays not only with marbles, with blocks, with dolls, but also with ideas. No sooner does he master some idea than he is only too eager to make it his toy. (Chukovsky, 1963, p. 98)

The turning upside down in play – the misfit improvisations – are both self-congratulatory symbols of the child's new achievement and a means of reinforcing what he has learnt about actuality. The self-congratulation becomes more explicit when, as often happens, the absurdity is part of somebody else's behaviour – as when Simple Simon was stupid enough to fish for a whale in his mother's bucket. So, Chukovsky concludes, the function of such rhymes and tales 'is obvious; for every "wrong" the child realizes what is "right", and every departure from the normal strengthens his conception of the normal.' (Chukovsky, 1963, p. 102)

Play with sounds and with ideas – rhyming, punning, making outrageous statements or teasing jokes or other kinds of nonsense – these occupy a considerable place in many children's talk of all kinds. One other and favourite form of play remains to be considered.

Make-believe play is an increasing preoccupation for a child as he grows from about two to about five. It is a kind of play in which his construction or representation of the world might be said to take over from reality: in other words, the process of construing what happens (and perhaps, as we have just seen, playfully exploiting the gap) gives place in this form of activity to a process of virtually *making things happen*, at his own choice and in accordance with his own desires. It is an enactment of his own construction of events. He selects from the whole of his past experience: in fact it would not be a gross distortion to assign to such play, at this stage, the role of maintaining a child's view of the world in a condition in which he is happy to live with it.

Piaget explains it thus: 'Just as practice play reproduces . . . each new acquisition of the child, so "imaginative" play reproduces what he has lived through, but by means of symbolic representation.' As he reproduces it in play, Piaget finds, he may work upon it, 'assimilating reality to his desires' in order to come to terms with it or compensate for it or reduce its threat. (Piaget, 1951, p. 131)

Such play does not, of course, disappear when the child reaches five: but by then its make-believe has become more realistic and so less and less distinguishable from constructive and creative activities that have grown up around it and occupy the seven- or eight-year-old in a way which is difficult to characterize either as 'work' or 'play'. The child from two to five is at his busiest as an explorer – if we are to judge merely by the rate of increase of his discoveries about the world: it is at this stage that make-believe games are at their peak. To use a rough analogy, it is as though the immense data-collecting task necessitated an equivalent in intensive data-processing sessions. Or, more decorously, look at T. S. Eliot's description of the infant:

> 'Issues from the hand of God, the simple soul'
> To a flat world of changing lights and noise,
> To light, dark, dry or damp, chilly or warm;
> Moving between the legs of tables and of chairs,
> Rising or falling, grasping at kisses and toys,
> Advancing boldly, sudden to take alarm,

Retreating to the corner of arm and knee,
Eager to be reassured, taking pleasure
In the fragrant brilliance of the Christmas tree,
Pleasure in the wind, the sunlight and the sea;
Studies the sunlit pattern on the floor
And running stags around a silver tray;
Confounds the actual and the fanciful,
Content with playing-cards and kings and queens,
What the fairies do and what the servants say.
The heavy burden of the growing soul
Perplexes and offends more, day by day;
Week by week, offends and perplexes more
With the imperatives of 'is and seems'
And may and may not, desire and control . . .*

The perplexity and the pressures on him when so much of his view of the world is what *seems* rather than what *is* – fanciful rather than actual – it is this that goes some way towards explaining why a young child devotes so much energy to make-believe play, to the continual refashioning of his representation of the world.

But in make-believe play, the representation is not a language product pure and simple. Enactment is in terms of human behaviour as a whole, not talk in isolation. Talk indeed plays an organizing role – in fact the relation of language to the total form is the relation that exists, as we have seen, between language and all other forms of representation that play their part in behaviour. Because speech remains embedded in its context of situation it is in a form more accessible to a young child than narrative speech. Luria's work with the twins showed that the regulatory role of language – paradoxically enough at first sight – is essential to make-believe play. When a chair must feature in the activity as a boat and the carpet perhaps as a lake, their imagined roles must be to some extent kept constant or the activity breaks down. Children, when they play together and even when they play by themselves, will normally use

*From 'Animula', *Collected Poems of T. S. Eliot*, p. 111.

words to assign these roles: not till language has some power to regulate activity can they be persisted in and the imagined situation allowed to develop.

A child improvising experiences in accordance with his own desires is obviously not in a situation that makes cooperation with other children easy. A good deal of make-believe play is solitary – often with the help of dolls or other toys who are born, nursed, schooled, married and buried as occasion arises. Often enough children will pursue such games alongside each other, but the only social contact likely to arise will be over something each wants to incorporate into his game. However, there is of course also a good deal of combined make-believe play. Up to the age of four or so this is likely to mean that one child uses others as though they were dolls – and they submit to the situations he plays out. 'Turn and turn about', give and take, and then the genuinely joint adoption and execution of a single project are common enough after that age. Stories they have all had read to them often provide common material. In families with children of different ages several kinds of compromise are found: a three-year-old will often play second fiddle cheerfully to a four-year-old: and a five- or six-year-old on the other hand will sometimes fill roles to please a younger child.

We have in this section looked at a number of ways in which speech enters into the kind of behaviour we call play – sometimes providing its substance, always in whole or in part its means. Let us close the topic with Michael Oakeshott's commentary on the language of childhood:

Everybody's young days are a dream, a delightful insanity, a miraculous confusion of poetry and practical activity in which nothing has a fixed shape and nothing has a fixed price. 'Fact' and 'not-fact' are still indistinct. To act is to make a bargain with events; there are obscure longings, there are desires and choices, but their objects are imperfectly discerned; everything is 'what it turns out to be'. And to speak is to make images. For, although we spend much of our early days learning the symbolic language of practical intercourse . . . this is not the language with which we begin as children. Words in everyday use are not signs with fixed and invariable usages; they are poetic images. We speak an heroic language of our own invention, not merely because we are incompetent in our handling of symbols, but because we are moved not by the desire to communicate but by the delight of utterance. (Oakeshott, 1959, p. 61)

VI

With every word that he speaks within his parents' hearing, a child reveals to them who he is. Before he could speak they knew him by what he did: but what he says is able to reveal much more. By what he says he shows what he makes of the world, and his interpretation is open to further interpretation by them, but what is being construed in this latter case is not the world in general but a single infant. The process is, however, two-way (though obviously not in equal proportions) and can moreover be channelled into deliberate inquiry. Here, for example, is Clare at the age of two years eight months cross-examining her father:

CLARE: What did your Daddy do?
FATHER: He worked in an office.
CLARE: You haven't got him now, have you?
FATHER: Who told you?
CLARE: I just knew. Well, now you haven't got him, have you?
FATHER: No, Darling.
CLARE: What's your Daddy done?
FATHER: He's died.
CLARE: Why?
FATHER: Because he was very old.
CLARE: He wasn't very old when you were a little boy.
FATHER: We get older.
CLARE: After you've had some children, do you?
FATHER: Yes, Darling.
CLARE: Why didn't you have a little sister boy to play with?

FATHER: I did.

CLARE: What's he done then? Who's it?

FATHER: You know him – you know uncle . . .

CLARE: But why did he die? How old were you when he died?

FATHER: Thirty-five.

CLARE: Why were you a man? It might have been when you were fifteen. You'd have been quite a big boy, wouldn't you? Why weren't you a big boy when he died?

Obviously, there are a great many things for a child to talk about when his parents can listen. What they can do then is probably something that can never be done at any other time by anybody else. The Russian psychologists we have quoted believe that the higher forms of human mental activity begin their development as a process shared between two people – a child and an adult: that qualitative changes take place in a child's mental processes as a result of speech and cooperation with his parents in infancy. There is, on the negative side, some evidence to connect apathy in a child with the hamstringing of his curiosity at an early age – the effect of lack of answers, for one reason or another, to his questions.

Piaget saw that one of the first steps towards mature thinking lay in the child's learning to see things from other points of view as well as his own. He found that, for this to happen, they needed, for different reasons, both contact with adults in the family and contact with other children. In their adult wisdom parents have most to offer in the way of 'other points of view'; yet the parent–child relationship is itself likely to be 'child-centred'. Talk of parent with child alternates between 'communion' together and exploratory questioning from the child, rather than constitutes a 'meeting of minds'. In Piaget's words: 'The adult is at one and the same time far superior to the child and very near to him. He dominates everything, but at the same time penetrates into the intimacy of every wish and every thought.' (Piaget, 1959, p. 257) In these circumstances a child's egocentricity is likely to be at its greatest in relations with his parents. With another child he will at first make little contact, as we have seen – neither being able to stray from his own viewpoint far enough to take into account the other's. As relations develop in shared activities, however – and that would include quarrelling over a toy – the challenge of the differing viewpoints is taken up and this results in a move in the direction of 'a meeting of minds': just as we saw the twins developed speech to meet the challenge of playing with other children. Then there is a final stage in which the two processes – interactions with parents and interactions with other children – produce one effect. In Piaget's words:

As the child grows older, his respect for the superiority of the adult diminishes or at least alters in character. The adult ceases to represent unquestioned or even unquestionable Truth and interrogation becomes discussion. It is then that all that makes up a socialized attitude towards others, developed in the give and take of exchanges with contemporaries, prevails over a feeling of intellectual submission and thus constitutes that instrument so essential to the individual of which he will make ever-increasing use and which will serve him throughout his life. (Piaget, 1959, p. 258)

'That instrument' is what Piaget would call 'a socialized intelligence' – a mind capable of meeting other minds.

With George Kelly, I believe that every child begins with the drive to explore the world he is born into, that curiosity is indeed 'native'. Speech becomes its principal instrument. (A. N. Whitehead pointed out long ago that the zest for naming things was merely a continuation of the zest to explore.) For the infant, the family constitutes his whole theatre of operations: to cooperate more fully with his parents, to participate more fully in the activities of the household – these have for him the fundamental 'satisfaction of progress'. Again, speech is a principal means by which he gains this satisfaction. As we look at him and listen to him in these early years, 'learning', 'growing' and 'living' seem alternative names for the same process, and – though there are exceptions* – it is to a surprising degree an audible process.

Since it is by talking that a child learns to talk, the best way of helping him to learn will take the form of fostering his explorations and his participation in family activities. One kind of fostering lies in the opening up of new fields – and the world to be explored through stories and books in general need not wait till he can read for himself. Another kind of fostering lies in modifying the pattern of family activities in order to accommodate what he can contribute.

The exploring and the participating are interdependent. It is not for long that the home itself provides space enough for the exploring, nor the family an adequate social environment. Thereafter, the courage to explore further afield and the confidence to form relations with other people will rely upon the security he feels in his home base.

VII

'Make-believe play' and the 'running commentary', the 'spiel' and the 'pre-sleep monologue', 'family activities' – is not all this something of a luxury when you think of 'ordinary families' in their thousands? Mothers who work all day as well as fathers; meals at odd times, in a hurry, with no time to talk; a family routine that seems to leave little time for contact even between adults?

A survey made by an American psychologist called Samuel Kirk reported some interesting research into the language ability of 'disadvantaged children'. Twenty-four children of one-and-a-half to two years old, living in an orphanage, were divided into two groups, matched for 'measured intelligence' – as far as it could be measured at that age: what is clear is that both groups showed *low ability*. Each of the twelve in one group was sent to be looked after

* See p. 317

by an adolescent girl living in a mental home: the other group was left at the orphanage. After two years the group that had been living with the girls showed extraordinary increases in so-called 'measured intelligence' (well over twenty points), while those in the orphanage showed a *decrease* of similar proportions. What is more astounding still is that after *twenty-one years*, the experimenter was able to trace the children and discovered that the average of the final school achievement of the group looked after in infancy by the girls was twelfth grade (work normal for seventeen- to eighteen-year-olds) whereas the average for the other group was fourth grade (work normal for nine- to ten-year-olds). Samuel Kirk reported also that a check on the abilities of children under school age in the poorer black districts of New York revealed a small number of children of distinctly higher ability than the rest. When these were followed up it was found there was in each case a grandmother living with the family.

This is not a plea for importing grandmothers (nor for farming out infants to weak-minded girls): it is important as evidence that suggests that talk in infancy with an older person may make all the difference: and not necessarily the intelligent talk of educated parents. Evidence from the same survey proved that timing is crucial: the advantage of providing a talking environment is greatest around two years of age and falls off sharply after five. (National Council of Teachers of English, 1965, pp. 250–67)

Sociologists have shown that families differ considerably from each other in their social structure, and that one of the major effects of such difference is upon the linguistic development of the children. Families where the members are interrelated primarily in accordance with the family status of each (as for example 'father', or 'elder brother' or 'youngest child') will tend to get along together by communicating in a form of language that provides limited choices of utterance. Since utterance reflects status, and status has a defining function and is assigned, only certain kinds of utterance will be appropriate – or necessary. The infant in such a family will learn to respond to language appropriate to the status of other members and to use those forms appropriate to his own. Families, on the other hand, whose members are related as persons, as individuals rather than as 'occupiers' of an assigned status, will tend to use a much less restricted language, because speech is expected to be a principal means by which they reveal individuality, unprescribed differences from each other.

Viewed from the outside, the interlocking relationships of a 'status-organized' family make for a closely knit unit: the comments of any one member of it in a given situation are likely to represent the reactions of all. Coherence in the 'person-organized' family, on the other hand, relies upon continued consultation or discussion – the purpose of which is to reveal 'individual intent'.

Looking now at internal relations, a child in a status-organized family who says 'Why?' to an instruction is likely to have as an answer, 'Because I tell you to'. In the person-organized family he is more likely to elicit a reason, an explanation – 'Because if you don't you'll have nothing to spend when you go on your holiday'. The second kind of answer usually leads on to more talk: the first acts as a full-stop to discussion.

This is a much over-simplified version of important ideas put forward by Basil Bernstein (1965). Their relevance as a postscript to this chapter will be obvious.

CHAPTER THREE

Participant and Spectator

═══

I

'O H I see, it's *this* that's doing it!' is a remark that was perfectly intelligible when it was made to me, as an opening gambit, some time ago. It was intelligible partly because of the *immediate situation* in which it was made; partly because items in the situation were indicated by the speaker's gestures; and partly because the speaker and I shared in common certain *previous experiences*. The utterance, the present situation, actions within it, and a shared context of past experience – these were required to make up the total intelligible speech event. My reply was an *action*: the situation, my action within it, and the shared context of past experience combined to produce an *intelligible event*; but there was no speech. My wife watched me and soon pulled a wry face, and I knew what she meant: she meant 'don't do that, you'll break your thumb-nail'. Then she said, 'Wait a minute, I'll get a –' 'No, it's all right', I said, and went on to 'explain' why it was all right by picking up a nail-file from a lcdge nearby. The explanation satisfied her, evidently, because she stopped going to fetch whatever it was. And with the nail-file I took the protruding nail out of the back of the chair I had been sitting in, and that was the end of the 'conversation'.

A great deal of our speech is like this interchange in these two respects: first, the speech is dependent upon the situation and accompanying actions for its interpretation; second, the speech is part of a chain of mingled utterance and action. As Sapir puts it, 'In those sequences of interpersonal behaviour which form the greater part of our daily lives speech and action supplement each other and do each other's work in a web of unbroken pattern.' (Sapir, 1961, p. 9) Structurally, items of speech and items of action are interchangeable in these sequences. To take an obvious example from 'our daily lives', if you go into a shop the girl behind the counter may approach you and say, 'Can I help you?' or she may simply step forward and look expectantly in your direction. You might do one of three things: you might pick up a bar of chocolate and hand it to her in silence: you might pick it up, hand it to her, and say, 'I'll take this please': or you might stand with your hands in your pockets and say, 'Twenty-p Bournville please'. Again, to give a somewhat different kind of example, if you have a bulky parcel to get through the door, you may manipulate the door somehow, or you may use speech to keep the door open by somebody else's agency.

Such use of speech is indeed so common that linguists sometimes give to other forms the name, 'displaced speech'. In displaced speech language is used to *refer to* or *interpret* or *recount* an experience (or experiences) and not as an embedded part of the here and now of the experience concerned. It is speech about other times and other places. Anyone who has been the infuriated partner of a garrulous bridge-player will be fully aware of the difference between embedded speech ('Was it two *spades* you said? Mm – then I shall say three diamonds') and displaced speech ('Do you know, I saw Joan the other day – haven't seen her for months. She was taking David to nursery school and she said she'd call in on the way back . . .', and so on.)

If I were to say, 'I always lose when I play with Mrs Smith – she talks too much', I should be referring to experience, and to experience that I am not now engaged in, using speech about other times and other places: but rather differently from the way Mrs Smith herself did in the example I have attributed to her. My statement is generalized from repeated experiences: she was recounting, or narrating, a particular experience. I think it will be clear that the term 'displaced speech' makes a less useful distinction as we move away from accounts of particular events towards generalizations upon events. We spend a good deal of our time using one or other of these forms of displaced speech. A serious bridge match would find little room for anything but embedded speech, and the same would be to *some* extent true of any occasion where people meet to *do* something, something observable, something with *things* – whether cards or skittles or race-horses or vaulting horses or weaving looms. But the social round goes much further than this.

It does not seem at all odd to us, I believe, that our social institutions should place such stress upon talking that we organize most of our encounters with each other as talking occasions: tea-parties and cocktail parties, at homes and conversaziones, mothers' meetings and invitations to meet so-and-so, teach-ins and study-groups and conferences. We may meet to talk without eating, but whoever heard of an invitation to eat – out or at home – in which host and guest ate in silence? If we are with people we know, or people *like* the people we know, it is in fact an oddity and a growing strain if we do *not* talk.

By no means all of this talking is necessary: and if that sounds an odd remark, let the fact of its oddness bear out the point I am making. We talk, of course – quite unnecessarily – for pleasure.

It is this simple distinction between necessary and unnecessary talk, between getting things done by talk, and talking for the pleasure of it, that I want now to elaborate. We have already seen (p. 21) that Susanne Langer calls man a 'proliferator of symbols' and finds that only some of these are worked upon to any purpose, while the others 'vapour off'. It is within a particular kind of symbol-making, a particular kind of talk, that I want first to make the distinction. Within social speech, then, take displaced speech: within that, take not the generalized but the particular end of the scale – recounting or narrating particular events: and further limit that to the case of a speaker recounting his own past experiences.

99

It is a natural enough occupation. Our minds tend to dwell on what has been happening to us, and when we have nothing particular to think about we respond to our environment often enough by summoning up past experiences associated with whatever in it catches our attention. And these preoccupations are likely to spill over into words when we find ourselves in the company of someone disposed to listen.

From time to time a friend and neighbour of mine catches the same train as I do in the morning. We meet on the platform and the whole body of past experience of each of us offers to each of us a vast area from which to choose a topic to start the conversation. Since neither of us is a complete bore, we shall not choose what currently preoccupies us unless it happens to be something that would be likely to interest the other. Initial silence probably indicates that our individual preoccupations were not in an area of common interest. In that case we are likely to cast our minds back to the last time we met: as a result of this, he may say to me, 'How did your date with X go? Did you find him in the end?' and I shall then embark on the story of my meeting with X, perhaps bringing out all the difficulties and frustrations I had in tracking him down. If it is anything of a *cause célèbre* for me I may have told the story often enough before to other people, but tell it again with relish and feel better for having done so. Further, as I retell it, I may find I have altered my perspective on it a little and especially so if, as I relate it for this particular listener, my relations with him and my conception of the sort of person he is, influence me in the way I construe it. As I finish my story and we arrive at our destination, that altered perspective, that new construction of the event, might constitute what any recording angel would have to record as the outcome of my narration and my encounter with a neighbour.

On the other hand, we can suppose a different situation with a different outcome. Suppose I have failed to track down X and am still concerned to do so: and that I therefore recount all my

frustrated endeavours as a deliberate way of working up to saying, 'Well look, you've been in touch with X more recently
than I have. Do you think you can do anything to help me?'
Tracking down X is my concern, it is something I want to get
done, and in narrating my past experience in this case I am
using language in an attempt to 'get things done'. As a member
of the human race I could claim that my concerns are a part of
the world's concerns and that in pursuing them I am participating in the world's affairs. (It is helpful to think in this con-
glomerate way of 'the world's affairs' in order to distinguish in
general between getting things done and its converse – in spite
of the anomaly that ten people trying to grab a single seat in the
train must be seen as all participating in the world's affairs!)

In the first hypothetical case, on the other hand – that is,
when I recount how I did see X – whether or not I find a new
perspective in the telling, I tell the story for the pleasure of it. I
go back over the experience, not in any way to get things done,
not participating in my own and the world's affairs, but as a
mere *spectator*. Moreover, in offering the story for my friend's
enjoyment, I am inviting him to be a spectator of my past
experiences.

This last observation extends the area of application of the
distinction beyond the one I started with. If someone listening
to me takes up the role of spectator of my experiences (just as,
in agreeing to help me make contact with X he would be
participating in that particular experience) then I am similarly
in the role of spectator of *other people's* experience when I tell
the story of how my grandfather, with thousands of others,
once watched for the appearance of a notorious 'ghost' on the
banks of the Trent, or of how Columbus discovered America,
or Newton sat under an apple tree.

But not so fast. Imagine a party – and the party is over: you
and your fellow-hosts sit around discussing the behaviour of
your guests in order to deduce who it might have been that left
a ring by the wash-basin. This is helpful – it is part of the

world's work, it is being useful to somebody. But you would probably find that the conversation soon drifts from the participant to the spectator role: you begin discussing the behaviour of your guests in order to *enjoy* it in a way you could not while they were still behaving. This is not useful – but it *is* very enjoyable. Most groups that have undertaken any joint enterprise – producing a play for example – will be familiar with the quite characteristic kind of pleasure they derive from going over it all when the enterprise is finished. In talk like this after the last performance, even the gross blunders and ensuing panics, looked back on, are tremendously entertaining.

On such occasions, the members of the group take up jointly the role of spectators of their common experience. In going back over it, as we have already noticed (p. 19), they enjoy it, savour it, interpret it. Indeed it seems to be part of the nature of man's experience that both in prospect and in retrospect he can respond to the quality of events in a way he is unable to do at the time of their happening. Some people particularly seem to measure out their lives in remembered rather than ongoing occasions. Perhaps this is a part of what Piaget meant when he said that the sharpest division to be made in experience is that which divides the whole of what has led up to a moment from that moment of experience itself.

The distinction we are making between participant and spectator roles can now be further extended to cover prospect as well as retrospect. I may take up the role of spectator of my own future as well as my own past. Day-dreaming is a common form in which to do so. If I *plan* a future event, on the other hand – say a camping holiday – then I am in the role of participant: if I talk to you about the coming event, in order to find out what you know about good sites or good routes or in order to borrow a Primus stove from you, then I am bringing you in as a participant. But if I relax and describe how marvellous I think it will be to lie in the shade of pine trees on the edge of the sunburnt beach – then we are both in the role of spectators of my future. Part of your pleasure may arise from anticipating with me the delights in store for me, but no doubt – since the pleasure of such day-dreaming is in any case not very closely related to the probability of realization – you will change the roles from time to time and see yourself in the centre of the picture.

This leads us to the final extension of the area of application: if I may take up the role of spectator of my own past or future experiences, of other people's experiences, past or future, then I may also become spectator of events that have never happened and could never happen. I do so, in fact, whenever I read – or hear or tell or write – a fairy story or its adult equivalent. The satisfaction I have in the story is the kind of satisfaction I derive, not from having an experience, but from looking back on one I *have had*: it is as though I were to go back over an experience I have *not* had!

Freud has said somewhere: 'Every imaginative product be it art or dream comes as experience to the participant'. I bring that in here for two distinct reasons. First, in support of my last paragraph, to use it in an amended version – 'Every imaginative product be it art or dream comes to us as experience' – and with the suggestion that it comes in the guise of experience *recalled* and not experience in the act. Secondly to take up the obvious point that where Freud says 'participant' I should need to say 'spectator'. An explanation here, I believe, would not only serve to resolve the discrepancy apparent on the surface between Freud's statement and my thesis, but would also clear up a number of doubts that may have been growing in your minds throughout the last few pages. When Freud says 'participant' he means, clearly, someone who participates in the imagined experience of art or dream: that is to say one who is in the role I have been labelling 'spectator'. Certainly I would not want to question for a moment the fact that response to a recounting of past experience, a day-dream, or a story of any kind, includes the reader's *participation* in the account, the dream, the story.

Or, putting it from the other side, to be a spectator does not mean to remain aloof, uninvolved, detached: a spectator is 'disinterested' only in the *outgoing* sense of that word – his self-interest has nothing to gain or lose, he has no axe to grind, no iron in the fire of this recalled or imagined experience: he is certainly not 'disinterested' in the *incoming* sense of that word – that is, 'uninterested'. Both 'spectator' and 'participant' then are used in a special and restricted sense: 'participant' is the key word to mark out someone who is participating *in the world's affairs*: 'spectator' is the label for someone on holiday from the world's affairs, someone contemplating experiences, enjoying them, vividly reconstructing them perhaps – but experiences *in which he is not taking part*.

Let me illustrate very briefly with an example I have already used elsewhere. A mother of young children will quite commonly relate to her husband when he comes home in the evening the events of the children's day. She does it because they both enjoy the rehearsal: they are both in the role of spectator. Though what he hears may sometimes provoke in him vague dispositions to act or to decide, they are too weak to switch him from his role. If he knows that the children are safely tucked up in bed, he will savour the excitement of the hair-breadth escapes and the daring escapades: his wife enjoys them in the telling – in a way she was not free to do earlier in the day when she was a participant: as a participant she was liable at any moment to be called on to act or to decide – she is free now to savour, to appreciate, to interpret. But occasionally the husband will come home to a different situation: the wife goes about her story tactfully, preparing to break the news. She is still a participant in the event she must describe because its consequences in action and decision have not yet been consummated. And her husband must master his feelings and summon his judgement in order to bear his share in the action and decision.

Remember it is the language we are concerned with. In participating in the children's day, the mother would use language to direct, persuade, cajole, warn, help, comfort and amuse the children: heaven forbid that I should be taken as implying that all this may not be *enjoyable*. (It won't always be enjoyable, but she will go on doing it.) But as spectator, she recounts, embroiders, interprets, comments upon the *events* and what she enjoys then is not the company of the children but the events themselves, as events, and the telling of them, as narrative – an enjoyment she shares with her listener. There is no reason for its existence unless it is enjoyed – were it done dutifully on demand it would become the language of the examination room which is certainly in the role of participant and not spectator!

The need to act and decide characterizes the participant role – to act and decide in response to the social demands of human co-existence. At the moment we have characterized the spectator role simply as a freedom from those demands, but we shall go on in section II to look at the way this freedom is used, what other characteristics develop. I have laboured the distinction between language in the role of participant and in the role of spectator because I believe it will prove important for a proper understanding of the manifold ways in which language works.

II

In considering language as a mode of representing experience, our main stress has been upon its use in turning confusion into order, in enabling us to construct for ourselves an increasingly faithful, objective and coherent picture of the world. In looking at the way young children sort experience as they learn words, the classification we had in mind was primarily a classification in accordance with 'the way things are'. We did observe, however, that our representation of the world is affected also by the projection of our individual feelings, our needs and desires: let us regard this now as involving an alternative mode of classifying – a classification in accordance with 'the way I feel about things'. There will, of course, be striking differences in the way objects fall into classes in the two systems. Classifying 'the way things are', 'puss', the domestic cat, will fall into a group – the cat tribe – that includes also the tiger: by 'the way I feel about things', the two creatures are in widely different classes.

Though not a great deal is known about the process of establishing these feeling-based categories, it is clear that learning is involved. Or to put it another way, we influence each other in our feelings about things, and nobody is more amply or more rapidly influenced in this respect than the young child. The basis of classification remains essentially 'the way I feel' rather than 'the way people feel', but over a very broad range of experience children born into the same social group come to feel in many ways similarly by the time they are adults. The British psychologist, D. W. Harding (whose work is to figure a good deal in this section), considers that our main form of social satisfaction lies in 'knowing that our interests are shared and our sentiments and attitudes given sympathy . . . the satisfaction of knowing that the scale of values expressed in what we do is sanctioned and supported by other people'. (Harding, 1966, p. 15) And Piaget puts the very general point that 'spontaneous feelings between one person and another grow from an increasingly rich exchange of values'. (Piaget, 1968, p. 35)

Children are avidly curious about the way their parents feel towards things and will do their best to penetrate the fog-screen of 'general goodwill' that parents often maintain 'in front of the children'. They will demand to be told 'someone you *hate*' or 'someone really *horrid*' or ask 'Who are you really afraid of?'. And they will sit silent and absorbed for hours, if they are allowed, while parents gossip with friends and neighbours. Clearly at this stage they seek social satisfaction mainly by ascertaining and to some degree taking over the sentiments and attitudes already acceptable within the family. Piaget has shown the importance at a later stage of transferring the source

of this social sanctioning from the family to the group of friends
– their 'equals' in the school and neighbourhood. (Piaget, 1932)
By this time they have become as avid as gossipers among
themselves as they were listeners at an earlier stage – and for
similar reasons.

D. H. Lawrence has commented on the connexion between
gossip and the way we feel about things. Mrs Bolton in *Lady
Chatterley's Lover* was in the habit of retailing the local gossip
to Sir Gerald Chatterley, and Lady Chatterley (Connie) would
sometimes be within earshot.

Connie was fascinated, listening to her. But afterwards always a
little ashamed. She ought not to listen with this queer rabid
curiosity. After all, one may hear the most private affairs of other
people, but only in a spirit of respect for the struggling, battered
thing which any human soul is, and in a spirit of fine, discrimina-
tive sympathy. . . . It is the way our sympathy flows and recoils
that really determines our lives.

But the passage does not end there: alongside gossip, as a
form of speech in which our sympathies reveal themselves,
Lawrence brings in the novel:

It is the way our sympathy flows and recoils that really determines
our lives. And here lies the vast importance of the novel, properly
handled. It can inform and lead into new places the flow of our
sympathetic consciousness, and it can lead our sympathy away in
recoil from things gone dead. Therefore, the novel, properly
handled can reveal the most secret places of life: for it is in the
passional secret places of life, above all, that the tide of sensitive
awareness needs to ebb and flow, cleansing and freshening.
(Lawrence, 1928, p. 104)

This brings me directly to my point. It seems to me that for
the spoken form of language in the role of spectator we must
use, as the nearest we can get, the term 'gossip'; and for the
written form of language in the role of spectator, the word
'literature'. We are notoriously lacking in terms by which to
distinguish kinds of talk – a reflection of the scant attention

until recently we have paid to it in our thinking. 'Gossip' is a suitable word in that we sometimes refer, with satisfaction, to 'a good gossip' and in the role of spectator, as we have seen, we speak for the pleasure of it: it is an unsuitable word in an implication that still lurks behind it that gossip is malicious. Speech in the role of spectator may be as malicious or as un-malicious as any other kind of speech. About the term 'litera-ture' I am happy, though the claim to have defined it at all may seem extravagant, and this particular definition requires a good deal of further examination and qualification.

I think it is helpful to have a way of defining literature which refers to the sort of thing *it is* rather than one which brings in the judgement as to how good it is of its kind. It is not that I feel the question 'how good is it?' is not a highly important question, but I think it should come *after* and not instead of the question, 'what is it?'. (Picasso is a better painter than an average child in the Infant School, yet they both *paint*.) If we operate only with a normative definition of literature – one that begins to apply above a certain threshold of excellence – we are left with the difficulty of deciding what a piece of writing is that tries but fails to rise above the threshold. It must be *something*. We have only to think of the kind of writing done every day by thousands of children in school to see that this is not an entirely frivolous objection.

However, it is not an entirely serious one, either. What is important is to see whether 'written language in the role of spectator' aptly describes the kind of thing literature is – literature in its usual normative sense – and then go on to see its wider application to writing that might be produced by Tom, Dick or Harry.

It was D. W. Harding who first looked closely at the relation-ship between gossip, literature and the role of spectator. In his article on 'The Role of the Onlooker' in *Scrutiny* in 1937 he considers first the case of someone who is literally a spectator, an eye-witness of the things going on around him in which he plays no part; someone 'merely looking on'. His response to what he sees is, in Harding's view, 'mainly evaluative'.

At a street accident the spectators are thrilled or horrified, pitying, or perhaps ironic; they may judge one or other of the participants to have been at fault, they may reflect on the stupidities of modern transport. In all this they remain 'detached'. But though they make no direct operative response they still assess the event in the light of all the interests, desires, sentiments and ideals that they can relate it to; and they feel it to be noteworthy, commonplace, agreeable or disagreeable, tragic, funny, contemptible, heroic – to mention a few of the cruder responses. (Harding, 1937, p. 250)

In participation we evaluate, necessarily, in preparation for action; but 'detached evaluative responses [that is, those of the spectator] though less intense, tend to be more widely comprehensive than the evaluation which preceded participation. One views the event in a more distant perspective and relates it to a more extensive system of information, beliefs and values.' It is for this reason that Harding concludes: 'if we could obliterate the effects on a man of all the occasions when he was "merely a spectator" it would be profoundly to alter his character and outlook'. (Harding, 1937, pp. 252–3)

The spectator, then, freed from the necessity to act, to meet the social demands made upon a participant, uses his freedom to *evaluate* more broadly, more amply: and Harding words his statement carefully to indicate that in the process of evaluation* assessment according to 'the way I feel about things' plays a considerable part ('the spectators are thrilled or horrified, pitying . . .' etc.). Moreover, evaluating – relating the event to his system of values – cannot in operation be kept distinct from the process of relating it to what he knows (his system of information), and to what from experience he has come to take

* For a fuller description see D. W. Harding, 'Psychological Processes in the Reading of Fiction', *British Journal of Aesthetics*, II, (2), 1962.

on trust (his system of beliefs). In ordinary usage, I think, we use either 'evaluating' or 'judging' in speaking of a similar process, the first putting the stress on the feeling aspect and the second on the knowledge aspect. What is important here is to note that in spectator role activities we are concerned to set up, test out, modify categories according to 'the way I feel about things'.

Spectators, in fact – at a building site or a street accident – are not usually solitary in their occupations; and the responses of any one of them to what goes on around them will be influenced by those of other people: they will be likely to enjoy the social satisfaction of having some part of their system of values sanctioned, sometimes challenged, and perhaps modified. Harding goes on to point out that in contemplating our own past or future experience we take up in privacy the role of spectator, *representing*, as we do so, and, at one and the same time, *evaluating* those experiences or possible experiences. Further, that in gossip there is communication both of experiences (seen in the spectator role) and of the evaluations put upon them by the narrator. As we retail our own or other people's experiences we communicate also our attitudes towards the events and the people concerned, and there is opportunity for immediate response, of agreement, qualification, disagreement, to be made by our listeners. Finally, Harding brings in literature:

The playwright, the novelist, the song-writer and the film-producing team are all doing the same thing as the gossip. . . . Each invites his audience to agree that the experience he portrays is possible and interesting, and that his attitude to it, implicit in his portrayal, is fitting. In the less developed levels of entertainment the process is chiefly one of reinforcing commonplace values in a trivially varied array of situations. In the representational arts, most obviously in literature, the author invites his audience to share in an exploration, an extension and refinement, of his and their common interests; and, as a corollary, to refine or modify their value judgments. (Harding, 1937, pp. 257–8)

And taking up the theme again in a later article, he speaks of 'make-believe, whether it takes the form of play with companions, of drama, or of fiction', as 'imaginary spectatorship in a social setting' and claims for it:

The result is a vast extension of the range of possible human experience that can be offered socially for contemplation and assessment. . . . True or fictional, all these forms of narrative invite us to be onlookers joining in the evaluation of some possibility of experience. (Harding, 1962, p. 138)

Within the many forms that 'imaginary spectatorship in a social setting' may take, we have been accustomed by tradition to mark off for special treatment a body of tried and approved writing we call 'literature'. Now it has been said of literature over and over again in a variety of ways that, in common with other arts, it seeks no practical outcome. This would mean, in the terms we have used, that it is not a participant activity. Wordsworth seemed to imply something of this sort when he wrote to a 'lady from Sheffield' who invited him to contribute to an anthology of anti-slavery pieces and said (by way of declining):

Poetry if good for anything must appeal forcibly to the imagination and the feelings: but what, at this point, we want above everything is patient examination and sober judgment. (Lewis, N.B., 1934, p. 14)

Coleridge, still speaking of poetry, put it more bluntly: 'The immediate object of poetry is pleasure, not truth'; and W. H. Auden in his poem, 'In Memory of W. B. Yeats' gives this very elegant version:

> For poetry makes nothing happen: it survives
> In the valley of its saying where executives
> Would never want to tamper.

There is similarly a great deal in 'the literature' on the subject to support a close connexion between literature on the one hand and feelings and evaluation on the other. Prudence suggests, however, that we leave it more or less at that bare statement: one view on the vexed question of *how* literature relates to feeling could barely be found that would support another. By one, literature excites feelings, by another it allays them. ('It is life that shakes and rocks us, literature which stabilises and confirms', said a one-time Professor of Poetry at Oxford.) (Garrod, 1929, p. 9)

The most developed theory of recent origin is probably that of Susanne Langer: 'Art, in the sense here intended – that is, the generic term subsuming painting, sculpture, architecture, music, dance, literature, drama and film – may be defined as the practice of creating perceptible forms expressive of human feeling.' And again: 'In a special sense one may call a work of art a symbol of feeling, for, like a symbol, it formulates our ideas of inward experience, as discourse formulates our ideas of things and facts in the outside world.' (Langer, 1962, pp. 76 and 80)

Pursuing our consideration of the role of feeling, let us turn back now to the activities of 'imaginary spectatorship' in general. Harding has suggested that a spectator uses his freedom from the demands of participation for the purpose of evaluating experiences, and we have seen that this includes commitment to, and modification of, emotional responses.

That feeling can be a spur to action is a commonplace, known for example to every propagandist and publicity writer: As Coleridge put it, 'the property of passion is not to create, but to set in increased activity'. Thus, in terms of familiar experience, while the persistent *knowledge* that we owe a letter to someone may be an insufficient stimulus to get us to write it, revival of feeling towards him – occasioned perhaps by re-reading his letter or by happening to talk to someone about him – may be a sufficient one. It seems likely, then, that when we are participants in an experience, feeling will tend to be sparked off in action, or where this is frustrated, eked out in anxiety. When, however, we go back over that experience, as spectators, we are free to savour *as feeling* the feeling that entered into it. This may help to explain why a tragic event on the stage is enjoyable, and why, though we experience fear vividly in the theatre we do not normally need to resist any impulse to get up and run away: and, again, the experience is exhilarating rather than debilitating. It may, moreover, be part of what is meant by 'psychic distance' – insisted on by some aestheticians as a necessary condition in an observer's relationship to a work of art.

The point under discussion is one that we have already glanced at once or twice in preceding pages: we saw that it was a pleasurable experience for members of a stage team to look back at the moments of panic in their performance, and for mothers and fathers to look back at the hazards of the children's day. To say that a spectator is able to 'savour feeling as feeling' is to claim that he is more aware of its *quality* as feeling. Let us go further now and see that this awareness enables him, as he looks back, to perceive the sequence and arrangement of feelings – the relation for example of fear to anger and anger to pride that might not inconceivably afflict a mother when her small child tries the fearfully impossible and achieves it. (The participant, vibrating to the particular emotion of the moment, has in any case no possibility of perceiving it in perspective, for the rest of the 'context' has yet to take place.) The crudity of the example, the gross terms for the emotions, do no justice to what is probably a highly delicate and intricate kind of response. There can be no doubt that the pattern of suspense and release of tension built up in even a simple story is a powerful part of its effect upon a listener. Beyond that, I can only refer to the experience of listening to music as something that seems to me analogous.

Finally I want to suggest that a spectator uses his freedom for the purpose of paying attention, in a way a participant is unable to, not only to the pattern, the form, taken by the feelings of the participants in an experience, but also to *forms* of other kinds.

There is, to begin with, the form presented by the events of the story as it is told, an arrangement given to them by the narrator. It is easy to overlook the degree of choice that is offered to him and to suppose that a form inevitably arises with the events themselves. It was found that children with particular language difficulties, on being asked to describe 'how we make a cup of tea', would sometimes begin with putting the sugar in and end with putting the kettle on! Inclusion and exclusion are necessary before 'an event' is derived, as we have seen, from the flux of sense data: and further selection among events creates a narrative – though the two processes are not so independent of each other as that wording suggests. The form of events in a story depends in part, it will be clear, on what is left out: and then on the arrangement of what is included. When something dramatic happens to us, something worth repeated telling, we may be aware not only that we make a fresh selection and a rearrangement of events in our account to create effects suited to different listeners (a parent, a child, an admirer, a rival), but also that some arrangements are in general more effective than others: or putting that another way, we may ruin even the best story in the telling. That quite young children may possess a highly general sense of the form of events is suggested by the summary Clare gave, when she was three, of the story of Cinderella: 'A bit sad book about two ugly sisters and a girl they were ugly to.'

Gossip, again using the term broadly, is a kind of talk that very readily throws up the amateur expert: we are likely to have among our acquaintances people known to be 'good talkers', lively *raconteurs*, or good to listen to on certain areas of their experience.* And this, I think, hints at the fact that part of our enjoyment of gossip is appreciation of the *way it is done*. (Since the alternative to gossip is often, not silence, but the banality of 'small talk', there is little wonder that we appreciate such advice beforehand as, 'You ought to get Smith on to his

* For an example, see Chapter 4, p. 172.

experiences in so-and-so'.) By 'the way it is done' I mean here the *forms of the language used*, the speaker's choice of a word or an intonation or a tone of voice or a tempo – his ear for 'how it sounds' in a quite literal sense. Part of what is involved here also, I think, is the expressive nature of such talk: the speaker is not only putting a story across but also putting himself over. It is what is *characteristic* in his way of talking that in this connexion we enjoy – characteristic of him, and differentiating one contributor from another. Part of the glow that we come away with after listening is the feeling that so-and-so's 'a card', or 'a comic' or 'a sweet child' – or whatever formula we use to epitomize our relations of feeling towards people. Transatlantic tape-swappers say that even the disembodied voice has formal features that revive such feelings in a way written communication cannot.

The written language has its own forms, different from the forms of the spoken language and performing different functions. Overriding these differences, however, they are similar in the respect we are now considering. In the written language in the role of spectator there can be no doubt that the arrangement of forms and the response of a reader to the arrangement are essential features. Art – and with it literature – has been defined at one time or another as 'created form', 'significant form', 'expressive form'. The definition quoted from Susanne Langer on p. 112 bears out this central notion. It seems likely that the principal difference between the work of gifted writers – literature – and the spectator role writing of the less gifted and the young, will lie in their differing ability to handle linguistic forms and control the effects of formal arrangements. This is a matter we shall take up fully in a later chapter.

III

Our interest in other people's lives is a primary one. The young may show particular interest in those who seem to represent people they might become, the older in those who seem to represent people they might have been, but this is merely part of a concern in general for people whose many motives may one day affect us, and whose activities seem to probe possibilities of experience unexplored in our own lives. We 'catch up' with the lives of friends and relations in gossip when we meet them, or by letter from time to time: we keep up with the lives of public figures through newspapers, radio, television: and beyond that, if we read stories or watch films or plays, we are moved to do so above all by a desire to extend our own lives into the lives of others. Susanne Langer, emphasizing a point we have already taken from Freud, calls the substance of fiction 'virtual experience'. As participants we have only one life to live: as spectators, an infinite number is open to us.

The sharp distinction at any moment between our own first-hand experience and anything that may happen to anybody else – and it is, I believe, a distinction upon which our mental health depends – is a distinction *of the moment*. Looked back on, the experiences others have related merge into the experiences we have had ourselves: as a basis for making generalizations, judgements, evaluations, decisions, we call upon both. We become experienced people, in other words, as a result of the fusion of other people's experiences with our own. All this claims no more than we have already claimed when, with Martin Buber, we say that it is by experience 'as we' that we build the common world in which we live. Clearly, however, we cannot 'take over' the experience of others and add it to our own by simple addition. The fusion is something we must engineer each for himself: but how?

'The reader's mind,' Burt has said, 'is the author's box of paints'. (Burt, 1933, p. 282) In other words, what the writer communicates to the reader is made out of the raw material the reader already possesses – and the statement applies equally to speaker and listener, of course. We are pushed back to recognition of the primacy of first-hand experience, the data delivered by the senses. But having already glanced at the way this sense material requires processing before we arrive even at what might be called 'an event' in our own experience, we are prepared to find the operation both complicated and, in our present state of knowledge, mysterious. We can only add here that, if the organization required on the part of the perceiver to make sense of his perceptions is a complex one, making demands, on the one hand, upon his already processed record of past experience, and, on the other, utilizing the agency of language, then we can more readily conceive that an altered mode of organizing could enable him to reconstruct to similar effect the experience of another communicated to him in language. Or, putting it even more approximately, if the way a man 'takes over' his own fresh experience is seen not as one of simple addition but as one of modifying a total past in recognition and accommodation of the new, then the process appears not so dissimilar from that by which he might also modify a total past in recognition of something other than his own first-hand experiences.

Both processes concern us here – the not-so-simple addition of new experience, whether our own or somebody else's – for both are particularly active when we take up the role of spectator. The new experiences are interpreted, structured in the light of the old, and in that modified form incorporated: the body of experience, the world representation, is modified, re-interpreted, in the light of the new, and its comparative unity and coherence as far as possible maintained. What we said in Chapter 2 about the role of make-believe games is in fact true of all these 'imaginary spectatorship activities': it is their function to preserve our view of the world from fragmentation and disharmony, to maintain it as something we can continue to live with as happily as may be. It is for this purpose that we take a holiday from the participant role – or, to pick up a phrase we have used earlier (p. 20), we cease operating in the actual world *via* the representation, and begin instead to 'operate directly upon the representation itself'.

Remember that in all this re-interpretation and modification, we are primarily involved with organization according to 'the way I feel about things'. Evaluation is central to the process. Our enjoyment of the stories of other men's lives cannot be explained simply in terms of *knowing*, but must always have a strong element of feeling – including, 'How would I have felt if that had been me?'. And the impact of other men's experience upon our view of the world, through the medium of gossip or make-believe or fiction, is likely to challenge our value system in a way it does not challenge our system of information. It is, however, in looking at what goes on when we are spectators of our own past experience that we see most clearly the central importance of evaluation.

As participants we generate expectations from past experience, put them to the test of actuality, and modify our representation of the world (our predictive apparatus, the basis of all our expectations) in the light of what happens. As we go back over the same experience, now in the role of spectator, we may make further and probably more far-reaching adjustments – for, as we have seen, we are likely to refer to a more extensive set of values than we are free to do as participants. But occasionally, what happens is *so* unlike our expectations that we are not able to achieve even an initial adjustment 'in our stride', as we participate. Events do not wait for us, so we participate as best we can, but when the experience is over we are left with a *positive need* to take up the role of spectator and work upon it further – in order, as we say, 'to come to terms with it'. We may make repeated approximations towards adjustment, gradually over a period of time regaining harmony: or we may, if we choose, make no such effort and merely *reject* the recalcitrant experience, go on basing our expectations upon a representation of the world in which such things 'simply don't happen'.

Among his observations of young children's make-believe

play, Piaget records this one of a girl aged three years eleven months:

She was impressed by the sight of a dead duck which had been plucked and put on the kitchen table. The next day I found J. lying motionless on the sofa in my study, her arms pressed against her body and her legs bent: 'What are you doing, J? Have you a pain? – Are you ill?' – '*No, I'm a dead duck.*'

And this one of the same child at four years six months:

I knocked against J's hands with a rake and made her cry. I said how sorry I was, and blamed my clumsiness. At first she didn't believe me and went on being angry as though I had done it deliberately. Then she suddenly said, half appeased: 'You're Jacqueline and I'm daddy. There!' (She hit my fingers.) 'Now say: "You've hurt me".' (I said it.) 'I'm sorry, darling. I didn't do it on purpose. You know how clumsy I am, . . .' etc. In short she merely reversed the parts and repeated my exact words.

Piaget comments:

These forms of play, which consist in liquidating a disagreeable situation by re-living it in make-believe, clearly illustrate the function of symbolic play, which is to assimilate reality to the ego while freeing the ego from the demands of accommodation. . . . In the case of the dead duck, it was merely the unpleasantness of a disturbing sight that was liquidated in this way. (Piaget, 1951, pp. 133–4)

For young children, as we have seen, going back over experiences in the role of spectator ('freeing the ego from the demands of accommodation') typically takes the form of make-believe play – a representation in action with words as appropriate. For us, talking and writing will perform a similar function. A friend of mine once when he was on the way to a week-end conference had his luggage stolen while he went for tea in the train. He spent a good deal of his week-end coming to terms with this minor misfortune by telling the story to anyone who would listen. It is common belief that talking about distressing experiences 'does one good'. The sympathy of our listeners may be some comfort to us, but experience proves that an audience of any kind is better than none at all.

However, it is not only the unfortunate who are in need of a listener: take for example someone in love. The fact is that experiences may be so unexpectedly *wonderful* as to overwhelm us as well as so unexpectedly distressing. The need is similar, though we may talk of one as 'worshipping' or 'paying homage' and the other as 'coming to terms'. It is not irrelevant to point out here that there is just as much poetry of love and worship – secular and divine – in the English language as there is poetry about death and separation and rejection and the transience of happiness. W. H. Auden has defined poetry as 'paying homage by naming', and suggested that we all possess from time to time in our lives 'sacred objects' to which (or to whom) homage is due. (Auden, 1956, p. 30) Gossip after the event – of the kind we instanced in referring to the party-after-the-performance – has something of the aspect of paying homage to the event, though the *need* to do so will not always be strong enough to bring it into this category.

As far as the written language in the role of spectator is concerned, it is appropriate that we should think of poetry at this point, for it is probably in poetry that the processes of 'paying homage' and 'coming to terms' are at their most intense. Poetry arises when something *needs to be said*, and the need is satisfied in the mere saying. It is a need on the part of the writer: but it is one that a reader may share, and where this is so the reader may come to terms with his own experience as he responds to the writing. If this seems a haphazard affair, remember that poetry will tend to deal not with the trivial, conventionally social aspects of experience but with what Coleridge referred to as 'the all in each of every man'.

Notice finally that the needs we have been referring to arise from the challenge experience may present us with to re-evaluate, to make changes in our value systems, the organization of our feelings about things. What we have been saying, then, is that though usually we take up the role of spectator for the pleasure of it – 'for fun' – there will be times when there is a stronger pressure upon us and we do so 'from need'. Mercifully, it is very difficult in any instance for an observer, and even for the speaker or writer himself, to determine how far it is fun and how far it is need that is operating. I remember one simple poem written by an eleven-year-old girl setting forth the ordinary happiness and security of bedtime in an ordinary home: it was only by accident long afterwards that I discovered how precious the thing of words must have been to the writer – a token of a reality which she had never experienced.

If action and decision are the keynotes of the participant role, how shall we characterize the spectator role? We have suggested that freedom from a participant's responsibilities allows a spectator to evaluate more broadly, to savour feelings, and to contemplate *forms* – the formal arrangement of feelings, of events and – let us now add – of ideas, and the forms of the language, spoken or written, in which the whole is expressed. But it is not enough to say that freedom from certain activities makes others possible: to characterize the role of spectator we must attempt to explain why these particular activities should be appropriate to it.

Piaget would say that the key-note was 'assimilation', a very useful but difficult idea. Let us say – as we began to say in looking at make-believe play – that in contemplating the new (the experience of which we are spectators) we are *more than usually concerned with our total world view*. We may expand this statement in three ways, all of them I believe relevant.

1. It indicates a concern to incorporate the new into the total. Since this is essentially a matter of *organizing* (organizing the new and reorganizing the total, each in the light of the other) it does not seem surprising that we should choose a way of using language that puts more than usual stress upon its *forms*, and

that we should concern ourselves with the formal arrangements of events, ideas, feelings.

2. It indicates an underlying concern for our ability to anticipate events: our world representation is the storehouse of our expectations about the future. That we should enjoy entering into other people's experiences, and imaginary experiences, and working upon our own, reflects our concern to explore to the limits the possibilities of experience. Moreover, as material from which to predict, the patterns taken by events are more powerful than their random particularities.

3. It indicates an underlying concern not only for life but also for the person who lives it: the view of the world with which we face each new encounter must be, as far as possible, one we can 'live with'. The kind of reorganization of the total that the new will demand, to satisfy this requirement, will be predominantly re-evaluation, a modification of the way our feelings are organized. Hence the importance of the opportunity to savour feeling, of the attention to the formal arrangement of feelings, and of a use of language (as for example in poetry) in which feeling is expressed by the manipulation of linguistic forms.

Informing people, instructing people, persuading people, arguing, explaining, planning, setting forth the pros and cons and coming to a conclusion – these are participant uses of language, uses of language to get things done. Make-believe play, day-dreaming aloud, chatting about our experiences, gossip, travellers' tales and other story-telling, fiction, the novel, drama, poetry – these are uses of language in the spectator role. Persuasion as a participant use may cause us some difficulty, for part of the art of persuasion is undoubtedly that of working upon the feelings of our listeners, and to this end we may employ many of the means used by the raconteur, the dramatist, the novelist, the poet. Imagine there was once an Indian chief who gathered his tribe together by the lake's edge and solemnly and ceremoniously harangued them to the effect that, having exhausted the supply of fish in these waters, they must gather up their belongings and set out in search of another home by another shore. If at the end his people applauded and *did nothing more* and if he was nevertheless content – then that was language in the role of spectator. But, of course, he would not be content: it is decision and action he is after. However, we might conclude the fable by conceiving that the same day a year later finds the tribe prosperously re-settled by a lake teeming with fish and the chief repeating by request his moving oration, the people applauding, and all being content to leave it at that! No doubt, works of persuasion will sometimes possess a secondary role, will live on in the spectator role when their task in a participant sense no longer operates. Churchill's war speeches are often quoted in this category; and it is certainly true that the kind of literature we call satire refers very often to causes that if not lost are won.

Another distinction that may be difficult to make is that between informing people about our experiences (which would be a participant activity) and inviting them to share in the process by which we pay homage to, or celebrate, or gloat over our past experiences – an activity in the role of spectator. I once saw a note-book in which a six-and-a-half-year-old boy in an Infant School had scribbled vigorously all over one page with brown chalk and on the opposite page had written:

> Exploring the rocks
> a place called Cromer
> I knocked the loose lumps of mud.

The teacher liked this, but she liked it better still when with the aid of her red pencil it had become: 'Exploring the rocks *at* a place called Cromer, (*comma*) I knocked the loose lumps of mud.' I would suggest – though I admit the distinction is a very fine one – that the boy wrote something in the spectator role, and the teacher turned it into something in the participant role. By her version, he was using the kind of language we use in telling people what they want to know, or what we want them to know: what he was doing in his version was, I believe, the same thing as he had done in his drawing – *gloating over* his holiday – or celebrating it, or paying homage to it as 'a sacred object'. To the teacher he was saying, 'here it is, you can share it with me'.

When we use language in the participant role we select and order our material according to the demands made by something outside ourselves, something that exists in the situation: information may be true or false and independent observation of all the circumstances could be used to determine which it is: instructions may be precise or vague, clear or confused and their usefulness to people carrying them out provides the basis for determining which they are: argument may be proved illogical, persuasion may prove ineffectual. But in language in the role of spectator we operate on a different principle. We select and arrange our material first to please ourselves: and secondly, not to please other people but to enable others to share our pleasure – which is not the same thing. (Imagine that as I walk on the sea-shore I pick up a pocketful of shells and come home and arrange them. I could select them and arrange them according to two different principles. The unlikelier one shows me to be a biologist: I have picked up shells I needed to complete my showcase and when I get home I arrange them as part of an exemplification of related species of marine life. If you were a better biologist than I was, you might come up behind me and say, 'You've got that wrong – you should put *this* one in *that* place'. The more likely situation – in which I am myself again – is one in which I come home and arrange the shells on my mantelpiece. My principle of arrangement is to make a display, a pattern, that pleases me. You could not then come up and say, 'You've got that wrong', because there is no right and wrong beyond the pleasure or displeasure I feel. My criterion is one of 'appropriateness' – the appropriateness of each item to the other items and to the whole of the design *as it appears to me*.)

Lawrence said, 'It is the way our sympathy flows and recoils that really determines our lives'. Let us broaden that for our present purposes to: 'we act and decide in accordance with the sort of people we are'. In participant activity it is the construction we place upon the *new* – the current encounter with actuality – that we attend to: as spectators, it is essentially the *total* – the accumulated view of the world that makes us the sort of people we are – that we are concerned with. Thus, though we have assigned a function, a use, to the language of spectatorship, it is a use which is clearly distinguishable from that of a participant. 'Language to get things done' remains intact as a criterion for the one role, and the language of being and becoming may roughly describe the other.

CHAPTER FOUR

Now that you go to School

═══

I

MICHAEL OAKESHOTT, in his commentary on the language of young children, quoted on p. 90 above, implies that as the child grows older he handles language symbols more competently but also that he becomes more and more moved by 'the desire to communicate' and less and less by 'the delight of utterance'. There is an echo here of the familiar notion of 'the shades of the prison house', the change from what is essentially play to what is essentially work. D. J. Enright in the following poem sees entering school as the point of change – change from a delight in things, and in words that stay close to things, to 'a proper respect for words', words that come to stand between us and the nature of things:

Blue Umbrellas

'The thing that makes a blue umbrella with its tail –
How do you call it?' you ask. Poorly and pale
Comes my answer. For all I can call it is peacock.

Now that you go to school, you will learn how we
   call all sorts of things;
How we mar great works by our mean recital.
You will learn, for instance, that Head Monster is
   not the gentleman's accepted title;
The blue-tailed eccentrics will be merely peacocks;
   the dead bird will no longer doze
Off till tomorrow's lark, for the letter has killed him.
The dictionary is opening, the gay umbrellas close.

 Oh our mistaken teachers! –
It was not a proper respect for words we need,

But a decent regard for things, those older creatures
      and more real.
Later you may even resort to writing verse
To prove the dishonesty of names and their black
      greed –
To confess your ignorance, to expiate your crime,
      seeking one spell to lift another curse.
Or you may, more commodiously, spy on your children,
      busy discoverers,
Without the dubious benefit of rhyme.*

There seems to lie behind that poem a conception of language as having three forms: first, the language that comes from dictionaries and that teachers teach, a language that takes us away from things: second, the language of poets which seeks to rediscover (in Lawrence's phrase) 'the thingness of things', so becoming a spell that lifts the curse of ordinary language and its 'mean recital'; and third, the language of children – referred to both at the opening and the close of the poem – the language of discovery, a language for exploring a world full of things, and a language as yet undivorced from the concrete reality of things.

That there is some affinity between a young child's speech and the language of poetry is a point we shall take up later in this chapter. I am concerned here with the distinction between the first use of language referred to above and the other two: that is to say, between language that takes us away from things and language that stays close to things.

Peacocks are game-birds and, so to speak, accustomed to being eaten – certainly from as far back as Roman times. I have never seen a recipe for peacock pie nor an order to a game-keeper or a poultry-monger for the delivery of birds. However, it would I am sure have been a mere inconvenience to the buyers and sellers and cooks if at each transaction a lively sense of the actual creature in its pomp and finery and 'style', in its

*From: D. J. Enright, *Bread Rather than Blossoms*, Secker & Warburg, 1956.

'thingness', had interfered in the dispatch of verbal business. Yet when the chronicler in the Bible wished to describe the wealth of King Solomon and wrote of him, 'For the king had at sea a navy of Tharshish with the navy of Hiram; once in three years came the navy of Tharshish, bringing gold, and silver, ivory and apes, and peacocks', it is appropriate that we should invest the word with some vividness of recollection of the living creature. And, despite Enright's complaints, given the encouragement of a suitable context, we are able to do so: the word 'peacock' will produce a flash of particular colour and movement and style on the screen of the mind as readily as will 'the thing that makes a blue umbrella with its tail'.

The point is a simple one indeed – and it constitutes no criticism of Enright's poem (else we should be in danger of mistaking what is a poem for a recipe or an order to the poultry-monger). It allows me to comment, however, that I see the beginning of school in a different light from that represented in the poem: not as a closing in of the work-a-day, but as the *development of difference* in language usage: a continuation and refinement, on the one hand, of language in the role of spectator, preserving the delight in utterance, providing for the contemplation of things in all their concrete particularity; and on the other hand the development by gradual evolution of language in the role of participant – language to get things done, the language of recipes and orders to the poultry-monger and of other more intellectual transactions.

II

The idea that learning is something you do sitting in a seat is a highly sophisticated notion and, to a young child, a very peculiar one. It symbolizes, probably more sharply than anything else, the long-standing traditional distinction between school learning and the kind of learning we all undertake from time to time at home, in the street, in strange cities, in the countryside – and many other places. Yes, we may also visit a library and learn a good deal without stirring from the seat, but to do so betokens a high level of verbal sophistication on our part.

It is to our national credit, then, that only in very rare instances do children in our infant schools spend the day sitting at desks. Rather, they are here, there and everywhere, up and about; going off to ask somebody something or tell him something else; going off to see for themselves; standing at a bench or a table, moving round to get a better grip or take a longer look; working or playing in different parts of the room or the building in accordance with what is to be found to do there. And the area given over to these operations, indoors and out, tends to grow greater and more diversified as the advantages of such active learning become clear to the people who control the design of schools.

The point itself is far from trivial, but it is here to introduce an even more important general principle: that in school we cannot afford to ignore all that has gone on before. So often in the past we have tried to make a fresh start, at the risk of cutting off the roots which alone can sustain the growth we look for. It is not only that the classroom must more and more merge into the world outside it, but that the processes of school learning must merge into the processes of learning that begin at birth and are life-long. We can no longer regard school learning as simply an interim phase, a period of instruction and apprenticeship that marks the change from immaturity to maturity, from play in the nursery to work in the world. School learning must both build upon the learning of infancy and foster something that will continue and evolve throughout adult life.

We have seen that talk is a major instrument of learning in infancy; that the infant *learns by talking* and that he *learns to talk by talking*. In trying to explain why it is that normal children succeed in this astonishing task of learning to talk we suggested it was because the two tasks – learning in the most general sense, that is, making sense of the world, and learning to talk – are so closely enmeshed. When we arrive at the school stage we must add writing and reading to talking, but the stress upon the operational value of language use remains the same, and teachers should rely on a similar motive – on the dividends that language learning pays.

Putting this at its simplest, what children use language for in school must be 'operations' and not 'dummy runs'. They must continue to use it to make sense of the world: they must *practise* language in the sense in which a doctor 'practises' medicine and a lawyer 'practises' law, and *not* in the sense in which a juggler 'practises' a new trick before he performs it. This way of working does not make difficult things easy: what it does is make them worth the struggle. It is, of course, subject to a good deal of criticism: it has been called 'language learning by osmosis', or 'learning by soaking' and the like. Teachers need to defend themselves against such criticism in two ways: in theory, by insisting that learning is an evolutionary process in which the fullest possible development at any stage is the best preparation for ensuing stages; and in practice (or 'more commodiously') by ensuring as far as they can that the operations undertaken by their pupils offer genuine challenge, and result in the extension and deepening of their experience. And where classes of young children are so organized that 'there are forty feeding as one' (as Wordsworth said of cattle), this is all but an impossibility.

The talk that goes along with the activities I referred to at the beginning of this section is essential to the learning, and it is a direct continuation of the small child's talk in his family. In due course, moreover, writing will grow from that talk: by 'grow' I do not mean to suggest that it comes without effort on the part of the child and of the teacher, but that their efforts are directed towards that growth from those roots. Yet no longer ago than 1925 teachers were exhorted by their advisers in one instance to 'make a fresh start' when the time came to teach their children to write. A Board of Education publication entitled

General Report on the Teaching of English in London Elementary Schools, 1925 (H.M.S.O., 1929, p. 19), drawn up by His Majesty's Inspectors, has this to say:

As long as children are expected to write for the most part upon subjects which afford them no opportunity for imitation of what has been well done in speech by their teacher, or in writing by the authors they are studying, they are not likely to express themselves well. And when the subjects are such as deliberately throw them into the atmosphere of their out-of-school life, it is almost certain that they will express themselves in the language of the home and the street, which, teachers constantly assure us, is ever in conflict with the language the school is trying to secure. And this language cannot be corrected by talking about it; a more correct language must be built up by the imitation of better models of speech and writing.

If this view is accepted, it is important that in the earlier stages the child's exercises in writing English should be based upon what he reads and hears in school, and not until he has acquired some familiarity with the language, which the school is trying to build up, should he be asked to express himself upon other topics.

The writers of this report, in spite of the wise things they say in other sections, could not have held an 'operational' view of speech: not appreciating its essential role in bringing a child from helplessness at birth to a five-year-old's grip on his world, they are prepared to discount it as 'incorrect', antagonistic to a teacher's purposes. An inevitable consequence of this would be to discredit a child's speech in his own eyes, at least in so far as his school career was concerned. (It is perhaps worth noting that the Inspectors were not so sure of their position as they make themselves out to be: why otherwise do they hedge over that last half-sentence? To state their case logically, it should have read: 'and not until he has acquired some familiarity with the language which the school is trying to build up should he be asked to express himself upon other topics'. That would have been to distinguish 'the language which the school is trying to build up' quite clearly from the language the children possess: by enclosing the words 'which the school is trying to build up' in commas, they make it a non-defining clause – an explanatory addition – so implying that what they referred to is 'the language' – the English language. This constitutes a quite unsupported claim that what the teachers teach is 'the language' whereas what the children use is *not*!)

We cannot afford to be in doubts over this matter: what the children speak is an operationally effective form of the English language. We may not like their speech, but if this is the case we should at least be clear on the grounds of our objection. Effective communication is a social good: for that reason it is desirable that the forms of our speech should be appropriate to the occasion and intelligible and acceptable to our listeners. But such a statement goes no way towards justifying the absolute judgements of right and wrong we have so often applied: it calls instead for judgements that are *relative* to particular circumstances. Speech cannot be effective if it is unintelligible: but the chatter of two West Indian children over a game of five-stones is none the worse for being unintelligible to me as I walk by. Oaths and blasphemies that offend one regional group or one generation are often acceptable currency in another. And grammar – that King Charles's head of any talk about talk – must be seen for what it is, a system of relationships that makes language possible: something therefore that is to be found in any and every dialect or variant of any language. As Henry Sweet put it in 1891, 'Whatever is in general use in a language is for that very reason grammatically correct'. Thus the grammatical features that we may find unacceptable in a child's speech are not examples of 'bad grammar': they are the grammatical features of a *language we find unacceptable*. I need not labour the point that it is no solution in such a case to attempt to 'teach grammar'. The forms of speech we find acceptable will be adopted by children only as they gain experience of them by listening and only as they are disposed (for one reason or another) and encouraged (by one means or another) to imitate what they have heard. And in this respect a grammatical feature ('them strawberry ones') is in no sense different from a vocabulary item (say a four-letter word), a mode of address, a pronunciation, or any other speech form.

When we speak of acceptable forms we probably have in the backs of our minds the variety of English that has been labelled 'Standard English'. It has been defined as 'that type of English used by educated people when carrying on their affairs publicly, in writing and in speech'. (Cassidy, 1966) What is important is to recognize that the term indicates in fact not one but many varieties of English. The Standard English used in Glasgow differs from that used in Edinburgh, that of Boston differs from that of San Francisco – and so on for Melbourne, London, Toronto and the rest. Over and above differences in vocabulary and – less prominently – in syntax, Standard English is spoken in a great variety of regional accents. Nevertheless, all these differences are of far less importance than the common intelligibility and the common functions of Standard English – and this of course is seen at its greatest in the written forms.

Standard English will be the mother tongue of some of the pupils in our schools: others will have acquired it, in addition to the language of their homes, by the time they leave school. On the other hand, in some situations the question of whether or not they should acquire it simply will not arise: other matters will be of obviously greater importance.

All living languages are subject to change and Standard English is no exception. Though we change our speech habits in the course of a lifetime, nevertheless there is likely to be a greater difference between speakers of an earlier and a later generation at any one time than there will be between, for example, my speech at the one age and my speech at the other. Educators have often ignored this difference between the generations and wasted a good deal of energy over battles they were destined to lose: battles to preserve – so it seemed to them – decent standards of speech: battles that were in reality attacks on quite trivial changes from the forms of their own speech (for example, 'different to' where they said 'different from', 'due to' where they said 'owing to', or 'disinterested' where they said 'uninterested'). 'Change and decay in all around I see' is what the hymn says: the real pedant sees change in everything that leads to the language as he learnt it, but regards all subsequent changes as decay.

Let me suggest one way of approaching the problems of this confusing situation. In ordinarily favourable circumstances no one has a greater influence than the teacher in determining what speech is acceptable in his classroom: the language of that group in that situation will evolve in the light of the standards of acceptability set by the teacher. Clearly a great deal depends therefore upon his own speech, to which the children listen: again, even from this limited point of view of 'acceptable forms', it is important that no child in the class should be a non-talker, for the listening and the producing need to interact. Given such a situation, the first thing I would say is that we must begin from where the children are: in other words there can be no alternative in the initial stages to total acceptance of the language the children bring with them. We cannot afford to 'make a fresh start'. From there I would go on to develop an awareness of difference among forms of speech: at a fairly explicit level this might lead to the recognition of interesting differences in the way different people speak and the way they speak for different purposes. Much less explicitly, it will enter into dramatic improvisation – the need for a king to talk like a king and his wise men, perhaps, to talk like a book. An acceptance of differences seems to me more important throughout the whole junior school age-range than any sense that approval narrows down upon one form, the socially acceptable. And from awareness of differences can grow, without anything of the sort necessarily being formulated, the habit of adapting speech to suit different purposes and occasions.

However, a teacher must in the end face for himself the com-plexities of our present social situation and make his own decision with regard to the children he is responsible for. We have moved quite rapidly in recent years away from the public dominance of the 'B.B.C. voice'; we can all point to individuals whose lack of acceptable speech does not appear to have held them back. Yet the ordinary child who grows up to apply for one of a range of jobs may well need to call upon his listening experience of Standard English – as things are today. Perhaps it is patience that a teacher needs most: opportunities for his own speech to influence that of the children arise mainly in areas where new experiences demand new language, and in particular where problems are discussed in a way that is more *general* and more *abstract* than talk in many homes is likely to be. Again, as children grapple with the written language, first by listening to stories read to them, and later in their own writing and reading, they move more directly into the sphere of influence of Standard English. Above all, patience is required in the form of trusting to the total process of schooling – despite its evident failures. If in the early stages we can increase the range of a child's choice, encourage acceptance of difference and adaptability to changing situations, and at the same time leave him in unimpaired command of the speech of his home, then I believe we shall have produced the best possible foun-dation for all his later uses of language, including that of taking over – if and when he feels the need for it – some spoken form of Standard English.

III

Language, as we have seen, is one way of representing or symbolizing our experience of the world. Sapir points out that it has 'an almost unique position of intimacy among all known symbolisms' and suggests as a reason that it is 'learned in the earliest years of childhood' and learned 'piecemeal, in constant association with the colour and the requirements of actual contexts'. (Sapir, 1961, p. 10) This is to say that, because early language is tied to the here and now, it grows its roots in first-hand experience, and, secondly, that it is by virtue of this characteristic that it continues to represent experience intimately, recalling here-and-now aspects of remote experiences as we represent them verbally in our speaking and writing, or call upon them to *realize* what we are reading.

As adults, we rely upon language as a means of making other people's experiences our own – and, through our reading, a vast field of secondary experience lies open to us by this means. The quality of the experience we gain must rely upon the effectiveness of the instrument we use, that is to say upon the vitality of the connexions between our language and our primary experiences, our encounters with reality via the senses, emotions, intuitions. And this vitality probably derives above all from early experiences of words with things.

Luigi Meneghello, an Italian writer and scholar, has this to say about words learnt in childhood, words in the home dialect as distinct from those acquired later:

There are two layers in the personality of a man; the top ones are like superficial wounds – the Italian, French and Latin words: underneath are the ancient wounds which on being healed have formed scars – words in dialect. On being touched the scars set off a perceptible chain reaction, difficult to explain to those who have no dialect. There is an indestructible kernel of *apprehended* matter, attached to the tendrils of the senses; the dialect word is *always* pegged to reality, because they are one and the same thing, perceived before we learnt to reason, and never to disappear even when we have been taught reason in another language. This holds good, above all, with names of objects.

But the kernel of primitive matter (whether in connexion with names or any other word) contains uncontrollable forces because it exists in a pre-logical sphere where the associations are free and fundamentally unstable. Dialect therefore is in certain respects reality and in others instability.

> I feel an almost physical pain in the nerves, deep down inside me, which produce words like *basavéjo* (sting of a bee) and *barbastrijo* (bat), *anda* (snake) and *ava* (bee), even *rùa* (wheel) and *pùa* (doll). It comes shooting up through me like a *lamposgiantizo* (flash of lightning), I feel conscious of that ultimate fusion of what we call life, that indestructible core, the very bedrock. (Meneghello, 1967, pp. 90 and 91)

'Instability' is at first sight difficult to reconcile with 'the very bedrock': I think it is a *rational* instability that is intended, indicating the absence of a systematic or logical framework, and 'the very bedrock' suggests the kind of conviction that multiple associations forged in successive first-hand experiences might convey.

Be that as it may, I would put forward the notion that much of the later detail of a man's world representation, filled in by relating idea to idea, or one verbally communicated experience to another, may retain its intimacy with actuality, its fidelity to things as they are, by virtue of the fact that elements in his individual language have remained from childhood 'always pegged to reality' – and enough of them to act as focal reference points for the structure as a whole.

All this goes to support the claim that talking-and-doing must be given major stress throughout the Primary School. Language must continue to grow roots in first-hand experience. The headmaster I heard of recently who said uneasily as he began to show his American visitor round the school, 'I don't know what's the matter – it isn't usually as quiet as this', was splendidly unaware that his comment might sound odd! Most of our Primary School buildings were not planned for the kind of work that goes on there today, so if the tide of busy and talkative children washes right up to the door of the headmaster's room, that may be taken as a good sign. For the smaller the working groups – down to a pair – the greater the total of relevant talk that can go on at any one time. And the more experienced the class in this way of working, the greater the amount of useful consultation between groups, and with the teacher. What in a traditional curriculum would have been history or science or geography or number-work or painting or English – all this may go on without distinction and all equally capable of contributing to the forging of links between language and first-hand experience.

Talk in a participant role provides also the most efficient schooling in *listening*. Young children, in their egocentrism, have to learn to cooperate and they have to learn the language of cooperation: if talking is to assist cooperative doing, it must move out of egocentrism towards reciprocity, and success in a joint undertaking is a built-in incentive. It has too often been assumed in the past that young children without any such schooling were capable of listening to the sustained monologue of a teacher. A London Junior Schoolgirl knew better when she commented recently upon a visitor in some such words as, 'Yes, I liked some of what she said – but she talked so much that there wasn't any time to learn'.

Much that is shared between children in this cooperative talk, however, will not be practical but expressive. (Sapir referred to the 'colour' as well as the 'requirements of actual contexts'.) Such talk will express in fact 'the way I feel about things' as well as communicate 'the way things are'. And if we are to pick up the implications of Meneghello's statement the expressions of feeling may well be of particular importance, contributing strongly to the 'ultimate fusion of what we call life'.

But talk is quicksilver. It is all very well to record that a joint activity may generate both practical and expressive talk, each with its own importance. The truth is that almost any sort of talk, given favourable circumstances, may break out at any time. The children in the following example were gathered round the teacher's desk, with the bits and pieces they had been working on, ostensibly to consult her:

E.C. I could buy a whole sack of potatoes with the money I've got at home. (*Referring to a bill he was working out.*) This isn't really a shopping list it's more a grocer's list. It's two sacks of potatoes. I'll need a five pound note.

P.S. In the olden days they didn't spell penny with a 'p' but with a 'd', didn't they?

G.H. You know carrots, those brown things on the top. Well my friend told me how to do it. You cut it off and wet the cotton wool and put it on and all the flowers grow out. You're the best lady I met in my life.

P.S. I wonder why rhinos are so fat yet they can run sixty miles an hour?

E.C. I'm going to live in a castle in the south of France in the summer. It was before gunpowder was invented and it's livable, but it's got dungeons and arrow-slits and gallows.

P.S. I can run sixty miles an hour in these shoes.

G.H. You know Little John in Robin Hood, well I thought he was little but he's about ten feet tall. (Rosen, 1966, p. 3).

The teacher receives what each has to say and needs, on this occasion, to say nothing in return.

A great deal of the most useful talk arises in connexion with events and activities that *have* taken place, inside or outside the school. Much of this will be in the participant role – talking to piece together the history of an old building or the accurate record of a pond-hunt, to make sense of facts and figures about the weather, or arrive at a solution to some such problem as 'how did they get the chains across the gorge to build the suspension bridge?' And much of it will be in the spectator role – individuals recreating in story the events of the day, or celebrating some precious moment of it – some notable find, or triumph, or disaster or even – occasionally – grief. Such talk merges, in the spectator role, with all the talk that arises from poems and stories, read or heard, told or written.

Two final points remain to be made in brief. It can hardly be doubted that the talk of young children is the direct precursor of their later thinking. Much of our thinking as adults seems to us to bear the guise of an inner debate: the 'voice of reason', the 'voice of conscience', the 'voice of ambition' – these *dramatis personae* have often enough been named, figuratively of course, but the figure seems right. In an earlier chapter we have considered Vygotsky's suggestion that 'speech for oneself' becomes internalized as 'inner speech' and then, by a further metamorphosis becomes verbal thinking. James Moffett, of the Harvard School of Education, elaborates on this point with some conviction: 'In order to generate some kinds of thoughts, a student must have *previously* internalized some discursive operations . . . Elicitation [e.g. "asking stimulating questions"] has a place certainly at some stage of instruction, but more basic is to create the kinds of social discourse that when internalized become the kinds of cognitive instruments called for by later tasks.' (Moffet, 1968, p. 70) We shall inquire into the nature of these instruments within the context of Chapter 5.

Connie Rosen, from whose article I quoted the example of talk with a teacher given above, introduces my second brief point with these comments on the talk in her own class of nine-year-olds:

. . . I'm not the type to say to them, 'Look here, I'm terribly sympathetic and understanding and you can tell me anything you like, my dears. Was that your mummy in that nice car? What a pretty dress you have on!' I know some people can and produce some kind of nice, warm conversation with young children, but I can't.

I can only aim at making a triangle of myself, the children and the activities outside both of us, but in which we are both involved for different reasons. We must make and do things, paint and stick and cut, go for walks, collect things, feel things and discuss them together. In some ways there is too much talk that needs pruning and trimming, and too little of the purposeful reasoning talk. The talk I am aiming for is the talk that arises from shared experiences, experiences enjoyable and interesting to all of us, organized and yet allowing the children freedom to express themselves. Talk that will encourage comment and criticism and lead them to think about what is happening to them. In the course of such activities I would hope to build a relationship where they could feel safe to talk about anything that concerned them, and then because they had learnt to talk in class in a particular way, we might produce the kind of remarks and questions and individual approach that Stephen can make. (Rosen, 1967, pp. 27–8)

It had been Stephen who, on the first day of the new term in a new school, had created the right orientation for the whole class by asking the question that lay buried in everybody's minds: 'When are you going to tell us the names of the teachers?'

Yes, the talk that constitutes learning of so many varieties is at one and the same time the means by which we must spin in the class-room the web of human relations. To this aspect I shall return in the last section of this chapter.

IV

Make-believe or dramatic play is a special form of talking-and-doing: dramatic speech is a special form of speech-with-action. As a way of dealing with other times and other places it is, as we have seen, more accessible to a child than verbal narration, and herein lies its importance. In narration, an event has to be verbalized if it is to feature at all: in dramatic play the situation and the actions within it are themselves represented, and the speech thus remains embedded, in context. In the earliest forms of such play a child simply speaks as though the enacted situation were in fact his present one. But soon, in order to get help, or to play with other children, or merely to be sociable, he may need to use speech in order to call up the scene or establish the course of the action: as for example, in the play of the two-and-a-half-year-old recorded on p. 52: 'Open door! Open door! Want to go shopping. Want to go shopping this way, Dad!... I've gone shopping. Could you have any spouts today?' So long as the child remains master of his own game these demands are likely to be easy to meet, but when a situation is corporately built up and developed they become less so.

One might say, then, that what is being manipulated in dramatic play, its medium, is human behaviour; and at the other end of a continuum, that is the medium in which the dramatist creates his work of art. In dramatic play as it develops in the primary school, author, players and audience are one: with the dramatist's stage play, they are three.

All kinds of psychological theories have been developed to underline and explain the educational importance of dramatic activity. Some of these stress the continuity of drama in school with the public art of drama on the stage; others stress the differences. There is pretty general agreement, however, that the scripted play made into a performance for an audience of parents and friends is not only the least appropriate form of activity for the primary school but would tend, in fact, to militate against those aspects of dramatic work that are of educational importance at this stage. The psychological theories about drama that seem to me most relevant to education as a whole are those that stress *spontaneity* and *exploration* – and neither is likely to flourish easily in a produced presentation of a dramatist's play 'using' young children. What will concern us in this section, therefore, is what might be described as the movement from make-believe play to dramatic *improvisation*.

I think young children appropriate other people's roles mainly as an expression of their admiration or envy. After a visit to a colleague and his family when Alison was three she established what might be called a 'routine' – a routine that survived throughout the summer. It went more or less like this: 'Dad, 'tend to be you're Taffy. I'm Gwynneth. . . . Taff! What are you doing, Taff?' (I'm chopping down a tree.) 'Can I help you, Taff? . . .' and so on. There is usually plenty of scope for a young child's admiration and envy of other people's lives – especially of older children or grown-ups. But if the impulse to behave in this way is – in a neutral sense – self-seeking, acquisitive, the behaviour itself results in a reduction of ego-centricity: from trial of other roles the child returns less firmly enclosed in his own point of view, his own set of feeling relationships. And a dramatic situation that really takes hold in a group propels the members of it more forcibly out of their own skins into somebody else's than any other form of representation can do at this early stage.

In the early stages of the primary school, play goes on much as it did at home. Singly, or in small groups, set going or assisted by toys, clothes, odds and ends of furniture and materials, and perhaps a miniature room they can sit in, children play at mothers and fathers, doctors and nurses, school, weddings, funerals, tea-parties and the like. Among the observations recorded in the Department of Education and Science report *Drama*, are the following:

Most of the play-corners that were seen were equipped with tables, chairs, dresser, often a cooking stove, a bed, and so on. The setting is usually structured towards domesticity. . . . In a Yorkshire school a boy dressed up as a girl had just married a girl dressed up as a boy and the whole class had participated in a dramatic reconstruction of a wedding. . . . When [the boys] begin to play in groups they use bricks, boxes, packing cases, anything that comes to hand that will enable them to build trains, ships, fire-engines, locomotives. In a school in the south-west the boys and girls were playing, as so often, apart. The boys who were sailors in a splendidly built ship joined the girls in their domestic play-corner only when they were invited to tea. . . . In a school in the north-west an infant had made a boat out of a corn-flake packet and two toilet rolls – 'and may God bless her and all who sail in her', he added. (H.M.S.O., 1968, p. 7)

As the play becomes more sociable, that is to say less and less the device of one child or of a succession of individuals in turn and more and more a corporate product, it becomes more demanding. 'Puppets' in the game become contributors, co-producers; and now planning talk may enter in to initiate the game or change its course. It becomes more demanding as more children are drawn in. But it is above all each child's increasing willingness and ability to respond to the play of other children that brings progress. Taking examples again from the Department of Education and Science report, *Drama*:

In the centre of an adjoining classroom four boys wearing cloaks and horned Viking helmets made out of cardboard were sitting one behind the other in a boat made out of bricks. The teacher said that they had heard a story of a Viking raid, they had painted an episode in the story, made a collage, and now they were acting it. They were rowing up the Thames to raid the city. . . . The 7 and 8 year olds were acting the story of Polyphemus. . . . They chose the story because they had heard it on the radio; but the selection of episodes was their own. . . . Their use of words was perfunctory, their mime was desultory. Yet of those aspects of the story which they did tackle, they made something individual: the storm that drove their boats onto the island, the search for the cave, the flock of sheep, and the final escape. . . . The older juniors were working on the story of Childe Rowland. They were dressed in costumes they had made themselves and used for text an interesting mixture of verse spoken in chorus for the narratives, and improvised dialogue for the action. . . . A third year class had pushed back the desks and in the few square feet that were clear in front of the blackboard they improvised a cross-channel swim with a bland and observant radio commentator. There were five English supporters at Dover and fifteen French for the interesting reason that the children found 'magnifique' more fun to yell than 'hurrah'. (H.M.S.O., 1968, pp. 8–11)

Clearly, the increasingly cooperative nature of the activity is not the only dimension upon which progress is made: it is accompanied by an extension in the range and complexity of the themes explored. It is here that the teacher has his opportunity – in making suggestions and providing material. Explorations of family life are likely to continue but they will be joined by improvisations upon less familiar experiences, improvisations calling upon knowledge newly acquired, and perhaps acquired specifically for the sake of the enactment. There may be historical themes – perhaps related to the history of the locality: themes of adventure and work and crime – loosely related to the contemporary social environment: and heroic themes, incidents from myth, legend and fairy-tale. The world of myth provides a rich source: its men and women are 'in outline', psychologically uncomplicated, and their deeds arise out of powerful motives: and the one world – that of Greek myth for example – can accommodate many stories. Children become familiar with its highly characteristic 'paraphernalia' – its chariots and temples and war-ships, its banquets and beggars and heroes in disguise – and its powerful gods. Perhaps it is simply that since the myths themselves are the handiwork of generations of improvisers they lend themselves to further improvisation.

Among these thematic extensions we can distinguish two kinds: first the comparatively open-ended situations such as the Viking raid or the cross-channel swim, and secondly – as in the Polyphemus incidents – the acting of a story that has a preordained course towards a preordained end. Clearly this is an important distinction in the bearing it will have, at a later stage, on the relationship between improvisation and the scripted play. I must begin by endorsing Dorothy Heathcote's pronouncement: 'Drama is *not* stories retold in action. Drama *is* human beings confronted by situations which change them because of what they must face in dealing with those challenges.' (Heathcote, 1967, p. 30)

There is no doubt that improvisation as some teachers organize it does turn out no more than a 'story retold in action'. Success or failure is measured in terms of 'getting the story right' and this often descends to trivial detail – remembering to close the (imaginary) door or step over the (imaginary) parapet. On the other hand, there is ample room for exploration in the face of a situation in which much is fore-known: the exploration is a realization, a bringing to life. And when one boy, as David, faces another boy, as Goliath, the confrontation may be a sharp one, a challenge that has to be dealt with. One of the most teasing problems we have to meet in studying the way language works is still that of understanding how utterances come to have meaning for the hearer. And that is at the root of what concerns us at the moment. Were the Bible stories more meaningful to the medieval townspeople because, in the mystery plays, they set them forth in their own dress – in the terms of their own habits and occupations and environment? And can it be that the children who improvised upon the theme of Macbeth in such words as 'This banquet is too good of you' – 'Nothing is too good for you. You are my king.' and 'Murder Duncan? But I always thought women were gentle people.' – 'Now you know.' (H.M.S.O., 1968, p. 12) – can it be that they may sometimes come nearer in broad outline to Shakespeare's view of the human condition than the scholar does as his eye passes over a page of Shakespeare's words?

In the final analysis, I think the story that has been read or told, the historical facts and ideas derived from reading, visiting places, talking, and the talk of any other kind that has gone into the preparation of a dramatic improvisation – these all have a similar status. They are necessary preliminaries to setting up a dramatic situation: when the improvisation gets going there comes a point at which the *situation takes over*. Since it is the situation that is being explored, its demands will be not for histrionics, not for audience response, but for greater penetration by each of his role, and by all of the developing action as a whole – in fact for a more sensitive and energetic exercise of insights.

A group of ten-year-olds from a school in a particularly depressed part of County Durham had read and talked about the Great Plague: they went on to improvise a scene in which villagers found themselves threatened by the spread of the disease northward. A young man has been taken ill and carried into the village: Margaret, reputed to be a witch, Joanna, the young man's mother, the Beadle and other villagers are discussing the situation. What authority has the Beadle? What rights has the young man – or his mother? What should be done to protect the village and yet to care for the sick man? These are matters that the children might have considered in a class discussion – and there would have been various points of view to put forward. But when the scene is enacted, the physical situation itself – the sick man lying there – pushes them to the point where something must be decided, something must be *done*. In interacting with each other it is to the *demands of this situation* that they are responding. These are extracts from a tape-recorded transcript lasting over thirty minutes:

MARGARET: Ooh! Oh, that's the plague.

VILLAGER: The what?

MARGARET: It's the plague.

VILLAGER: It can't be! (*General talk* – Is it? Is it the plague?

JOANNA: Stop telling lies, Margaret.

MARGARET: I'm not telling lies. Who's seen the plague here, then, tell us?

VILLAGER: I have. That's the plague all right.

JOANNA: I won't believe *you*, for a start.

VILLAGER: But the plague can't have come here!

MARGARET: Can't it? Well it can.

JOANNA: It can't be the plague. She's telling lies, that's what she's doing.

VILLAGER: Well it was the plague in London. We heard the messenger come round.

JOANNA: Yes, but this isn't London, this is here.

VILLAGER: Could have spread to here, couldn't it?

MARGARET: What can we do? Look at him . . .

JOANNA: You keep out of it, I'm his mother, not you

MARGARET: I won't keep out of it.

JOANNA: I bet she's put a curse on him, that's what she's done.

MARGARET: A curse on him! How could I put a curse on him?

JOANNA: 'Cos you're a witch, that's why.

MARGARET: A witch! I'm not a witch and you're not going to say I am!

★

VILLAGER: What are we going to do about it?

BEADLE: We'll have to have him locked up, won't we?

JOANNA: What do you mean you're going to have him locked up?

BEADLE: Well if he's got the plague we can't have him wandering around the streets. (*All talking together.*)

JOANNA: And where is he going to go?

VILLAGER: Yes, she thinks more about her son than us.

JOANNA: Yes. Maybe I do.

VILLAGER: And it's better that one person dying than the whole village.

VILLAGER: We're not talking about that.

JOANNA: It wouldn't bother me if the whole village *did* die.

VILLAGER: No, you don't care about anyone, do you?

BEADLE: Look – where are we going to put him?

VILLAGER: It's no good arguing here.

VILLAGER: That's Joanna's job. She's his mother.

VILLAGER: Yes – you find a place to put him.

JOANNA: He's going to my house – that's where he's going.

VILLAGER: He's not going to your house – not next door to me, he isn't!

JOANNA: He's going in my house, that's where he's going!

VILLAGER: He's *not* going in your house.

JOANNA: Why isn't he then? You can't stop me putting him in his own house can you?

VILLAGER: Not next door to *me*.

BEADLE: Yes, he has his rights; he probably might get the plague.

VILLAGER: I bet I will – if you go in there.

JOANNA: So have I: I pay taxes on my house so I have a right to go in it, haven't I?

VILLAGER: He'll have to go somewhere.

VILLAGER: Yes. In an old place, somewhere away . . .

JOANNA: Why should it be an old house? He's a *human being* not an animal!

148

BEADLE: Well he has the plague, he's not an ordinary human being.

JOANNA: That makes him different does it? So that means you can just kick him about and put him anywhere you want to? Well it doesn't to me.

BEADLE: I am the Beadle.

(*In the end, the Beadle orders two men to carry the son to an outlying hut.*)

BEADLE: Joanna has taken my orders. So *you* will take my orders.

VILLAGER: (*Pause*) Come on, Peter. Let's take him.

VILLAGER: I hope you get it first.

VILLAGER: I doubt it, if you had hold of him.

VILLAGER: Joanna, you're not going in there are you?

JOANNA: Why shouldn't I go in there?

VILLAGER: Well, he's got the plague!

JOANNA: Yes, and he's my son.

VILLAGER: I said: Are you coming in?

JOANNA: Yes.

VILLAGER: Then come on in.

BEADLE: You'll have to stay in there!

JOANNA: Who says I'll stay in? If I want to come out I will do!

BEADLE: *I* say you will stay in there.

VILLAGER: Yes, now *you* must take his orders.

JOANNA: I don't have to do everything he says.

BEADLE: It's written in the Plague Laws.

(*Whispering*): She's going in there! She'll catch the plague off her own son!

VILLAGER: There's nothing we can do, except paint the cross on the door.

VILLAGER: (*Pause*) Come on, Peter, let's go.

Improvisation of this kind relies upon spontaneity, sensitive interaction and cooperation: for this reason, such work acts as a kind of flux in the daily programme. In classrooms where drama is given prominence, talking, writing, reading, painting, movement, model-making, music-making both contribute to it and are generated by it.

V

When a teacher reads to his class, at least three important processes are going on at the same time. First, the class is functioning as a single group; and where most of the time is spent working as individuals or in small groups, such communal experience becomes particularly valuable. Listening is itself an active process, but the sense of a community activity may be heightened if the teacher reads something in which the children can participate – a ballad with a chorus, perhaps, or a story told in dialogue – material, that is to say, drawn from a limited repertoire with which the class is familiar. I know teachers who deliberately begin every session of individual work with a five- or ten-minute reading, sometimes of this familiar kind providing for participation and sometimes, of course, of fresh material. So that desks do not have to be moved or the materials of work in progress disturbed, the children simply gather round and sit on the floor. It is a simple ritual, an enjoyable group experience – and spreads its sense of harmony across the buzz of individual work that follows it.

In the second place, the children who listen are gaining experience of the written forms of the English language, and this aspect of the process is of particular importance to those who cannot yet read for themselves. There is an art of listening to reading that is very different from the process of listening to somebody talking to you – and this art contributes to the art of reading. Jean-Paul Sartre has described how he first listened to his mother, Anne-Marie, reading a story to him – a story that she had told him often enough before:

Anne-Marie made me sit down in front of her, on my little chair; she leant over, lowered her eyelids and went to sleep. From this mask-like face issued a plaster voice. I grew bewildered: who was talking? about what? and to whom? My mother had disappeared: not a smile or trace of complicity. I was an exile. And then I did not recognize the language. Where did she get her confidence?

After a moment, I realized: it was the book that was talking. Sentences emerged that frightened me: they were like real centipedes; they swarmed with syllables and letters, span out their diphthongs and made their double consonants hum; fluting, nasal, broken up with sighs and pauses, rich in unknown words, they were in love with themselves and their meanderings and had no time for me: sometimes they disappeared before I could understand them; at others, I had understood in advance and they went rolling on nobly towards their end without sparing me a comma. These words were obviously not meant for me. The tale itself was in its Sunday best: the wood-cutter, the wood-cutter's wife and their daughters, had acquired majesty; their rags were magnificently described, words left their mark on objects, transforming action into rituals and events into ceremonies. (Sartre, 1964, pp. 33-4)

Telling stories to his class, a teacher can of course adapt his presentation to their responses – spoken or unspoken. And a child – even as a member of the group – may feel that 'the words are meant for him'. But the reading of stories by the teacher is, amongst other things, a stage on, a step towards reading by the children themselves. The reader can still do a great deal in interpreting the written words – tone of voice, tempo, intonation, stress, gesture – all these enable him to give what the silent reader must take for himself. Listening is for this very reason valuable preparation for later reading.

If my second process was that of gaining language experience, my third is, in the simplest terms, that of gaining life experience. It is, in fact, satisfaction of the major incentive behind most of the reading we do. Taking the limited objective, that of encouraging a child to acquire the skill of reading, there is more sense in building up a strong incentive for him, a solid satisfaction derived from listening, than there is in denying that satisfaction in the hope that this will drive him to read for himself. Taking the broader view, for reader and non-reader alike, experience from books is a natural and necessary extension of all those experiences – his own and other people's – that have nurtured the child so far: we cannot wish to withhold it while he develops the skill to acquire it for himself.

Before considering the nature of the process of reading itself, let me make some comment upon the material – upon the educational value of stories and poems. What needs to be said is so germane to all that has already been said in this book that I need not labour it. The stories and poems read in school – by teacher or by children – the stories and poems the children write, together with the dramatic activities, and the talk that accompanies and mediates all this – these form a unified body of activity in the primary school – activity in the spectator role. Of course they mingle with activites of another kind, activities that present (or more accurately develop in course of time into) a second unity, activities in the participant role. They mingle because experiences, individual or communal, may be followed up in either role, and because an activity in the one role may spark off activity in the other.

When we think of 'curiosity' and 'exploration' and 'learning from experience', I believe we think first of activity in the participant role; of the development of practical and cognitive skills, of problem-solving and data-handling; of number work and environmental studies, scientific, historical or geographical. Certainly theorists sometimes speak as though this were all that could be called *essential*.

The essential, I believe, includes the two modes. An education limited to activity in the participant role is in the last analysis an attempt to produce men and women with the efficiency of machines. It must fail, because men and machines operate on different principles – or to put it another way, because a man is a poor machine. We suggested in Chapter 3 that activities in the two roles could be distinguished as follows: in the participant role, the stress is upon interpreting the new, ongoing experience in the light of the sum total, the world representation: in the spectator role, on the other hand, the principal function is to work upon the world representation, reorganizing it in the light of experiences not now engaged in but contemplated; and that it was by this latter process that a man's world representation was maintained in a condition of harmony such that he could bear to 'live with it'. Man carries with him the world derived from his past experiences – it is one aspect of what we mean by 'consciousness' – a major feature in the difference between a human being and a machine.

But in the second place, if a man is to operate efficiently in the participant role, he must generate appropriate expectations: and his expectations are drawn from his world representation – the corpus of the experiences he has had himself or has made his own. Making other people's experiences our own and so extending and complicating our world representation is, as we have seen, something that we may do in our stride in participant activity, but something that forms a major preoccupation when we take up the role of spectator.

Our memories of past experiences are in story form, are narratives. We so readily construct stories out of our past experiences that it is difficult to perceive that anything has been 'constructed' at all. Imagine the view Nelson might have, looking down upon Trafalgar Square on a Sunday afternoon: a space crawling with people, a mass in movement – like maggots on an upturned spit of earth. Yet at ground level, to each man in the crowd, his own life is a story – he has made it that way.

To represent what happens to us we derive a narrative from the flux of sense impressions: if we represent what we should like to happen or what we fear might happen, the result, again, is likely to be in story form – and fiction this time. And prominent among fictions is narrative as an art form – the novel or the short story. Thus, as Barbara Hardy has put it, narrative is 'a primary act of mind transferred to art from life'.

We often tend [she says] to see the novel as competing with the world of happenings. I should prefer to see it as the continuation in disguising and isolating art, of the remembering, dreaming, and planning that is in life imposed on the uncertain, attenuated, interrupted, and unpredicatable or meaningless flow of happenings. (Hardy, 1968, pp. 54–6)

When we read stories to children, it is not, then, to turn their faces away from life, to offer an alternative; and as the stories grow less like their own unpremeditated recollections and more 'formal', more 'artistic', they are encouraged to remember or dream or plan with a greater intensity of perception and feeling.

More simply, as children read stories they enter into the experiences of other people. There is no dearth of material for them, and they may continue to take up the role of spectator with increasing satisfaction for the rest of their lives – even within the scope of what is written in the English language. But there is another future in it too. A child approaches the facts of history by involving himself in the lives of people of past ages, and the facts of geography by involving himself in the lives of people in other countries. It is through sharing their experiences that he moves towards an impersonal appreciation of historical and geographical issues. Judgement on all human affairs – political, social, economic, educational – is built upon the sympathy and understanding derived from both actual and 'virtual' experience. Cassirer reminds us of this when he says, with reference to the historian's task: 'If I put out the light of my own personal experience I cannot see and I cannot judge of the experience of others.' (Cassirer, 1944, p. 187)

When words are used to produce a work of art – whether story or poem or drama – their formal disposition or 'artistic arrangement' is a deliberate part of what is afoot. Thus, the physical properties of words as sounds are taken into account in a way in which they are not in everyday uses of language: and this is particularly true of poetry. For everyday purposes we become accustomed to looking *through* the substance at the meaning. But, as we have seen, young children's concern with words is more like that of the poet, since they too are more than usually aware of the physical qualities, and show this by the way they play with sounds, making jingles and rhymes and puns and mixing in nonsense sounds.

There are other similarities between poetry and young children's speech. Poets tend to look for significant, evocative detail – something straight out of life – to carry their meaning, and to avoid the vaguely general or abstract term. (It was T. E. Hulme's view that: 'poetry always endeavours to arrest you, and to make you continuously see a physical thing, to prevent you gliding through an abstract process'.) With young children it is not a matter of choice: their ideas must take a relatively concrete form of expression because they have not yet mastered the art of making and handling abstractions. A five-year-old boy in an infants' class once said to a colleague of mine, 'Oh yes, I know Geography. It's polar bears at the top and penguins at the bottom.'!

More generally, a great deal of children's speech seems to be uttered for the pleasure of speaking rather than in order to communicate anything to anybody. And in this it resembles poetry, for poetry is, broadly speaking, more concerned to celebrate, to mourn, to pay homage, than it is to inform or instruct or convince.

Finally, there is plenty of reason to believe that young children have strong feelings about the people and the creatures and the objects they meet: that a part of the process, indeed, of growing up into sane and sensible adults is to lose these particular passions or at least to so reduce them that they do not prevent their owners from keeping appointments on time, holding down a job, behaving decently and tolerantly to all and sundry. Psychologists explain this change as a process of organizing our emotional activity, subjugating it to the system of habits that enables us to operate in society. But it is one of the functions of poetry and the arts in general to break through this organized decency, these well-ordered sentiments, and bring back a little of the fire of undomesticated emotion. This may sometimes take the form of a grand passion, but it may also appear as an expression of feeling towards some object or creature – or person or event – that ordinarily we might take for granted, entertain no feelings towards. Van Gogh has painted, with evident concern, a kitchen chair: the upshot of what I am suggesting here is that a child is likely to respond to such a painting without any of the puzzled head-scratching that many adults display. I was reading some poems to a class of eight-year-olds on one occasion: I had read them a poem by de la Mare about a nightwatchman on a winter's night, then one by James Stephens called 'The Wind' and then this fragment by Emily Dickinson:

> The moon was but a chin of gold
>   A night or two ago,
> And now she turns her perfect face
>   Upon the world below.

By the time I came to the end of it, there was a small boy in the back row hugging himself like a cabman, and saying, 'Please sir, would you read us a *warm* one!'

For the reasons I have given, some of the writing done by primary school children will be nearer to poetry than it is to prose statement: what concerns me here is that, for these same reasons, primary school children are capable of being more responsive to the work of poets than many of their teachers give them credit for. I believe in fact that the period up to about eleven years of age constitutes a golden age for listening to poetry.

A final word on stories and poems – those read to the children, and also at a later stage by the children. I think we can make a rough general distinction between the two kinds of material: among writings offered by their authors for strangers to read, poetry is the most personal, the most individual kind. In reading a poem we turn, as it were, inwards: and while there are a number of stories, especially perhaps among folk-tales and fairy stories, that we would in this respect class with the poems, the general run of stories encourage us to look out and around. It is from the stories read in school, therefore, that other activities, both practical and symbolic, in both participant and spectator roles, are likely to arise; it is the stories that will spread as they merge with the interests of the children, sparking off inquiries, investigations, expeditions, projects, and even at times culminating in a display of work. A poem will certainly give rise, often enough, to talk and the talk will relate to the children's interest and experiences – but from such starting points it will tend to move *into the poem* rather than into life interests in general. A poem may be read by an individual, read in chorus, read in 'orchestrated' parts, acted out, painted, and so on: but such performances and products will tend to represent isolated 'moments of contemplation', individual gestures, rather than form links in a general chain of activity.

VI

There is a good deal of support these days for the idea that the next stage on from listening to the teacher's reading should be to tackle at one and the same time both reading and writing. Traditionally, learning to read came first. One of the most promising of these innovatory methods is the one devised by David Mackay and Brian Thompson as a part of the Programme in Linguistics and English Teaching at University College, London. By their method children in infants' classes learn to compose sentences, and read what they have composed, before they learn to write the symbols of the written language for themselves. The materials they use are of two forms – cards bearing printed words (or in some cases affixes) systematically stored in a 'word folder', and cards bearing printed vowel and consonant symbols, stored in a 'spelling folder'. I am sure the uses made of these two forms will vary a good deal in accordance with the methods of teaching reading employed. It seems to me that the advantage of working first with the word folder would be considerable: composing and reading would be more directly related to a child's spoken language and the contexts in which that occurred. In other words, the context of events, situation, upon which his ability to speak so heavily relies can more readily support the comparatively rapid composition of whole words into sentences than it can the building first of words and therefrom of sentences. (That the second folder is christened 'spelling folder' suggests to me that the authors regard it as of secondary value, a later refinement as compared with the composing and reading processes.) On the other hand, some concern with phonics, with the relation of individual sound to individual written symbol, has been proved valuable in learning to read since it enables a child to generalize from one situation to another – from mastery of 'of' and 'on' for example to tackling 'fight' and 'night' – so that most teachers will use in fact a mixture of the two basic methods, the phonic and the 'whole word' (or 'look and say'), varying the mixture in the light of an individual child's progress and problems. I hope the word folder and the spelling folder will in a similar way be variously used, but also in such a way as to exploit all that the word folder can offer.

As children compose sentences in this way, they are exploring the systems that govern written English: their efforts are illuminating, and not only to themselves, as this statement by the authors will illustrate:

We found that the child's use of the word folder helped us to observe the outcome of some of the thinking and rethinking he might go through before reaching the solution to a problem. We strongly recommended that the teachers using the trial materials observe the children in order to note sources of difficulty as well as areas in which the children worked with confidence. The purpose of this can best be shown by describing one typical incident. A group of four children were making sentences and the teacher was helping them. Another child, a boy aged four years nine months, joined them. He asked the teacher if he could join in, got his folder and stand and said 'Can I make a sentence now?' He selected four words and made, correctly, *I am a boy*. He read it to the teacher, studied his word store for a moment and asked 'Can I make "I am a big boy"?' He couldn't locate the word *big* so the teacher helped him find it. He placed the word *big* after the first word in the stand so the sentence now read: *I big am a boy*. His teacher asked him to read it to her and he read quickly 'I am a big boy'. She said 'Look at the words and read them again'. The child began 'I am . . .' and stopped. 'Oh no, that's not right.' He found the word *am* in the sentence and took it out. He returned his attention to the stand and tried to read what remained there, *I big a boy*, but knew it to be wrong and stopped again. He said, 'I need another *am*' and it was obvious at this point that he was disorganized. He had started by making something he was confident of: the sentence *I am a boy*. He tried to add to it the word *big* without first deciding where the adjective belonged in the text, realized he had done it incorrectly and, for a moment, was unable to sort out the problem. He picked up the word *am*, studied it for a while, looked at the words in the stand and then suddenly beamed and said, 'I see where it has gone wrong', and ordered the sentence very quickly to make *I am a big boy*. This child was discovering, consciously for the first time, the importance of word order in written English. He was able to achieve the correct word order in spoken language without thinking about it but through his attempt to add a qualifier to a nominal in written English he was probably made partially conscious of this part of the grammar for the first time. (Mackay and Thompson, 1968, pp. 116–17)

What is important is the marriage of the process of composing in written language to that of reading, and the relating of both to the learner's spoken language resources. Doubtless teachers have devised and will go on devising a variety of ways in which this co-ordination can be achieved in teaching. Mackay and Thompson's analysis of what is involved will provide them with a linguistically sound basis and orientation.

But the process of learning to read is one that has appeared to grow longer and longer as we have come to understand more fully what is involved in reading itself. I. A. Richards goes so far as to say 'we are all of us learning to read all the time'. (Richards, 1942, p. 20) Certainly we go on learning well into adult life. It is quite false to think of reading in terms of a reader receiving on a blank page of his mind the impression of the writer's message – a sort of photo-copying of a crude and approximate kind. It would be better, in fact, to think of a person, the reader, as a highly complicated collection of on-going processes, and ask what changes are brought about in these processes when he takes up a book. And then to remember that the writer, as he wrote, was also a highly complicated collection of ongoing processes and it was these that determined the words he used. The reader then uses the words in order to reach behind them and set up an interaction between his own processes and those, at that earlier time, of the writer. Those of the reader's processes that are most relevant to the reading he is about to engage in he is likely to be aware of in the form of *expectations*: but there is evidence (Luria and Vinogradova, 1959) that these conscious expectations are surrounded by a wider area of 'unconscious expectations', aspects of past experience that have been 'alerted' to the anticipated event. What a reader perceives in his reading and what he fails to perceive, and the further organization he gives to what he takes from the reading, will vary in accordance with these expectations. Put very simply, this is to say that the meaning we take from a reading lies in the modifications it imposes upon our expectations. A very firm expectation may lead us to mis-read – or mis-hear: late one evening, when the bar was crowded after a function of some kind near by, several of us recognized a large and noisy party, and I mentioned casually to the bar-maid that they were, 'Our colleagues'. It was from the confused look in her face that I realized she had mis-heard me: what she had understood was 'Alcoholics'!

Clearly the expectations we take to a book are likely at the initial point to be very general: and their first modifications are likely to be the sharpest. Thereafter what we anticipate has been shaped with particular respect to the individual text. A general interest in novels, in novels by this author, in the kind of novel this title suggests, in novels of the length this appears to be – all this may be focused into much more specific expectations as we read the first few lines. The process, after that, might be described as follows:

1. With every sentence we read, the pattern of focused expectations is filled in with detail; grows better defined as it grows more complex. The meaning is an *emergent pattern* of relationships – more like a negative in the developing-dish than it is like a train coming out of a tunnel.

2. We may test this pattern in its broad outlines by comparing it with familiar patterns of thought, by translating it into concrete examples, by referring it to our own experience, and so on. Approval and disapproval begin to influence our responses. Even a minor flaw is likely to seem a 'discoloration' of the whole rather than a misplaced piece in the jigsaw.

3. We anticipate, and are reassured by, elements that easily fit into the emergent pattern: we are checked or jarred by elements which do not appear to fit, or by gaps caused, for example, by words we do not understand.

4. But we shall probably read on, suspending judgement: what follows may reflect back and enable us to fit in what had 'jarred' before or supply what seems a satisfactory meaning of the word we could not interpret; or may satisfy us that the flaw or the gap was merely trivial and to be ignored. On the other hand, as we read on, the ensuing statements may increase the sense of misfit, be less and less in keeping with the pattern of our expectations: and in this case we shall probably go back to some plain-sailing point earlier in the chapter and re-read, reinterpret – where necessary seeking help with the difficult unfamiliar words.

Such a view of the reading process is consistent with I. A. Richards's advice:

A certain querulous questioning tone – 'What *can* it mean?' – is an enemy of comprehension. Read it as though it made sense and perhaps it will. (Richards, 1942, p. 41)

'Read it as though it made sense' is advice that we can hardly introduce too early in the process of learning to read. At the same time, what is available for children to read must be stuff that makes sense, and can make sense to them: easy enough to say, but behind it lies a whole vexed question – the question of 'graded readers' versus 'real books'. Graded readers, as a species, are notorious for providing a kind of language that is found nowhere else – language that does not make sense as language. At the heart of the problem lie divergent views about 'vocabulary'. A reading scheme that concentrates upon phonic generalization in learning to read will tend to stress a 'sight vocabulary' in comparative isolation from a 'speech vocabulary'. This leads to severe restriction of the items used, both in order to ensure rote learning by repetition and in order to ring the changes upon a limited number of written symbols. Where, on the other hand, the effort is made to provide a written version of *what a child says* for him to read (either when the teacher writes it or the child composes it in the way we have seen), these severe restrictions on vocabulary cannot be imposed, and are no longer necessary since the child's whole speech vocabulary is being treated as potential sight vocabulary.

But the whole notion of 'vocabulary' as a reservoir at the child's disposal is somewhat misleading to my way of thinking. It cannot be denied, of course, that a text containing more than a certain proportion of words unfamiliar to the reader is one that he cannot make sense of. Nevertheless, when the proportion is not disabling, to succeed in making sense of a text containing unfamiliar words is the *normal way* of enlarging one's linguistic resources. In other words, it is from reading (or more completely from reading and listening, reinforced by talking and writing), that we learn to *interpret the various contributions* that a given word may make to the meaning of an utterance. Even the Plowden Report, which had so many welcome things to say, misrepresented the truth of this matter when it claimed that

one of the most important responsibilities of teachers is to help children to see order and pattern in experience, and to extend their ideas by analogies, and *by the provision of suitable vocabulary* [my italic]. (H.M.S.O., 1967, p. 197)

The notion of 'providing vocabulary' is a limited and misleading one, suggesting an all too static conception of language. Language in use is a flow, a current of activity, and not any sort of reservoir. The words a child can come by in this deliberate fashion at the teacher's providing – in the course of a vocabulary lesson – will tend to be those of limited use, necessary at times but with little power to vitalize the current of speech. Teachers need to care about the flow – about reading 'as though it made sense', and writing and talking – and when they do, the reservoir will look after itself. To put it another way, it is from successive experiences of words in use – words used for some actual profit or pleasure – that a child builds up his resources, and there is little point therefore in our dragging things in by their names.

The most powerful words, as Richards takes pains to show, are not words of relatively fixed meaning – 'semicolon' for example, or 'quadrilateral' or 'potassium' – but those for which no single out-of-context definition can do very much. He cites 'make, get, give, love, have' and 'seem, be, do, see' and 'mind, thought, idea, knowledge' and 'reason, purpose, work' and a great many more. They grow in usefulness first as, in our listening and reading, we search for coherence, for the emergent pattern of meaning, and secondly as in talking and writing we experiment with them, testing out what they will do for us and our purposes.

That there should be available, from the earliest possible stages, plenty of reading matter that feeds a child's interests, material that stretches his powers of making sense of what he reads, that relates to the world he really lives in, has talked about, and continues to talk about – this will by now be a postscript that I need hardly add.

VII

I am inclined to believe that young children rely upon speech for all that they want to communicate and that when they write before going to school their writing takes the form of a 'construct' or a performance. I have seen many examples of stories written, illustrated and decorated, the pages stitched or clipped together to make little books. They exist as objects in the world: miniature or even make-believe objects. I have in fact one such production made when the child could write only a word or two (she was under four years old): its six pages, each about an inch square, are filled with saw-tooth lines of mock writing in which at rare intervals there stands out a word: WWWW THE MMMM

We have already noticed a parallel between a poet's use of language and a child's speech, both exemplifying 'the delight of utterance'. That delight dovetails here with the joy of making an object; and puts the writing firmly in the spectator role. Teachers have built upon this foundation, and a good deal of early writing in the primary school is not aimed at telling anybody anything but at producing 'written objects' – something to be mounted and displayed, or collected in a folder; something that deserves to be embellished, illustrated and to go along as part of the possessions of the group. This is spectator role writing: is it therefore a kind of poetry, a kind of literature, or are there other defining characteristics to be accounted for?

Postponing any answer to that question, let us first observe that writing begins as written down speech. It may take into its fabric words and phrases imported from written language the child has heard or read (as for example, the three-year-old boy who dictates stories for his mother to write down and recently included a use of 'for' which certainly comes not from his own speech but from hearing stories read: ' . . . for he had nowhere to go'). But the fabric itself of their writing remains written down speech. We would hardly expect a child to do otherwise than to draw upon his speech resources when he wants to write.

However, all forms of speech are not equally useful as starting-points for writing. Occasionally we have found stories written by children who seemed to have at their command only dialogue – social interchange – and this proves a very unsuitable medium for telling a story. Here is the beginning of one by a girl of ten:

Oh Mummy do you think it would be all right to go and watch daddy. Well I shall want some shopping. it will be closeing day tomorrow. All right I will go for you. But do you think you will come. this afternoon   daddy will not be fishing then will he   no. Oh here comes Robin Mummy can he do the shopping yes— dear. He can do the shopping if you get the things we will need we shall want the rugs, saddles, spaddes, buteckes, and the dogs lead. If you go and do that I will get some sandwiches and cake for tea on the beach. goodness me it twelve oclock I must get dinner daddy will be home soon . . .

I suspect that 'speech for oneself' (the running commentary and the forms of narrative and planning speech that develop from it) constitutes an important stage in the process of learn-ing to write. It is sustained speech, it becomes in due course internalized, and it does not rely upon feed-back from a listener. However that may be, it is clear that any more or less sustained narrative speech is likely to be a lead-in to writing. For this reason it has been suggested that children should be encour-aged to amplify their contributions to a conversation with their teachers: 'Yes, and then what happened?' 'Was there anything else you saw?' – and so on. Or, as James Moffett puts it:

. . . the first step towards writing is made when a speaker takes over a conversation and sustains some subject alone. He has started to create a solo discourse that while intended to communicate to others is less collaborative, less prompted, and less corrected by feedback than dialogue. He bears more of the responsibility for effective communication. . . . The cues for his next line are not what his interlocutor said, but what he himself just said. (Moffett, 1968, p. 85)

From this point on, we can envisage two parallel main lines of development. As the child becomes more familiar with diverse forms of the written language – forms adapted to different audiences and different purposes – he will draw more and more upon those forms in his own writing. We shall have more to say about this in a moment. At the same time, every new field of interest for him is likely to be investigated, explored, organized first in talk. The talk, as it were, prepares the environment into which what is taken from reading may be accommodated: and from that amalgam the writing proceeds.

'Ordinary speech', according to Edward Sapir, 'is directly *expressive*' (Sapir, 1961, p. 10), and since I want to apply the term, in some degree at least, to most of the writing that goes on in the Primary School, it is important to inquire more exactly what it means. Sapir opposes it to *referential*:

. . . in all language behaviour there are intertwined, in enormously complex patterns, isolable patterns of two distinct orders. These may be roughly defined as patterns of reference and patterns of expression. (Sapir, 1961, p. 11)

He goes on to say that language is

rarely a purely referential organisation. It tends to be so only in scientific discourse, and even there it may be seriously doubted whether the ideal of pure reference is ever attained by language.

Though the two patterns are 'intertwined in enormously complex patterns', it seems reasonable, and consistent with Sapir's views, to suppose that an utterance which was predominantly expressive might be distinguished from one which was predominantly referential; and this we propose to do, calling the one 'expressive' and the other 'transactional'.

The word 'expression' is used to name a variety of ideas and some of these, the most general, we can rule out as not contributing to the meaning of 'expressive' as we want to use it. 'Expression' may be used as equivalent to 'formulation' or 'externalization': in this sense the policy of a political party may find its *expression* in a manifesto. Again, 'expression' is used as a way of referring to a piece of language as such – as when we refer to a word as 'an ugly expression' or a phrase as a 'trite expression', 'a loose expression' and so on. On the other hand, when we say that a man 'reads with expression', this – in so far as it means anything at all – comes nearer to the meaning we require. If I read with expression a part of me, my voice, is giving indications of what I think the writer means by his words. In a similar fashion the expression on my face is likely to be giving such indications. But the expression on my face is likely, every moment of my waking life, to be giving indications *about me* – about my state of mind and mood and so on. And there is a sense in which, in the case of me reading, whatever indications my 'expression' gives are indications, at least in part, of the way I think and feel about the story or about the people, events, and everything else in the story.

If I exclaim when I am surprised or delighted or angry or hurt – either in words or by making 'purely expressive' noises – moaning or cooing or whatever else might be my counterpart of a cat's purring, a dog's growling, an infant's yelling – then that represents the extreme of what we mean by 'expressive'. With a full knowledge of the situation in which I am making such a noise, a listener is able to discover from it something about me. But in addition, as we have seen earlier, I continually declare the sort of person I am by the way I construe the world – by what I make of my encounters with people, events, ideas, works of art, fictions and all the rest. Whatever I talk about, therefore, I am likely to be at the same time signalling to a listener – intentionally or unintentionally – things about myself. The occasions when we deliberately try to avoid doing this are rare enough to be remarked upon: we say 'expressionless' either about a voice or a face (and I think the term is much more frequently translatable as 'not giving away his own attitude to what he is saying' than it is into 'failing to bring out the meaning of the words he is speaking').

As we have suggested, a mere grunt can tell us something if we know the person who is making it and can see why he is doing so; it follows that in different situations the grunt will tell us different things. Similarly, the more expressive my utterances about the world are, the more liable they are to mean different things in different situations; and in this case it is likely that the differences will be heightened by the way the words are spoken – the tone of voice, gesture, facial expression. 'So, you're home then!' could be an affectionate and excited welcome to a returned exile or the sarcastic opening of a family brawl.

Talk that is predominantly expressive, then, tells us a good deal about the speaker and relies heavily for its interpretation on the situation in which it occurs – that is to say, it draws heavily upon a common response to a shared situation, or it relies heavily upon the listener's knowledge of the speaker's situation.

Let us suppose someone is relating what happened to him on a past occasion. In a police court he is likely to do so in a neutral, even expressionless tone: as though to allow the bare facts to speak for themselves. But to an intimate friend he may reveal at each point his attitude towards what he is relating: and this is to bring to life the events as he experienced them – which is the only way they can be made to 'seem real', since the speaker is his listener's only link with those events.

When we chat with our friends in a relaxed way, our talk is likely to be mainly expressive: we verbalize what runs through our minds and with people we know well we do not need to fill in the background – we can speak as though we spoke to ourselves or even meditated silently and did *not* speak. If in the course of this chatter one of us says something that the other wants to question or dispute or explore further, then this sets up a demand for speech that pays more attention to 'things out there' – to facts or logical, causal or chronological relations; and at the same time we demand that the speaker take into account his listener's point of view. In both cases this constitutes a need to be more *explicit*, that is, a need to switch from predominantly expressive to predominantly transactional speech.

A young child's speech will be expressive for the very reason that in his egocentrism he finds it difficult or impossible to escape from his own point of view, to take into account his listener's – or indeed to suppose that 'things as they are' could differ from 'things as he sees them'. A child will take time therefore to learn how to respond to the demands of a situation requiring transactional speech.

But there are other situations that demand a change of another kind: a change from expressive not to transactional speech but to 'formal' or 'poetic' speech. And here we depart from Sapir's frame of reference and must justify ourselves for including what he omitted.

Let us begin by noting that the change from expressive to transactional speech comes when *participant* demands are made – that is, when language is called upon to achieve some transaction, to *get something done* in the world. The other change arises when demands are made from the opposite end – for a more powerful exercise of language in the spectator role.

We may gossip idly about our neighbours, or swap yarns

about war service, or the place we work in, or about holidays: all this will be expressive speech, and, with a few possible digressions, in the spectator role. If I grow interested in your chatter because I vaguely begin to wonder whether the place you went to might suit me for a holiday, I may move the talk from the spectator role into the participant – but at this idle level it would remain expressive speech. But if the possibilities really begin to be of practical interest to me – say for next year – then I may initiate a move from expressive to communicative speech. ('You say it's near Whitby. How far is it from the station?')

Suppose, on the other hand, I grow interested in the account of your holiday experiences *as a story* – become involved in the same way as I would become involved in a novel or a play: then I shall not want to shift your talk in the direction of things I want to find out – in fact, apart from making encouraging noises, I shall not want to interrupt at all. And you, as you warm to my interest, may begin to concentrate on giving your story a *more satisfying shape*: your talk becomes more and more of a performance, more of a construction, a verbal object. All this indicates a move away from the expressive and in the direction of the *formal* or *poetic*.

I believe something of this sort may be heard happening in the following conversation. The four people taking part knew each other well but had just met again on the first afternoon of a residential conference:

A: Wearing your stetson tomorrow?
  B: Yes, I thought so.
    C: Have you got it here?
  B: No.
A: Would *you* like to wear it?
      D: Don't, don't catch L.—'s eye, or . . . or . . .
  B: Oh, God, no . . .
      D: . . . if you want to . . .
  B: . . . draw the curtains. C., you're in a wonderful position . . .

marvellous . . . have the whole conference in your bedroom.

c: That'd be marvellous. I'll just hold up the window and beckon them in.

d: I'm not looking at anybody.

c: Draw it back, A. . . ., they've gone now.

(*Curtains drawn.*)

b: Look at all those strange shoes.

c: Did you see those two mountains arriving? I think . . . they must be huge . . . gardener . . . they were two such big ones.

a: What, two big gardeners?

c: Two big women.

a: Oh, well, I think they must be the Misses Jones.

b: . . . look like a French hotel. What?

a: The Misses Jones. No . . . oh . . . are they part of the staff?

b: No.

a: Well, they were very . . .

b: Students.

a: . . . matriarchal. They're not!

b: Well, delegates.

d: Delegates . . . um, um.

c: Delegates.

d: . . . good goings-on.

c: What do you mean, delegates?

b: Well, we're all delegates.

c: What do you mean?

d: I'm a delegate.

c: You mean somebody's paying for you . . . you're a delegate.

b: No, no, you're a delegate . . . oh!

c: You mean somebody's paying for you.

b: Pay to be a delegate.

c: Who do you represent then, B. . . . ?

b: I don't represent anybody.

a: He represents himself. He represents me and I represent him.

d: I see.

a: And its called Barnum and Bailey.

(*Laughter.*)

d: What about these murals?

A: Do you want me to tell a story. I think the time . . . the time has passed for me to tell that.

    C: No.

        D: Bar's open, tell us a story about the murals.

    C: Tell us the story of Muriel and then we'll go.

A: It isn't the story of Muriel, it's another story I was going to tell you.

    C: Well, tell us another story, then.

A: Um . . . about it. . . . It was when I was married you see and . . . me and me chap went . . .

    B: One of those.

(*Laughter.*)

A: And we came back from this party and we were very sober and we thought we'd get some Coca-Cola to drink.

    C: Coca-Cola!

A: Yes.

    C: What with?

A: There are two stories about this Club Paradise. Now this story is about . . . we went down into the bar to get some Coca-Cola and went to the bar and it was full of these strange people . . . and we bought Coca-Cola and we came to the top of the stairs and there were a group of young men standing at the top of the stairs and . . . and with a sort of little landing and there was a mirror. And . . . er . . . me chap who was a big hefty . . .

    B: Excuse me, but I must draw attention to . . . the delegate.

(D *clears throat significantly.*)

A: That's Brother Aiden . . . he's coming to you tomorrow.

    B: All the way from Lindisfarne.

A: Look, look, look, he's got wings.

        D: Is he in your group? . . . in your seminar?

A: He's a vulture.

    B: I don't know.

        D: Go on, A. . . .

    C: Go on about your chap.

    B: Yes, come on.

A: Yes.

    B: Ooh, stop . . . look.

(*Laughter.*)

A: B. . . . don't . . . B. . . . won't let me tell it.

B: Look, he's looking, he's . . .

C: B. . . . , stop it, I want to hear this story, pay attention A. . . .

B: Yes, I'm sorry.

A: Um . . . you'll be very shocked when you hear this story, are you sure you want to hear it?

C: We want to hear it, go on A. . . .

A: We emerged with our bottles of Coca-Cola and my husband . . . I think must have elbowed one of these chaps out of the way, when suddenly a lovely fight developed. One of the fellows broke a bottle against the mirror and smashed it and the next thing I knew was M. was forcing three of them down the stairs in a great flurry (*laughter*) . . . and then he had one of them up against the wall holding him by his shoulders up against the wall and he had his thumb in the bloke's mouth who was biting it furiously and I had another one . . . and I was pulling his hair, and there must have been some gentlemanly instinct in him because he . . . all he . . . he didn't hit me, he kept shouting, 'Get 'er off, get 'er off, get 'er orf me, get 'er orf me' . . . and then . . . er . . . we emerged again . . . they went and then . . . um, we were very cross, and we said the police should be informed . . . er . . . these blokes creating this disturbance and everyone obviously blamed us. . . . all our friends disappeared like magic . . . um . . . we . . . we went home and . . . er . . . we found ourselves sitting there with a very curious Irish fellow who, who kept on saying, 'Oi stood boi yer, oi saw them going after yer, oi had one of them, oi was looking after yer, M., yes . . . I was', and I was very upset because no one else had come to help us at all, and then M. took his coat off and the whole of the lining of his coat was completely stiff with blood.

C: Ugh!

It is perhaps easier to describe and to apply the categories when we turn from speech to writing: it was for the purpose of differentiating among writings that they were devised.*

* In the course of a Schools Council project on the development of writing abilities in children of eleven to eighteen conducted at the University of London Institute of Education.

The earliest forms of written down speech are likely for every reason to be expressive: among them we may distinguish writings in the spectator role and others in the participant role, but the distinction will not be a sharp one. It is when the demand is made for participant language that *any reader* can follow, or to spectator role language to satisfy an *unknown reader* that the pressure is on for a move from expressive writing to transactional and poetic writing respectively.

Children will not be able to comply fully with these demands at once. In fact, as we have suggested, it is by attempting to meet them that they gradually acquire the differentiated forms. In order to trace development therefore, we need to include two transitional categories along with the three we already have. Thus:

Transactional/◄———/Expressive/———►/Poetic/
    1   2   3   4   5

Most of the writing produced in the Primary School is likely to lie within the three central categories. I propose to explain the diagram in two ways: first by attempting to differentiate the two poles more clearly; and secondly by giving illustrations of Primary School work in the transitional categories.

By what contrasts, then, can transactional be differentiated from poetic writing? That an informative, scientific report is an example of the one, and a story or a poem an example of the other – this is something that may usefully be in our minds as we follow the contrasts in detail.

1. First, this by way of recapitulation: transactional writing is writing in the role of participant fully differentiated to meet the requirements of that role: and poetic writing is fully differentiated to meet the requirements of the role of spectator. Thus, what is said in Chapter 3 to distinguish the two roles is the background against which to consider the more particular points that follow.

2. Transactional writing is intended to fit into, to articulate

with, the ongoing activities of participants: poetic writing is a way of interrupting them - interrupting them by presenting an object to be contemplated in itself and for itself. Thus a piece of transactional writing - this present page for example - may elicit the statement of other views, of counter-arguments or corroborations or modifications, and is thus part of a chain of interactions between people. A response in kind - another piece of such writing - is always a potential of transactional writing. Poetic writing, on the other hand, demands a 'sharer', an audience that does not interrupt. A reader is asked to respond to a particular verbal construct which remains quite distinct from any other verbal construct anybody else might offer. A response in kind is not therefore inherent in the situation.

This very broad distinction has an interesting corollary: what is contributed to the ongoing activity by a piece of transactional writing may well survive when the writing itself is forgotten. Thus, for example, Lindley Murray's English Grammar could be shown to have contributed ideas that are found in many succeeding grammars. It is in fact common practice for informative books to be brought up to date: over a period of years Kirk's *Handbook of Physiology* became Haliburton's, which in turn became McDowell's - and no doubt somebody else will substitute his name in due course. Can one imagine, on the other hand, Charles Dickens producing his version of Fielding's *Tom Jones* - to replace the original - and that in turn being rewritten by C. P. Snow? Poetic writing, if it survives, survives as itself, in and for itself. (*Rosencrantz and Guildenstern are Dead* may so survive - and so will *Hamlet*!)

3. A reader 'contextualizes' transactional writing in the course of reading it - by segments, so to speak. Poetic writing is contextualized, not by segments but as a whole.

John Lyons has pointed out that the initial context for any utterance must be held to include . . . the knowledge shared by hearer and speaker of all that has gone before. More 'abstractly' it must be held to comprehend all the conventions and presuppositions accepted in the society in which the participants live in so far as these are relevant to the understanding of the utterance.

As a conversation develops, he sees this initial context as consistently building up, 'taking into itself all that is relevant . . . from what is said and what is happening'. (Lyons, 1963, pp. 83–5)

As we read a piece of transactional writing, we build in to our initial context whatever fits – piece by piece. We reject what does not fit, the things in fact that do not appear to interest or concern us. What we finally take – from, for example, an informative report – is the sum total of these pieces that we have 'built in' with the addition of anything we may have made of them by creating further connexions ourselves. We may have found much or little that 'fitted in' – as you may have found in reading this chapter.

But the writer who embarks on a piece of poetic writing, I believe, deliberately works *against* this process of contextualization by segments. It is internal relations, relations *within the construct*, that he tries to set up, and in doing so he has to resist the processes by which a reader might relate to parts of the shared context that lie outside his area of concern. It is a 'hard shell' he needs for his object. As readers, we must first recreate the object, in all its inner relatedness, and only then try to relate it as a whole to our own concerns, our own lives. If after reading a poem we think to ourselves, 'So they practise witchcraft in Peru', or 'I didn't know Yeats was a spiritualist' – we are framing responses that are inappropriate to poetic writing. Of course we make such responses, and can profit from them: but if they are not secondary to a response of the kind we have described above – the recreation of a verbal object and its contextualization as a whole – then we have missed the point of the poetic enterprise.

The distinction here, then, is between contextualizing piece-meal, in transactional writing, and contextualizing as a unique whole, in poetic writing.

4. Expressive writing becomes more public as it moves in either direction; but the means by which it seeks to reach a wider audience differ as between the two poles. As expressive writing more fully meets the demands of a transaction, it becomes *more explicit*. That is to say, some features that might be omitted from the expressive version because they are *implied* when we write for someone of similar interests and experiences to our own, have now to be brought into the writing. Again, some features that would interest a reader who was interested in *us* – and so enliven the writing – will be omitted in deference to the unknown reader who may be expected to want to know what it is we have to say but not what sort of a person it is that says it. Both these changes could be described as attempts 'to say X more explicitly' – whatever X may stand for.

As expressive writing moves towards poetic, however, it reaches a wider audience by quite another means; by heightening or intensifying the *implicit*. By the deliberate organization of sounds, words, images, ideas, events, feelings – by *formal arrangement* in other words – poetic writing is able to give resonance to items which in a less carefully organized utterance would be so *in*explicit – so minimally supported or explained in the text – as to be merely puzzling to a reader who was not intimate with the writer and his situation. For example; 'The grey girl who had not been singing stopped' (a) might not be baffling as an initial or isolated piece of expressive language – say a comment you make to someone who knows you well and is sitting beside you looking at the same things as you are; but (b) as the opening of a piece of public communication is utterly baffling: much prior identification and explanation is needed before it makes sense to a stranger seeking information as to 'what is going on'. And yet (c) it is the first line of a poem – a piece of poetic writing addressed to the world at large. ('New

Year's Eve' by John Berryman, in Alvarez (ed.), 1962, p. 34)
And as it finds its place in the precise and complex organization
of forms that constitutes the poem, it no longer baffles a reader.

It cannot be ignored that there lies behind these attempts to
distinguish the pole of transactional writing from that of
poetic a suggestion that the one 'has meaning' in a way the
other does not – and *vice versa*. If we ask 'What does it mean?'
of a piece of transactional writing, we shall not expect the
same sort of answer as we expect when we ask it of a poem or a
novel. For this reason philosophers have spoken of the 'meaning' of a transactional text and the 'import' of a poetic one.
And of the import of a work of literature, Paul Valéry, the
French poet, has this to say:

In sum, the more a poem conforms to Poetry, the less it can be
thought in prose without perishing. To summarize a poem, to put
it into prose, is quite simply to misunderstand the essence of an
art. Poetic necessity is inseparable from sensory form, and the
thoughts set forth or suggested by a poetic text are in no way
the unique and primary concern of discourse, but are rather the
means which move together *equally* with the sounds, the cadences,
the metre, the embellishments, to provoke, to sustain a particular
tension or exaltation, to produce in us a *world* – or a *mode of
existence* – altogether harmonious. (Block and Salinger, 1960, p. 35)

To turn now to illustrations of writing in the transitional
categories. Here is a piece by a ten-year-old boy:

How I filtered my Water Specimens

When we were down at Mr Haris's farm I brought some water
from the brook back with me. I took some from a shallow place
by the oak tree, and some from a deep place by the walnut tree. I
got the specimens by placing a jar in the brook and let the water
run into it. Then I brought them back to school to filter. . . .

He tells us exactly what he did, and then finishes:

The experiment that I did shows that where the water was deeper
and was not running as fast there was a lot more silt suspended as

little particles in the water. You could see this by looking at the filter paper, where the water was shallow and fast there was less dirt suspended in it.

This, I suggest, has moved a good way out of the expressive in the direction of the transactional. But it is still transitional: there are expressive features – things that tell us about the writer rather than form part of what he is intending to communicate. Thus, it was Mr Haris's farm – he had been there before and all his class-mates had been too: to refer to it meant something to the members of that group. And the shallow place in the stream *was* by the oak tree – he had been there and he knew: and the deep place *was* by the walnut tree. These bring the experience to life for him and enliven it for those who are interested *in him*. But they are not a part of the message he sets out to communicate.

I must hasten to add that far from censuring these as imperfections I welcome them at this stage for this writer. They indicate development upon what I believe to be the right lines. Expressive language provides an essential starting point because it is language close to the self of the writer: and progress towards the transactional should be gradual enough to ensure that 'the self' is not lost on the way: that on arrival 'the self', though hidden, is still there. It is the self that provides the unseen point from which all is viewed: there can be no other way of writing quite impersonally and yet with coherence and vitality.

My second example is a piece by a seven-year-old girl:

Class I had Monday off and Tuesday off and all the other classes had Monday and Tuesday off and we played hide-and-seek and my big sister hid her eyes and canted up to ten and me and my brother had to hide and I went behind the Dust-bin and I was thinking about the summer and the buttercups and Daisies all those things and fresh grass and violets and roses and lavender and the twinkling sea and the star in the night and the black sky and the moon.

This clearly is pretty close to expressive speech – and is familiar in another way – in the way it slips into one of those catalogues that small children love to write. I want to suggest here that in so far as the writer moves away from the expressive at all she moves in the other direction from the last piece – that is to say towards the poetic. I can prove nothing: it is in the reading aloud that I suspect this move. It seems to me that as the child wrote, the *sound* of what was written began to have some effect upon what she wrote next: she falls, so to speak, into a rhythm.

Such a submission to sounds is no extraordinary matter: most children who chant nursery rhymes or later reel off galloping verses show considerable skill at improvising in metre – sometimes 'off the cuff' at length. But it is not a galloping rhythm that takes hold in this piece, and its effect seems to me to be on more than simply the rhythm: what is said, I suggest, is chosen under the influence of a sharpened attention to the form.

Most of the writing in the Primary School is likely, as I suggested earlier, to be expressive or transitional between expressive and the poles of transactional and poetic. It is desirable that it should be so. What the children write in the spectator role will not therefore be 'literature': it will be moving out in that direction and the point at which we make the cut – the degree of formal organization required to merit the name 'literature' – this is a matter upon which we can speculate, and, mercifully, upon which we do not have to agree.

VIII

We have looked at a variety of things that go on in the Primary School – at talking, 'doing drama', reading and writing. In this last section we shall go back to think once again of talk – but talk as the means by which we spin in the classroom the 'web of human relations': talk therefore with the teacher very much in mind. In considering this aspect of speech, we become most forcibly aware of the educational revolution in course of progress – a revolution that it is no easy matter to interpret, let alone evaluate. Given that human life is above all a matter of transactions between people, what kind of relationships should be looked for in a group consisting of thirty odd children and one adult, the adult being charged with responsibility for the learning that brings the group together? Is the teacher to be Lord and Master, or society's plenipotentiary, or a third parent, or a chairman, or 'one of us' but wiser and more experienced? Or perhaps some combination of more specific roles – umpire, cheer-leader, quiz-master, compère, and master of ceremonies? Or is none of these adequate to describe his role?

There is an earlier tradition that survives – whether in debased form or merely anachronistically it is difficult to say – and has whole schools in its unhappy grip. Such schools may be recognized by characteristic forms of language used by the teachers. In the corridors and the playground speech is an offensive weapon, aimed one feels at 'keeping the children at bay'. ('Do you think I want *you* standing outside my door?') In the classroom, where a teacher has his own children, the tone he uses to the group is, at best, one of 'conditional approval'. After all we said about the young child's talk at home it will not, I think, be difficult to imagine how daunting such a situation in school must be, how blunting to questions and stifling to curiosity. It is an act of faith for a small child to address an adult he does not know; to do so across the silence of thirty-five other children can only magnify the difficulty; add to that the fear of rejection of what he offers and the picture is complete.

Children do learn, of course, in such circumstances, but it will be the ones upon whom approval settles that tend to make the progress, and they are likely to do so within limits laid down by the teacher, and at some risk of alienating themselves from the rest of their classmates. This story by a fourteen-year-old boy of a walk he took one winter's day throws some light on the situation:

The streets were overcast with cloud and it threatened to rain. I passed a derelict terrace of Victorian houses and then into the alley leading to the school. I don't know why I went this way, I just did.

I remember my first day at school, the christening it was called by the teachers. It was the day on which they picked their favourites and chose the ones they were going to needle. I was one of the latter. I was continually called upon to recite the eight times table, a thing which nobody else in the whole class could do, and was ever asked to do. It was always me, because I was the one they picked. I found myself sweating with a broken pride. It was not until the second part of my education that I found real joy in being educated. I found teachers who condemned favouritism and regarded their pupils as equals.

The characteristic roles realized in and maintained by the teacher's speech in these 'unliberated' schools are these: one of aggressive disapproval in casual encounters, one of unconditional approval towards certain children in the teacher's own class – an approval which may spread to include casual encounters with them – and one of conditional approval in the classroom, both to the group as a group and to the unselected individuals in it.

The revolution is one in the teacher's conception of his own role. The ideal of the enlightened Primary School teacher is at one level a relationship of simple reciprocity: between teacher and any individual child an acceptance of each by the other, as persons. This means of course that one may strongly disapprove of the actions of the other, but not in such a way as to destroy him – or destroy his ultimate self-respect.

Beyond that, the relationship is in two important ways not a reciprocal one. In the first place it is not reciprocal in that its effect is directed upon the pupil and not upon the teacher. Let me begin here by citing what Clare Winnicott has said about social workers: their relationship to those they look after is a *professional* one, and as such it harnesses 'the most highly organized and integrated part' of the personality.

Our professional relationships are more balanced and more reliable than our personal ones, and it is important that they should be. We look to our *personal* relationships for the satisfaction of our personal *need* for relationships – for instinct satisfaction. (By instinct satisfaction I mean the need to love and be loved in a personal intimate way.) Personal relationships are, therefore, less reliable because they are subject to our needs and demands, to our moods and our jealousies and rivalries. (Clare Winnicott, 1964, p. 12)

The case-worker uses this professional relationship in order to create a limited and reliable environment for his client – one which accepts all that the client puts of himself into it, and 'holds' it, so giving a chance for his own integrative processes to operate. For the client, then, the relationship is 'personal, because it contains all that [he] has put into it himself'.

Martin Buber recognizes the same sort of one-sidedness in the relation of teacher to child. He assigns the educator's function as he states what he means by education:

The world, the whole environment, nature and society, 'educates' the human being: it draws out his powers, and makes him grasp and penetrate its objections. What we term education, conscious and willed, means *a selection by man of the effective world*; it means to give decisive effective power to a selection of the world which is concentrated and manifested in the educator. (Buber, 1947, p. 89)

If the educator is to select widely from the world, the whole environment, he must live in the world: if he is to make his selection not arbitrarily 'from himself and his idea of the pupil' but 'from the pupil's own reality', he must 'have gathered the child's presence into his own store'. He must experience **the selection of the world from both sides: from his own, and** at the same time 'from over there', from feeling 'how it affects this other human being'. Thus, 'the educator stands at both ends of the common situation, the pupil only at one end'.

Looking back over the history of European civilization, Martin Buber sees that there was a time when the role of the teacher was that of ambassador, 'the ambassador of history to this intruder, the child'. Authority existed for the teacher to wield, that of the established beliefs of the society he lived in. Today – in this 'hour of the crumbling of bonds' – such a relationship is no longer possible, in Buber's opinion, and the teacher 'faces the child as individual to individual'.

The malady of that former system was a 'will to power' in the teacher which became more furious as the strength of traditional authority behind him grew less: the malady of the current system he calls 'Eros' – the deterioration of the relationship into one of reciprocity – a change from a professional relationship to a personal one into which teacher and pupil would enter equally. Eros, says Buber, desires to enjoy men and acts from choice or inclination. The educator, as far as he is able, must take on allcomers.

The rewards of Eros are clear – the pleasures of giving and receiving affection, of achieving intimate understanding and intimate partnership – and no one would deny that these contribute to a good teacher's daily wages, being damaging to his professional relationships only when they become themselves an objective. But what are the rewards proper to the teaching relationship? I think they are in essence those that Clare Winnicott claims for the social worker:

Briefly, we get a fundamental reassurance about our value and goodness – because people can take and use what we give. We get the chance to contribute to the world through our professional function and thereby relate ourselves to society and feel more secure in it.

This, as she says, is 'a very great deal, and fundamental to our well-being, and our continuing ability to do our work'. (Winnicott, 1964, p. 12) And the child, what does he gain from the relationship? Martin Buber, setting forth the ideal, puts it this way:

Trust, trust in the world, because this human being exists – that is the most inward achievement of the relation in education. Because this human being exists, meaninglessness, however hard pressed you are by it, cannot be the real truth. Because this human being exists, in the darkness the light lies hidden, in fear salvation, and in the callousness of one's fellow men the great Love. (Buber, 1947, p. 98)

This distinction between a professional and a personal relationship is one that a recent American writer on the subject fails to make. Jules Henry in *Culture Against Man* records teachers' views to the effect that in the permissive classroom it is 'love' that promotes order and cooperation: that the teacher has in fact taken on the role of a third parent and the classroom become an extension of the family. Henry is sharply critical and sees this system of relationships, in practice, as a device for inculcating habits of affection without commitment, habits appropriate to the 'buddy-buddy relations of contemporary business, government, and university' in America.

It is hard for us to see [he says], since we consider most people inherently replaceable, that there is anything remarkable in a parent-figure like a teacher showering the symbols of affection on a child for a year and then letting him walk out of her life, to be replaced next year and the next and the next by different children. . . . The fact that a teacher can be thus demonstrative without inflicting deep wounds on *herself* implies a character structure having strong brakes on involvement. Otherwise how could the teacher not go to pieces? If she became deeply involved in the children in her classes she would have to give up teaching, for the hurt inflicted on her as she lost her beloved children each year would be too severe. It must be, then, that the expressions of tenderness imply also, 'So far and no farther'; over the years, children must come to recognize this. It is a kind of mutual conspiracy of affectivity in which children and teacher hold themselves aloof, neither giving nor demanding more than the tacit rules permit. (Henry, 1963, p. 318)

Clearly, a teacher who could go to pieces at the loss of her beloved children exemplifies 'Eros'. Thus the alternatives Jules Henry envisages are the Eros relationship and its empty counterpart in pseudo-affection: both of them he rejects, the former as unworkable and the latter as unworthy. He goes on to hint at the possibility of a third alternative, a positive role for the teacher – that based upon 'Love of knowledge for its own sake, not as the creature of drive, exploited largely for survival and for prestige'. (Henry, 1963, p. 319) But the difficulty with a subject-centred role for educators lies in the fact that it throws off their shoulders the burden of deciding *what is to be learned*, and the burden is likely to land nowhere. The fact that a teacher is interested in and has expert knowledge of a particular 'selection from the world' provides no evidence as to whether that selection will be of value to one, some or all of the children for whom he is responsible. A succession of teachers, in fact, will teach what was chosen for them, each by his predecessor, until nobody who actually knows the children any longer selects for anybody (save at the level of detail). Moreover a young child's roving curiosity shows learning on a principle of choice: when he encounters a strictly subject-centred school programme he must summarily unlearn the habit of choice and forego the right to be interested. It seems to me that learning to choose is a part of learning to learn, and so, in the long run, more important than learning *x* or *y* or *z*.

Neither the subject-centred curriculum nor the *laissez-faire*, permissive, pseudo-affectionate régime that Henry observed (and that has sometimes passed for a 'child-centred curriculum') meets the requirements of education as we found it defined by Martin Buber; neither the 'subject-specialist' nor the pseudo-parent provides an adequate alternative to the professional role of the teacher as he described it.

I come now to the second of my reasons why the teacher is not reciprocally related to his pupils. What we have discussed so far is his relations to individual pupils, but he stands in a different relationship to the group as a whole – in fact, of course, in a series of relationships to various groupings, but on similar principles.

Cooperation always demands some sacrifice of individual freedom of action, and children – since they learn from co-operative activity – have to learn to cooperate. Sometimes they will be faced with an open choice: they may choose whether or not to pay the price in order to participate. But when a group's interests compete with an individual's, or with those of other groups, authority of some kind may be needed. Again, to look at the need for authority at its lowest level, if there is at any point something that everybody in the class needs to know, it is, in all common sense, the teacher's voice that must be heard! He is in fact responsible for securing whatever order or organization in the classroom is needed so that learning, of whatever form is appropriate, may go on. And here his relations with individual children are not the immediate means by which he discharges his responsibility – though of course they materially affect that means.

His authority over the group is in the long run derived from the group itself, and both the integrity of his concern for the group and the quality of his relations with the members as individuals authorize him to wield it. However, in a group that rejects the educational processes the teacher represents, no such authority exists: while he will continue to summon it from them as far as he can, and foster it in them for the future, he has meanwhile to draw authority from elsewhere. In favourable circumstances, where the school stands for the same sort of educational principles as his own, he draws it from more experienced colleagues and higher authorities in the school. Anyone who knows schools at all will recognize the importance of this corporate effort towards a common order based on the authority that derives from the whole community of human beings. Where circumstances are unfavourable, and a teacher has to seek such order in his own classroom, in isolation from the school community – then I think he has society on his side, but how to draw effectively upon that authority I do not know, and the mere knowledge that he has that support is likely to be of small comfort in the long and patient struggle he must undertake.

In whatever circumstances, and whether the going is hard or easy, the establishment first of a reciprocal person-to-person relationship and next of a professional relationship with individual children must be sought by any means, while at the same time the teacher's management of the group as a whole is conducted in such a way as to threaten least damage to these individual relationships.

It is true then that every word the teacher utters counts. We do not use language sometimes to establish relationships and at others to pass on information, for even the most neutral piece of instruction exercises some effect upon our relation with the listener. And there is some evidence from experience that a direct attempt to express warmth and sympathy (not so far removed perhaps from the pseudo-affection that Jules Henry observed) is less effective than Connie Rosen's was:

I can only aim at making a triangle of myself, the children and the activities outside both of us, but in which we are both involved for different reasons.

Finally, the teacher's relationships with those he teaches cannot be sustained in a vacuum. The homes and neighbourhoods of the children must remain a part of their life when they come into school – which means that we cannot afford to have schools that stand aloof in the communities they serve. As Bernstein has recently pointed out:

If the contexts of learning – the examples, the reading books – are not contexts which are triggers for the children's imaginings, are not triggers on the children's curiosity and explorations in his family and community, then the child is not at home in the educational world. . . . If the culture of the teacher is to become part of the consciousness of the child, then the culture of the child must first be in the consciousness of the teacher. . . . We should start knowing that the social experience the child already possesses is valid and significant, and that this social experience should be reflected back to him as being valid and significant. It can only be reflected back to him if it is part of the texture of the learning experience we create. (Bernstein, 1970, p. 120)

CHAPTER FIVE

Language and Thought

I

IT is fashionable at the moment for researchers to undertake what they call 'feasibility studies': and that, in a frivolous sense, is what this brief chapter should be. Can we see as feasible the claims psycholinguists have made regarding the influence of language upon thought? This is in any case an area of speculation rather than proof: we shall be more concerned with seminal ideas, ideas about possible relationships, than with explanatory data. Many of these ideas have already been alluded to or implied in earlier chapters of the book: looking at them now more directly, can we credit them as probable, if sometimes partial, truths?

The topic, language and thought, will inevitably bring us to a consideration of the relation between a man and the society he belongs to, between the behaviour of the individual and the behaviour patterns regarded as 'normal' in the culture he is brought up to share. 'Thought' – a name for the most advanced forms of a man's mental activity, inward, never wholly revealed; 'language' – something that is audible and visible in the infant's environment long before he can take any part in it: the inwardness of thought stands over against language, something 'out there'.

In order to consider this relationship we must look back once again at the obvious starting point – the state of the young child who has not yet acquired language. Susanne Langer sums it up:

Before speech there is no conception: there is only perception, and a characteristic repertoire of actions, and a readiness to act according to the enticements of the perceived world. (Langer, 1960b)

190

Yet we would judge this repertoire of actions to be purposeful, directed, exploratory: and to show changes, as the child grows older, towards an increasing mastery of exploratory skills. The behaviour has the appearance of 'learning' as we have described it. Unless we are to regard thought as so closely tied to language that the two cannot be considered independently at all, it seems feasible to regard these aspects of an infant's behaviour as evidence of the early forms of mental activity that we shall without hesitation call thought in their later phases.

When Piaget speaks of the period from birth to about two years as 'the sensori-motor' phase, this is to indicate that the infant at this stage uses movement and perception as means of making sense of his environment. In the earliest behaviour, perception relies heavily upon movement. Piaget exemplifies this in a series of observations concerning the distress an infant shows when a favourite object is taken away from him: a child of ten to twelve months protests only if he was actually holding the object: a few months later, also if he is reaching after it: and a few months later still, even if it is merely in view: and at somewhere around two years, when it is not in sight but he knows where it ought to be – or to have been.*

I don't think anyone who has spent time with young children will find difficulty in accepting that for them action and perception are interlocked: from small movements like poking their fingers into holes, patting or stroking or pushing things, to larger movements like climbing on to ledges or worming their way under chairs and into cupboards, they make it clear that they are far less able than we are to satisfy their curiosity by merely looking. And the tendency persists of course, for the three-year-old will pat the picture of his favoured object and the four-year-old will trace the lines on his more complicated pictures with his finger.

*These observations are reported in Bruner *et al.*, *Studies in Cognitive Growth*, Wiley, 1966, from which I have taken many other very useful things in writing this chapter. See pp. 203 ff. below.

Bruner makes a further distinction within this sensori-motor period since he sees it as the establishment of two systems of representation: first, the action-cum-perception, which he calls 'the enactive system' and then the action-free perception, which he calls 'the iconic system' (*ikon* being the Greek word for an image). He suggests that this second system is well on its way towards establishment by the end of the first year of a child's life. (Bruner *et al.*, 1966, Chapter 1)

As a way of representing the world the enactive system clearly has limitations. Internalized movement patterns – schemas of movement – may develop from simple isolated patterns into more complex and more connected patterns, but it is difficult to imagine that they could ever wholly escape from the limitations of their *serial* nature. We may roughly exemplify this by looking at some of our own activities that seem to remain at the enactive level. Thus for example, to recall a single-line extract from a poem I have learnt by heart I may well have to recite the poem from the beginning, recovering my line only when I reach that point in the *serial* performance. Again, suppose after a long interval we were not sure whether we still knew how to do a particular dive or a particular golfing shot – could we convince ourselves by reasoning about it, or visualizing it, or should we not in fact have to carry out the actual sequence of movements? When a representation is of this kind it can perhaps only be reactivated by the renewal of the actions: the infant could thus only 'know' his world at this stage by performing his repertoire.

With the sense image – the iconic system – comes a great gain in the *simultaneity* of our representation of the world. Alternative expectations are offered, alternative courses of action are open to us by its means. I believe we can roughly parallel this change by reference to the experience of car-drivers who, when they move into a new district, may for a time build up a repertoire of particular routes – enactive up to a point, since it is the stimulus of a particular building or landmark that causes them to turn right or left, and so on: and then at a later stage – and usually with the help of a map – they get a visual picture of the lay-out of the area. At this stage the particular routes, hitherto isolated, are related to each other and a new mode of finding the way becomes possible, one that is manifestly less dependent upon landmarks since it may involve turning off into quite unexplored roads. The spatial image puts a range of alternative routes at their disposal.

Bruner's third mode of representation he calls the linguistic or symbolic system. Since, with Cassirer, we have taken a broader sense of the word 'symbol' than Bruner does,* a sense by which all three systems are symbolic, we shall call this third one 'linguistic'.

A child learns to speak at about two years of age, but it is many years before his use of language enables him to exploit to the full the peculiar virtues of the linguistic mode of representation. His first uses of speech serve to regulate, organize, extend his representations made in the enactive and iconic modes: by stages the new, more powerful mode is added. We shall look first at the characteristics of the linguistic mode of representation – those peculiar virtues we have referrred to: and then go on to consider some of the stages by which a child takes on the mode.

II

To recall briefly our theoretical framework, the human individual builds a cumulative representation of his interactions with his environment: this representation is a predictive apparatus – a store of expectations concerning what may happen to him next. The capacity, or the richness, of his resources is obviously

* We have taken 'representation' and 'symbolization' as equivalents, a symbol standing for, or representing, something other than itself: by the definition Bruner uses, a symbol is an *arbitrary* representation: it represents something other than itself by *convention only* and not by *analogy*.

one measure of its value to him: the availability of any particular 'item' in it is another. And this flexibility depends, to put it crudely, on the efficiency of his filing system, the kind of organization built into his representation.

To have any expectations at all demands some kind of filing system – demands in other words the setting up of categories of experience. When a child begins to use words as labels for objects or people or events he has acquired a category-making tool far more efficient than anything he formerly possessed, or than any animal possesses. The dog who anticipates being taken for a walk has, as we have seen, formed categories of experience: but the child using words as filing pins rapidly multiplies the number of his categories.

If I put in one pile all the records I feel like listening to this evening, leaving the rest in another pile, my classification is of very temporary value: it will not accurately predict what I might want to have with me on another occasion. If I put together all the ones I like and make another pile of those I don't like, that classification – though likely to remain constant a little longer – is not much use to anybody else. The set of 'records I like' will, moreover, be a very mixed bunch, representing very different kinds of performance which I like (or dislike) for very different reasons. It is a poor filing system because it is designed to answer only one question, and that one only in my own case.

When we classify in accordance with the words that name objects (it might in the case of records be in such terms as 'symphonies', 'piano concertos', 'blues', 'folk-songs', 'pop-songs', though admittedly there are a confusing number of other possibilities), we are creating categories that are (1) on the same lines as those other people have made and (2) in accordance with describable general criteria. Two symphonies are put together, not on the grounds of many unexplored similarities (as is the case when I put together the records I like, and as would be the case if I chose two pictures to make a pair over my bookcase), but because they meet a specific and general criterion. It is specific because the qualifying conditions are clearly laid down: it is general because a wide range of pieces that differed from each other in almost every other way would qualify.

But it is even more important that the classes created should be related to each other. This is essential from the point of view of prediction: the class of event recognized as 'taking the lead off the hook' had to be related to that of 'being taken for a walk' before it could be of any use to the dog. And it is essential from the point of view of an efficient filing system – which again comes down to a matter of prediction in the end. Our counter-part of taking the lead off the hook might be a sudden increase in temperature in a car's cooling system and this might have many varied correlates in our past experience or (as we shall see) in our extrapolations from experience: our organization will need to be efficient if we are to muster the appropriate array of expectations.

As we have suggested in an earlier chapter, the categories created by using words to name aspects of experience are related to each other in a number of ways. We must look at one or two of these more closely.

1. The meaning we give to the word 'red' is, as it were, a value on the colour spectrum, a value related to the meaning we give to other colours – to 'orange', for example, or 'violet'. And the same principal works in some degree very much more widely. The physical continuum of the colour spectrum gives us a highly specific set of phenomena against which to place the values meant by the words, and we cannot usually be so specific. However, when Clare at three asked, 'Is delicious nicer than lovely?' she was clearly relating meanings in such a way as to construct a scale of values. Or to take a more complex example, we call one day 'a mild day' and another 'a cool day' where there was no difference in the actual temperature, but a difference in *context*, the winter or summer season: we have in

fact used terms related to *two different* scales, the one applied to winter and the other to summer. De Saussure has claimed that all language works on this principle. 'A linguistic system,' he says, 'is a series of differences of sound combined with a series of differences of ideas; but the pairing of a number of acoustical signs with as many cuts from the mass of thought engenders a system of values.' (De Saussure, 1960, p. 120)

2. It is the hierarchical relationship between word meanings that has the most evidently far-reaching influence upon our thinking. Anyone who has played guessing games where the answer is restricted to 'yes' and 'no' will recognize the strategy that follows hierarchical relationships somewhat after this fashion:

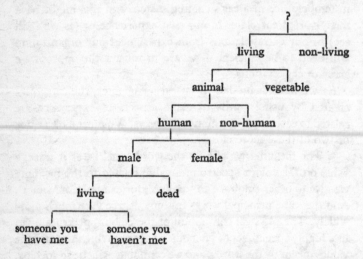

In the way scientists use language, hierarchies are usually very well defined. The fauna and flora of the world – teeming populations that make up the animal and vegetable kingdoms – are grouped into sub-species that are grouped into species that are grouped into genera, then into families, into sub-orders, into orders, into classes, into phyla, into sub-kingdoms – a vast comprehensive hierarchy. But of course particular classifications for particular purposes crop up at all points in the sciences.

And they lie behind most of our ordinary uses of language. As we arrive at a decision in a matter of colour – say, in talk with a friend – we may use words at descending levels of such a classification as the following:

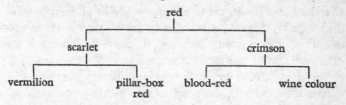

Or, to take something a little more complex, the organizers of a sports event may hold in the backs of their minds some such skeleton as the following:

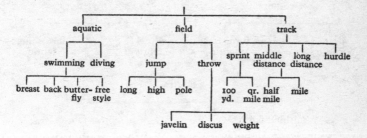

A very general exercise of this kind, however, does little to indicate the practical value of hierarchies. The form of a classification must depend in fact upon its purpose. For the purpose of buying and selling, for example, a shop might divide clothes into 'ready-made' and 'made to measure', but this distinction would have no relevance for a man who was organizing his holiday packing: we can conceive of a context in which he might think in terms of 'clothes for the journey', 'clothes for the evening' and 'ski-ing clothes'.

If we look around at the labels in a department store we are likely to find some labels that seem to belong to one hierarchy (say 'glassware', 'enamelware', 'tinware' and 'leather goods') and some that belong to another ('writing requisites', 'suiting', 'furnishing fabrics') and yet others that we might call *collections* rather than classes in a stricter sense ('kitchen equipment', 'gifts', 'fancy goods' and 'everything for the garden'). Certainly, as a result, the total array would be unlikely to sub-divide the articles sold in such a way that we were never in any doubt: in other words they are unlikely to constitute an exhaustive set of categories at a given level of generality.

Variations will arise partly because different purposes will dictate differences in the *order* in which divisions are made. Consider these alternatives:

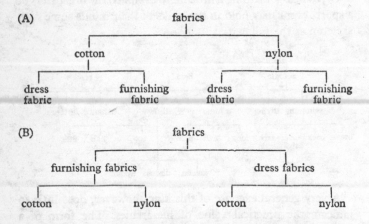

Filing orders to manufacturers might, one would suppose, be better done under (A); setting up wares for customers to choose from would certainly demand (B).

The multiple store will serve to bring us back to the point at issue in all this: hierarchical categories are important as means by which to organize expectations and regulate behaviour in the light of them: as I push my way through the crowded aisles

I have on the one hand a narrow range of expectations concerning the thing I hope to buy: and on the other, expectations of a general kind over a wide area called up in me by the labels I read. I do not have to think of tumblers and cocktail sets and vases in order to reject 'glassware', nor do I have to imagine what might go with a fountain pen – if that is what I want to buy – in order to make for the label 'writing requisites'.

3. A third way in which word meanings are related to each other is a feature of the place words occupy in the syntax of sentences. The relatedness is shown most clearly in such pairs of cognate words as the following:

man: manly	hope: hopeful	glory: glorify
sister: sisterly	bounty: bountiful	stupor: stupify
master: masterly	beauty: beautiful	beauty: beautify

glorify: glorification	sweet: sweeten
qualify: qualification	loose: loosen
mystify: mystification	hard: harden

However, the relationship we are considering does not rely upon such pairing: most words do not declare their class-membership or their kinship with words in other classes so clearly. It is a general relationship between whole classes of words that concerns us: that is to say the relationships by means of which we are able to encode aspects of experience either as *things* (using *nouns*) or as *actions* (using *verbs*) or as *attributes* (using *adjectives*). We may have the feeling that such distinctions are virtually dictated by experience itself, but this is certainly not as true as it appears. Think of the diverse situations and events that we draw together under the noun 'holidays': could we handle these circumstances in our minds at all if we did not 'reify', construct a 'thing' in this way? We are well aware of the dangers of 'reification' – regarding 'democracy' as though it were something we could lay a finger on – but we have to recognize also that the world of ideas would be an impossibility were it not for our habit of reifying. We must suppose that the internalizing of these grammatical distinctions between classes of words affects our thinking – that not only do we construct imaginary 'things', but that we entertain also a sense of movement – of time, say, *marching on*, of advancing and fleeing, of colliding, deflecting, oscillating, exploding and so on; and an adjectival sense, a sense of quality or condition – evil-smelling or fragrant, discoloured or crystal-clear, blurred or blunted or sharp, delicate or coarse: in other words that fictional things, actions and attributes attach themselves to even the most illusive of our half-formed judgements and ideas.

4. When we turn now to syntactical relationships in general – relationships expressed in the sentence as a whole – the picture is so complicated that we must select only the salient points. We shall be guided by Bruner who in turn takes his lead in this instance from one of the most influential of living linguists, Noam Chomsky of the Massachusetts Institute of Technology. It is suggested that all languages incorporate in their grammar three fundamental properties of sentences and that these are closely related to characteristics of mature thinking. They are (1) the *subject-predicate relation* by which what is named in the subject is shown, in terms from logic, to be 'a function of' what is said in the predicate. This is perhaps little more, in common-sense terms, than saying that the subject and the predicate are related in a particular way, a way that is constant from sentence to sentence; and that formulations of aspects of experience (predicates) are meaningful – can be believed or disbelieved – only when they are anchored upon some given entity (the subject); (2) the *verb–object relation* which expresses the logical relation of cause and effect, and (3) *modification* which represents what logicians call 'the intersect of classes': in 'a green hat', 'green' is a modifier of 'hat', and 'a green hat' represents the intersect of 'green things' and 'hats'. Thus, in Bruner's words,

The sentence *The man wore the green hat* contains the underlying relations ... of a man wearing something (or x being a function of y), a hat being acted upon (being worn, which is causing it to be worn), and a certain kind of hat at that (modification by green). (Bruner *et al.*, 1966, p. 43)

Then it must be added that all languages incorporate procedures by which simple statements of the kind we have just quoted may be 'transformed', re-written in various ways: for example in the passive (*The hat was worn by the man*), in the interrogative (*Did the man wear the hat?*), and in the negative (*The man did not wear the hat*). We omitted the modifier *green* from the example here because Chomsky, in setting out to describe in as economical and systematic a fashion as possible the relations between sentence structures, would explain *The man wore the green hat* as a re-writing, a transformation, of two basic sentences, *The man wore the hat* and *The hat was green*. But it must be noted that the abstract system he arrives at is a way of describing structures and not an explanation of how a speaker produces sentences.

If we bear in mind now the various relationships built into language, as we have briefly surveyed them, and add this last observation regarding transformation procedures, it becomes easier to accept the possibility that we might in fact, on occasion, represent actuality in language and then, going back to examine the language we have produced, discover from it something about the nature of relationships existing in actuality.

Furthermore, the possibilities of experience that we can represent in language are not limited to things we have experienced nor to things we take on trust from other people's experiences: we, in fact, *extrapolate* from experience. Or, as Sapir puts it:

It is highly important to realise that once the form of a language is established it can discover meanings for its speakers which are not simply traceable to the given quality of experience itself but must be explained to a large extent as *the projection of potential meanings into the raw material of experience* [my italic] (Sapir, 1961, p. 7)

He gives a simple illustration:

If a man who has never seen more than a single elephant in the course of his life nevertheless speaks without the slightest hesitation of ten elephants or a million elephants or a herd of elephants or of elephants walking two by two or three by three or of generations of elephants, it is obvious that language has the power to analyse experience into theoretically dissociable elements and to create that world of the potential intergrading with the actual which enables human beings to transcend the immediately given in their individual experiences and to join in a larger common understanding.

Let us consider a more complex example of extrapolation with the help of language. It seems probable that only from a symbolic system such as language could we ever derive a relationship of the kind that exists between 'red' and 'not red'. Our pre-linguistic judgements are almost certainly of the bi-polar or dichotomous kind that George Kelly has described: and, as he supposes, it is likely that these continue to be a principal means of operating even after, with the help of language, we are able to use more complicated methods. Kelly distinguishes the 'red' and 'not red' distinction from the bi-polar judgement as follows:

How does our notion of dichotomous constructs apply to such 'class concepts' as *red*? Is red a statement of contrast as well as similarity? We might point out that, according to one of the prevalent colour theories, red is the complement of green. But *red* is used in other ways also. When we say that a person has red hair we are distinguishing it from the non-redness of white, yellow, brown or black. . . . Similarly other constructs such as *table* express, within their ranges of convenience, both likenesses and differences. . . . Unlike classical logic, we do not lump together the contrasting and the irrelevant . . . it makes sense to point to a chair and say, 'That is not a table'. It makes no sense to point to

a sunset and say, 'That is not a table'. (Kelly, 1963, p. 63; see
also p. 66 and pp. 105–8)

While our behaviour may demonstrate that even in infancy
we comprehend both prohibition (the 'no' of authority) and
refusal (the 'no' of the worm that turns), yet the pure negative,
the logical relation of 'red' to 'not red', is one which proves
beyond our power until language provides us with the means.*
That we require it might be illustrated here by pointing out
that Kelly's idea of 'ranges of convenience' – that is to say, the
areas of experience to which a bi-polar distinction is applicable
– cannot be fully understood without invoking the idea of the
negative. (We agree with him that we may *operate* bi-polar
constructs within ranges of convenience without an explicit
understanding of the principle.) There will be more said later
about the way in our higher thought processes we employ this
'red'/'not red' distinction.

III

Vygotsky suggested that when a child of six or seven stops using
'speech for oneself', it is because that speech has become
internalized and continues to operate in the form of inner
speech. He supposed that as vocal speech for oneself became
abbreviated and individuated in its latest stages, so it was
probable that 'verbal thought' was even more abbreviated and
individuated than 'inner speech': in other words, it took up
forms of organization less and less like speech syntax, to arrange
'items' that bore a dwindling resemblance to word meanings.
Linguists, as we have seen, have referred to these items as
'post-language symbols'. They represent, that is to say,

---

*'The essential distinction between the verbal and the non-verbal
is the fact that language adds the peculiar possibility of the negative.'
(Kenneth Burke, *Language as Symbolic Action*, University of California
Press, 1966, p. 420)

symbols that have freed themselves from the restrictions of the language from which they were derived.

We have looked at some of the principal ways in which language serves to reduce to order the multiplicity and variousness of human experience: and we have suggested that these ways of organizing are fundamental processes in mature thinking. But what exactly is the connexion between these two processes – the organization in speech and the organization in thought? How far is one the simple consequence of the other? Is it a matter of the child learning to speak in a language which already embodies the means of organizing experience although he himself cannot yet so organize it? This would certainly be Vygotsky's view, and it seems to me an acceptable one. Then, once a child has taken in hand the right tool, he is in a position to learn how to use it. As he verbalizes what is happening, both the events, as he perceives them, and the verbalization are open to his examination. It might be that at this stage the possibility we have referred to of discovering relationships in actuality by examining the verbalization may be paying a very high dividend. Bruner describes and illustrates some such stage as this very helpfully: the gap between the linguistic formulation and what I have loosely called 'actuality' above, he sees as a mismatch between the deliverances of (a) the linguistic system and (b) the earlier systems of representation, enactive and iconic.

In essence, once we have coded experience in language, we can (but not necessarily do) read surplus meaning into the experience by pursuing the built-in implications of the rules of language. Until the time that this 'surplus meaning' is read off from our linguistic coding of experience, language and experience maintain an important independence from each other. A child can say of two quantities that one is greater than another, a moment later that it is less than the other, and then that they are the same – using his words as labels for segments of experience. It is not until he inspects his *language* that he goes back to his experience to check on a mismatch between what he sees with his eyes and what he has just said. He must, in short, treat the utterance as a *sentence* and recognize contradiction at that level. He can *then* go back and reorder experience, literally *see* the world differently by virtue of symbolic processes reordering the nature of experience. (Bruner *et al.*, 1966, pp. 51-2)

These inconsistencies of judgement were demonstrated in experiments he carried out with children of five to eleven. They are characteristic of the stage of mismatch between the linguistic and the earlier systems: he found them more frequent in the seven- to eleven-year-olds than in the younger children. (Bruner *et al.*, 1966, p. 179)

As a child's powers of thought develop they might be seen to go through the stages of first drawing level with and then surpassing his powers of speech. Or, putting it crudely by numbers:

1. He speaks a language which embodies powers of organization he cannot achieve in thought.

2. He achieves the ability to organize in thought what is organized in his speech.

3. He extends the range of his powers of organization in thought by first verbalizing more complex experiences and contemplating these verbalizations.

4. His powers of organization in thought come to exceed his powers of organization in speech.*

This no doubt is an over-simplified statement, but it is one Bruner seems to endorse when he suggests that man's innate ability to handle symbols enables him first to learn language and later to achieve powers of conceptualization beyond those of speech. Nor do I find in Vygotsky anything fundamentally inconsistent with this view.

As Bruner puts it,

language comes from the same basic root out of which symbolically organised experience grows. I tend to think of symbolic activity

* Notice that this relationship held *in general* would not preclude the possibility of reading off 'surplus meaning' from our own formulations in language.

of some basic or primitive type that finds its first and fullest expression in language, then in tool-using, and finally in the organising of experience. It is by the interaction of language and the barely symbolically organised experience of the child of two or three that language gradually finds its way into the realm of experience. (Bruner *et al.*, 1966, p. 44)

Thus we see language and thought as two forms of behaviour, powerfully interacting but distinct in origin and with differing forms of development. Vygotsky imagines two intersecting circles, the area of overlap being 'verbal thought' and the distinct areas being 'non-verbal thought' and 'non-intellectual speech'. If this presents any difficulty at all I believe it is because when we use the term 'thinking' we usually have in mind our sustained, or even deliberate and strenuous mental activities – in other words, activity most dependent upon words or post-language symbols, the aftermath of words. If we try to exemplify to ourselves thought independent of language we have to go back to pre-verbal behaviour – the purposeful, adaptive, intelligent actions of an infant, or, attempting the more difficult task of identifying 'non-verbal thought' in mature people, to take Vygotsky's example of 'thinking manifested in the use of tools' or John Holloway's examples of 'intelligent overt behaviour on the part of ballerinas, sailormen, mountaineers, carpenters, cricketers, and many others . . .'. 'In these fields,' he says, 'it is possible to "think" (in the sense of "solve intelligently") with one's hands, or one's feet, or one's whole body.' (Holloway, 1951, p. 77) Language without thought is much easier to conceive of – we use so much of it in our daily routine exchanges, saying what we have said so often that no thought goes into the production.

IV

Experimental work by Vygotsky and his associates and by Bruner and his associates throws some light upon the stages by which language comes to influence thought – though it is a sequence about which more is to be discovered than is yet known. Recall that, in Bruner's terms, the stages refer to the establishment of the third system of representation – the linguistic system – upon the foundations laid by the enactive and iconic systems. Bear in mind also Bruner's point regarding the mismatch between systems: it is a kind of inequilibrium that will not let the child rest, but prompts him to further exploration, further growth.

Vygotsky used a set of twenty-two wooden blocks – toy-like objects of different colours, shapes, heights and sizes. Although there were five different colours and six different shapes, it was the two heights (tall and flat) and the two sizes (large and small) that his experiments were focused upon. He defined, in fact, a two-dimensional concept which divided the blocks into four categories: to each category he gave a nonsense syllable as a name. Thus, tall and large blocks were called *lag*; flat and large ones were called *bik*; tall and small ones, *mur*; flat and small ones, *cev*. (In a similar way a two-dimensional concept of sex and maturity would divide an assortment of human beings into 'man', 'woman', 'boy' and 'girl'.) The name of the category to which a block belonged was marked on the underneath, where it could not ordinarily be seen. The experimenter picked up one of the blocks, showed the child the name on the bottom, then asked him to put with it all the blocks he thought might be of the same kind. This could, of course, only be done at this first stage by some kind of guess-work, since the child could not see the names and had not been told anything about the reasons for choosing the block presented. (If it happened to be a red block, the child was not to know that the reason for choosing it was not its redness.) When he had made his attempt, the experimenter picked up one of the wrong blocks and showed him that it had not got the right name on it, and suggested that he should try again: and so it went on. The final task – for the survivors – was to sort all the blocks into their four categories. In observing what children did to arrive at a solution at each stage of the game, Vygotsky traced a sequence of different behaviours from random activity to logical reasoning.

The youngest children attempted the task by putting blocks together in heaps, seemingly at random. When a block was found to be wrong it was removed but no clue was taken from it as to which others might also be wrong; and further attempts were no less a matter of guessing than had been the first 'blind' attempt. A little later, 'heaps' seemed to be influenced by the way the blocks were placed in front of the child, their spatial relationships. The child *chooses*, that is to say, but in terms of what appears to him to form a pattern and not in terms of any likenesses or differences in the blocks themselves. His groupings, in terms of the blocks, are therefore still random. As Bruner has commented, the focus for the child at this stage is probably upon the *action*, 'a kind of grouping by doing'.

Now to step for a moment outside the experiment and look at the ordinary behaviour of a child at the stage we are concerned with, a child who sorts blocks into random heaps is a child who uses a word to name, successively, a range of objects that for a variety of reasons have 'rung the same bell' in his mind. I say 'successively' in order to suggest that each case is a more or less independent act of naming – of giving as it were a proper name to a particular object or event. This is a stage that begins with the first use of language. Vygotsky gives the example of a child who, over a period of months, gave the name *bow-wow* to a china figure of a girl, a dog, pictures of his grandparents, a toy dog, the clock, a fur with an animal's head, a fur without a head, a rubber doll – and so on. (Vygotsky, 1962, p. 70) Operations at this level may persist longer than we should suppose: we may find traces of them in the way a child handles unfamiliar areas of experience, and we may suppose that they give an indeterminacy to his use of more familiar words which, because the contexts in which he uses them coincide largely with our own, seem to us stable and specific enough.

What Vygotsky calls a second major phase comes when, in the series of experiments with blocks, the child groups the objects in accordance with perceived similarities between them. He employs in other words *concrete* and *factual* criteria for choice, not yet *abstract* and *logical*. His operations reflect his capacity to see what is there: they are in the iconic mode. Vygotsky gives to this principle of operating the name 'thinking in complexes' and he compares it to grouping by family relationships. In the earliest kind of complex, which he calls an 'associative complex', the first block may be added because it is the same colour as the given block, the second perhaps because it is the same shape. Thus factual concrete connexions between pairs of blocks control his selection, but no one principle of choice runs through the operations by which further selections are made, further blocks added to 'the family'.

The second type of complex Vygotsky calls 'a collection'; it is similar to the associative complex, being its converse: diverse objects are grouped by their perceived differences from the given block – for example if the block was red, one block of each colour would be added. Such complexes continue, of course, to interest and concern us: a collector's efforts are typically aimed at getting 'one of each' rather than 'many of a kind', whether it be stamps, coins or rare books he is after. Many of the more ordinary collections we value are in fact related to practical activities – the tool chest, the needlework box, the equipment of the chemistry lab. or the kitchen. And the stage at which the children in the experiment sorted the blocks into collections may well have coincided with a stage at which the use of 'kit' was important to them in their practical activities.

Vygotsky then describes the 'chain complex': the child will match the given block, say in colour, two or three times perhaps, and will then introduce a block for its resemblance, say in shape, *not to the given block but to the last added*. So, through a series of such shifts of basis, the grouping is a 'chain' of objects, each being capable of acting as the basis of choice for the next. Vygotsky regards this as the 'purest' form of thinking in complexes because the original, given block has ceased to present any basis of choice, and because each item enters the assembly *bearing all its attributes*, any one of which may become the link with the next item.

A complex does not rise above its elements as does a concept [he says], it merges with the concrete objects that compose it. This fusion of the general and the particular, of the complex and its elements . . . is the distinctive characteristic of all complex thinking and of the chain complex in particular. (Vygotsky, 1962, p. 65)

The last of the complexes is at the borderline between complexes and what Vygotsky regards as true concepts: he calls it a 'pseudo concept'. Experimentally it was found when children grouped the objects quite consistently – say, all the red blocks – but could be shown to have done so on the basis of their perceived similarities and not by the application of the abstract principle (redness). This is a particularly interesting example of the complex because it represents, as we shall see, what goes on very commonly in children's use of language. The difference between operating a pseudo concept and a concept was revealed in the experiment by what happened when the assembly of red blocks was shown to be wrong. (Recall that the right answer demanded an assembly of, say, tall/large blocks and had nothing to do with colour.) The child whose attempt had been controlled by the concept 'redness' would say at once, 'Oh, then it can't be colour', and would remove all the red blocks he had collected. But other children (who had ostensibly carried out the same procedure) did not see the necessity for removing any but the one block shown to be wrong: since they had not operated on a (consistent) principle, no principle was countermanded by the new evidence, only the admission of a concrete item. We should note here that the abstract principle concerned is that of the relation between 'red' and 'not red', and its further application (since red was the colour of the given block) to 'colour/not colour'. From such reasoning would arise further strategies, whereas the child who had worked by complexes could not use the new information as the basis for any further planning.

Most complexes in the thinking of the five- to eleven-year-old are, in the nature of the circumstances, pseudo concepts: that is to say, superficially indistinguishable from concepts. For the circumstances are, as Vygotsky points out, that word meanings already in the language govern the categories a child forms. Here then, in more specific form, is the process we referred to earlier: as a child learns words in association with the objects of his environment he sorts those objects into categories: those categories are complexes; but since the naming will be for the most part in accord with social usage – the uses he has heard in others – these complexes will be pseudo concepts. And in the course of handling complexes (in both speech and thought) to organize experience, meet the challenges of new experience, manage his practical undertakings, satisfy his curiosity, commune and argue with adults – in the course of all this the ability to think in concepts (at least for some of the time) is achieved in adolescence by most members of our society.

Bruner reports a series of experiments that bear out some of these findings and add others. Boys and girls from six years to eleven were engaged in a series of games of 'Twenty Questions' and the types of question they asked were classified in accordance with their usefulness in arriving at a satisfactory solution. In the first test they were given an array of forty-two pictures of familiar objects and told to find out which one the experimenter was thinking of. Broadly speaking, the six-year-olds asked unconnected, specific questions (e.g. 'Is it the hammer?'), while the eleven-year-olds asked 'constraint questions' (questions applicable to more than one picture, e.g. 'Is it a toy?', 'Is it a tool?') and they related their questions to the answers they had previously received. The eight-year-olds employed a mixture of both sorts of question, usually passing from constraint questions to specific ones.

A second test set a problem in words: a situation was described and the children had to arrive at an explanation (the cause of an accident). It was found that eight-year-olds performed conspicuously better with pictures than they could with words: in the second test they were closer in their methods to the six-year-olds; in the first test they had been closer to the eleven-year-olds. It would seem that language serves to regulate their use of iconic representation before they are ready to operate – with the same degree of efficiency – a linguistic system of representation. Eleven-year-olds not only asked general questions, often starting high in the hierarchy of generality (as shown in the example on p. 196), but were often able also to explain afterwards why they had done so; 'Well, to eliminate big things quickly . . .' (Bruner *et al.*, 1966, p. 99)

The set of forty-two pictures was used in another form of experiment with the same children. This time they were asked to select a group of pictures that were 'alike in some way', no limit being placed on the number included, and then to say how the pictures in the group were alike. Perceptual attributes, surface appearances, formed the basis of nearly half the groupings made by the six-year-olds, a quarter of those made by the eight-year-olds and about a fifth of those made by the eleven year-olds. Functional attributes (what the objects do, or what we can do with them) were the basis of one third of the six-year-olds' groupings, nearly half the eight-year-olds' and nearly half the eleven-year-olds'. Grouping according to the conventional names (e.g. 'They are all toys') accounted for a very small proportion of the six-year-olds' groups (six per cent), about a quarter of the eight-year-olds' and about a third of the eleven-year-olds'. The experimenters suggest that:

A first step away from domination by the perceptually salient comes when the child, at about age 9, takes himself egocentrically as a reference point for establishing equivalence among things. He does this by imposing upon the world what *he* can do to things, producing equivalence by reference to his own actions. In time he accommodates to more conventional definitions of how things are 'alike'. (Bruner *et al.*, 1966, p. 101)

It is discoveries such as this no doubt that prompted Bruner to speculate on the importance of tool-using as a transitional stage on the way to a full application of the organizing principle of language to the raw material of experience.

From the intricacy of experimental detail let us try to sort out some broadly common features. Enactive and iconic systems of representation provide the first bases for groupings: when purely subjective or random arrangements yield first to system, it is to systems based on surface features, appearances. The use of language leads to the establishment of many 'groupings by name', categories that have the conventionally accepted boundaries but which, in so far as at this early stage they are supported at all by strategies of selection, base those strategies upon surface appearances. Practical activities lead first to 'collections', the grouping of different objects that complement each other in some particular form of tool-using activity: and such functional collections pave the way for a functional grouping in which the criterion, 'I can use it for . . .', becomes the more abstract basis for a more theoretical category. The operation of such a principle leads in turn to the ability to form fully abstract categories, categories capable of dividing phenomena into the 'x' and the 'not x' at successive stages of generality, and so permitting the systematic pursuit of what Piaget has called 'the consideration of possibles'. This last is the achievement of the adolescent.

V

The theories we have been considering, and the evidence we have sampled, certainly go some way towards explaining how with the help of language we organize our representation of the world. But other modes of organizing that cannot be explained in the same terms – if at all – must also be taken into account.

We must take into account the fact that we shape the objects of our perception in the act of perceiving them: thus, we regularize, simplify, give a more satisfying shape to what we look at in the very act of looking at it: and this ordering is reflected in the way we speak and write about our experiences. We must take into account also the fact that an organization of our *feelings*, by some means or another, must always accompany the process of arriving at a logical conclusion by the means we have been considering. In 'taking into account' these two modes of organization, we have to admit that they are processes we can by no means fully explain.

'Logical' describes the form of the end-product arrived at by the discursive processes – those classificatory, generalizing, abstracting processes that have mainly concerned us in this chapter. If we now look for the end-product of these other non-discursive mental processes – that is to say, processes that feature the organization in perception and the organization of feeling – we shall identify, with Susanne Langer's help, the *work of art*. (Langer, 1967) A work of art, as she sees it, is not a sequence of systematically related symbolic items – as a logical verbal statement is, or an algebraic equation – but is itself a complete symbol. It has 'organic' shape, that is to say it reflects in some way the tensions and rhythms that are characteristic of every act of all living creatures. It achieves uniqueness and unity as a result of the way diverse modes of projecting experience interlock within its highly complex structure. It follows that it cannot be 'translated' into other forms or other media, and no alternative organization of the elements that compose it (or of other elements) could be in any inclusive sense its equivalent. Since it embraces both cognitive and affective aspects of experience, it is a less exclusive mode of representation than is the discursive, logical mode.

We must notice next that the processes by which we arrive at end-products of these two kinds – the logical statement and the work of art – are likely to be far less differentiated than the products are distinct. We do not arrive at a logical formulation by processes that are themselves simply logical. As Langer has put it:

There is much more to rational thinking than the highly general form which may be projected in written symbols or in the functional design of a machine. Thinking employs almost every intuitive process, semantic and formal (logical), and passes from insight to insight not only by recognised processes, but as often as not by short cuts and personal, incommunicable means. The measure of its validity is the possibility of arriving at the same results by the orthodox methods of demonstrating formal connexions. But a measure of validity is not a ground of validity. Logic is one thing, and thinking is another; thought may be logical, but logic itself is not a way of thinking. ... (Langer, 1967, pp. 148–9)

By the same token, most of our commonplace mental actions will result in products that are neither strict logic nor works of art. Indeed, it might be argued that the most highly organized expressions of a total response – affective and cognitive – that a particular individual is capable of do not ever achieve the status of a work of art. What is important is that such expressions of a total response are 'art-like'. Take for example the following piece written by a six-year-old girl: if I am right in supposing that in describing the witch-child she is in fact describing her own isolation, she is clearly using mental processes of the same nature as those that result in a work of art – mental processes that are not to be explained in terms of generalizing abstraction. In short, the piece displays, I believe, an intuitive perception of the organic shape of an experience:

There was a child of a witch who was ugly. he had pointed ears thin legs and was born in a cave. he flew in the air holding on nothing just playing games.

When he saw ordinary girls and boys he hit them with his broom-stick. A cat came along. he arched his back at the girls and boys and made them run away. When they had gone far away the cat meeowed softly at the witch child. the cat loved the child. the child loved the cat the cat was the onlee thing the child loved in the world.

'An intuitive perception': as Langer points out, intuition is the basic intellectual process by which man represents his experiences of the world, whether in images or in words, and recognizes the representations made by himself and other people. Being largely expressive, ordinary speech, both in adults and children, is a vehicle for many of these acts of intuition: only some of it is concerned with practical affairs or with 'the way things are', and much of it is an expression of the way things *seem* to us, the way we feel about things, the way things *might be* or we should like them to be. (See for example Alison's remarks about the bath-water on p. 73 and Clare's comment on the yapping dog on p. 72.) And perhaps the balance is particularly on this side with young children, for their practical responsibilities are few. It is these aspects of expressive speech, I suggest, that will undergo organization in the direction – ultimately – of verbal art, of poem, story or play. Formally, they are far from the condition and quality of art: functionally I believe they may be of value for the same sort of reasons as the arts are valued.

We have already looked at some of the stages by which discursive reasoning may grow from ordinary speech: we must recognize now the potential of such speech for development into the art of literature – and, dare I add, into the art of that kind of conversation that has been called 'communion', a linguistic form that is no more discursive than is the lyric.

There is little doubt that young children's powers of speech develop more readily in this direction than they do in that of discursive reasoning. The very fact that they are not yet in the habit of handling generalizing abstraction would tend to leave them both more egocentric in their interpretations of experience and more open to emotive aspects of events. Thus, for example, they are likely to make and express judgement in directly felt concrete terms which at a later stage they would handle discursively. Clare at the age of three, after listening one night to her favourite 'sing me to sleep' song – 'Away in a manger, no crib for a bed, The little Lord Jesus laid down his sweet head' – made her comment: 'I 'spect when the horses have eaten all the hay his daddy will make him a proper cot!' Is it wildly astray to suggest that she was making in her own terms a value judgement frequently paralleled in general and abstract terms by older people?

The embodiment of an idea in concrete particulars, whether as example or metaphor or analogy, provides an expression that is nearer to 'showing' than to 'telling': and in a limiting case, I believe young children may organize aspects of their experience into stories which set forth situations they could not 'tēll' and can only 'show'; situations that is to say that they could not handle at all in explicit terms. I do not for a moment believe that the six-year-old who wrote the story about the witch-child supposed she was writing about herself in any way: but I believe she was – in the only way possible to her.

On page 325 of his 326-page volume *Studies in Cognitive Growth*, Bruner makes reference to a recent work on the influence of emotional factors upon cognitive organization, and then admits that we may be in danger of overlooking man's emotional needs. The real danger, it seems to me, lies in imposing a disjunction between thought and feeling, between cognitive and affective modes of representation. Psychologists in general have traditionally concentrated upon cognitive organization and tended to regard emotion as itself disorganized and possessing a disorganizing influence. We need to recognize the value and importance both of the discursive logical organization and at the same time that of the undissociated intuitive processes, the organization represented in its highest form in works of art.

We will allow Susanne Langer to draw these threads together in a final quotation: let me add to what she says the rider that in my view her comments apply also to children using forms of language that are transitional in either direction, towards discursive reasoning on the one hand or towards literature on the other (Langer, 1967, p. 114):

Just as we may, in discourse, state a fact of which we are aware and then find that we have stated, by implication, further facts of which we were not aware until we analysed our assertion, so an artist may find that he has articulated ideas he had not conceived before his work presented them to him.

CHAPTER SIX

The Question of a Lifetime

To say that as young children grow into adolescence they exchange a world of objects for a world of persons is an over-simplification, but not I think a gross one. But 'objects' must be taken to embrace living creatures other than human beings, and 'a world' must be taken to mean the world to be explored, the theatre of operations of an active curiosity. For of course people are immensely important to young children – the objects of passionate feelings; but there is a sense in which they are 'given', and taken for granted, rather than seen to be objects of choice or matters for active intellectual curiosity. As adults I believe we regard objects (in this broad sense) as properties in the human drama, that 'web of human relations' that largely constitutes life; and adolescence sees the change to this view from its converse. (I think we can imagine ourselves, in talk with a young child, identifying a person as 'the one who gave you the beads', whereas with an adolescent it will more often be a matter of identifying the beads as 'the ones John gave you'.)

Let me illustrate by quoting Clare, who as a child readily committed her preoccupations to paper. At six she wrote her first story: it was about a Teddy Bear (her possession) who had a pony (his possession). 'I've got a pony called Snow, and I live in a little house with a thatched roof. I've got a little shed for Snow with lovely pink slates. . . .' At nine she wrote one story called 'My Treasures' which began:

It was wonderful that I got my treasures at all. It happened like this. I was staying with my aunt, and *her* great aunt suddenly died, and my aunt Winifred got a lot of funny little things, some carved in ivory. She let me choose six, and this is what I chose:–

An ivory elephant a red velvet pincushion, with a mother-of-pearl back to it, a measuring tape, which came out through a slit in a carved ivory box. To put it back you twiddled a knob on top. Then I chose a minuture wooden spinning wheel, about eight inches high. Then I got a brooch and, from a suitcase, some gorgeous tawny velvet. As that was on the morning of my last day, I packed them carefully, in some tissue paper, and a box which aunt Winifred said I could have. . . .

And in the same year a little essay in natural history (fictional) entitled 'The Roski'. It began:

The Roski is a cat-like animal, living in the trees. When full-grown it is black, with a sandy coloured tip to its tail, and this is ringed with ginger. Its eyes are golden, and shine in the dark. Its pointed ears are edged with white. It has 4 orange claws on each foot, which help it climb. The young, or raskis as they are called are light brown marked with lighter stripes. The ears are like an adult roski. . . .

Just after her eleventh birthday, she brought in a dead missel-thrush from the garden and wanted to keep parts of it for a museum specimen: however, when she was persuaded that it was too maggotty for that, she gave it honourable burial and wrote a death-ode. Later in that year, when the family moved house, she wrote a poem about her favourite tree, left behind:

> Oh! for the elm-tree at the bottom of the wood,
> Basking gold in the evening sun,
> The warm brown bark and sunlit leaves.
> There I used to sit when the day was done.
>
> I will never see that tree again,
> Its branches safely bore me.
> In the fork I would sit and gaze at the world,
> But never again shall I see my tree.

Then, on the eve of her fifteenth birthday, she comes explicitly to the point I am trying to make and writes:

Fourteen is an age at which one decides to become civilised, and the ancient beautiful, secret, Pictish things have to be given up in favour of a more sociable, sophisticated world where friends and people and laughing are all-important. It is a change from the outdoor world to the indoor. I can remember moments of such wonderfulness at the top of the sycamore and elm trees that I don't want to climb them again. I can't go back and I don't want to spoil the seriousness and the feeling that I am not a modern girl but something which fits in completely with the wind and the crisp smell of the air and the pattern of the leaves against the sun. I wouldn't be able to feel that again. There is only one thing that still works, and that is lighting a fire in the garden, in the evening, preferably twilight. Sunset used to be almost enchanted, when I was nine or ten. Now there is always part of me holding back and laughing at it.

When I was younger, I could afford to be, and was, lonely. Now people, and friends, and people such as teachers, with whom there is an unnatural sort of relationship, are much more interesting and vital. You have to learn to put up with one person's obstinacy, another's silliness, etc., and still like them, and also to decide what sort of image of yourself you are going to project. I used to hope that I would find some environment in which I would not have to cover some parts of me up, but I now think that the only one is my Pict state, when I am alone, and even that was influenced by what book I had just been reading. I know exactly where I am at home, at school, which are the biggest divisions, and at Guides, and so on. School is 10% learning and 90% being part of the intricate, rarely mentioned and yet, completely understood hierarchy which determines who is whose partner, who sits next to who, etc. This is constantly changing, and everyone follows the changes with interest, but otherwise it is like a flexible caste system.

At the moment the set of friends I have at school is the principal one to which almost everything is sacrificed, so although I would like a boyfriend for his own sake, it would also mean that I would be looked on differently at school – mainly, but not altogether favourably. We laugh at boy-mad girls, but approve of boy-conscious ones, which you can always tell by looking at. It scares me to think that while now a boyfriend would be an asset for the kind of girl I am trying to make people think I am, and want to be, in two years time it will be a necessity. I don't want to join the elite who band together to take refuge in the 'waste of time and daft' line, although they have just as much self-respect, and may last quite a long time, I don't know, because, projected images apart, I don't think I am that sort of girl. . . .

'Friends and people and laughing are all-important'. She might very well have added 'talking': when personal relations become a matter of choice, and people an area of exploration, talking becomes for obvious reasons a major preoccupation. It is above all by what we say and do in face-to-face groups that each of us declares his identity, his difference from others; and on the basis of these declared identities we go on to establish relationships within the group. Getting to know people can be a noisy business, and adolescents are great chatterers and gossips. What is afoot, it seems to me, even in these casual conversations, may be highly important. For adults, as Hannah Arendt has pointed out (Arendt, 1958), life means above all a 'web of human relations', but a changing web and one that is continually being spun and re-spun in daily contacts. By such means we come not only to know other people, but, by reflection from others, to know ourselves, and, by interaction with other observers, to know the world. Hannah Arendt puts this last point very forcefully:

For us, appearance – something that is being seen and heard by others as well as by ourselves – constitutes reality. Compared with the reality which comes from being seen and heard, even the greatest forces of intimate life – the passions of the heart, the thoughts of the mind, the delights of the senses – lead an uncertain, shadowy kind of existence unless and until they are transformed, deprivatized and deindividualized, as it were, into a shape to fit them for public appearance. The most current of such transformations occurs in storytelling and generally in artistic transposition of individual experiences. But we do not need the form of the artist to witness this transfiguration. Each time we talk about things that can be experienced only in privacy or intimacy, we bring them out into a sphere where they will assume a kind of reality which, their intensity notwithstanding, they never could have had before. The presence of others who see what we see and hear what we hear assures us of the reality of the world and ourselves. . . . (Arendt, 1958, p. 50)

Entering into such a talking relationship with their peers is for adolescents a new look at the familiar world, and a turning point. As the influence of adults upon their ways of seeing, thinking and feeling declines, these chattering consultations with their own age-group first fill the gap.

'Getting to know people' does not seem an adequate way of describing the purpose of talk in the classroom: yet it is evident that the most serious, the most task-oriented, discussion bears at the same time, favourably or unfavourably, upon the relations between the people taking part. Any contribution to the talk has, as it were, a value on two scales: its forwarding of the task in hand (an understanding, for example, of the role of Juliet in Shakespeare's play) and its effect upon inter-personal relations in the group (the fact, for example, that B's penetrating comment came as a flat contradiction to A's misguided but bravely self-revealing speculation). A very gifted teacher exemplifies this interaction in his comment upon a poetry lesson in his sixth form:

The whole lesson demonstrates the interaction of literary exploration with the personal relations of the set. Sometimes the relationships pull the purely intellectual pursuit out of true, sometimes they inspire discoveries; and this works both ways – the literary discoveries create a greater understanding of the personal relationships. (Stuart, 1969, p. 68)

Perhaps the most important general implication for teaching, however, is to note that anyone who succeeded in outlawing talk in the classroom would have outlawed life for the adolescent: the web of human relations must be spun in school as well as out.

II

A thirteen-year-old, on holiday with the family, was heard to say in exasperated tones, 'Oh dear! It's so difficult to know when to go with the crowd and when to be yourself!' When 'the crowd' is the family, the dilemma is a typical one for young adolescents. Some families do, of course, present the appearance of a 'family pudding', or – to change the figure – a little army on the march with its mind made up and not a breath of mutiny. But most of them, mercifully, do not so seriously hold up the processes of development by which a child becomes an individual: nevertheless, to the child at the point of disengagement, they may look and feel like any other 'family pudding'.

Roughly speaking, an active preoccupation with 'things' under the shelter of a stable set of personal relations enables a young child, by means that we considered in earlier chapters, to develop a physical/mental equipment adequate to the task of making something of his experience. The next phase, that of later childhood and adolescence, is – roughly speaking – a stage in which by *social interaction* he puts this equipment to wider and wider use in directions of his own choosing. As Piaget has put it: 'If the social milieu is really to influence individual brains, they have to be in a state of readiness to assimilate its contributions'. (Inhelder and Piaget, 1958, p. 338)

The notion itself of development by social interaction has within it the germ of the further notion of 'development of differences', that is to say, of becoming an individual. The process has been variously called 'the search for ego-identity' and the 'creation of the self-image', and it is generally agreed to be an achievement of the period of adolescence. Entering adolescence, a child has as it were many fragmentary 'selves', all of which are now to be thrown into the melting pot. He emerges from adolescence a more or less consistent and integrated individual, aware of himself as a person, having to some degree reconciled his description and evaluation of himself with the impressions he appears to make upon other people, and aware of the relationship between the sort of person he would like to be and the sort of person he thinks he is – or, more generally, between what he believes and the way he behaves.

This task constitutes a major undertaking, and a major preoccupation for him. It involves, as a start, the establishment of a difference between himself and the corporate identity of his family; and beyond that, the establishment of differences and likenesses between himself and fellow-members of the social groups he belongs to (it is a part of his 'individuality' to be identified with one or more groups and share some group characteristics); and the establishment of unifying links between the many roles he may continue to play in differing social situations. To achieve this degree of self-awareness demands intellectual powers beyond those of a child: demands those powers, in fact, we have already described as 'the achievement of adolescence'. An increasing ability to handle the *possibilities* of experience, to deal in terms of 'what *might* be', accompanies and maintains the ferment – the ferment of self-questioning, doubting, experiment and counter-experiment. As we shall see, the task, the preoccupation, is reflected in a great deal of adolescent behaviour and in particular in their talk, their writing and their reading. In the participant role they will discuss, argue, confess, explore, theorize: in the spectator role they are likely to intensify their improvisations upon 'the world as I have known it', whether in their day-dreaming, or in the reading and writing of poetry and fiction, or (where they have the opportunity) in dramatic improvisation – which has the advantages and limitations of being a concerted undertaking.

Carl Rogers, the American psychologist, would add that there is a crucial, positive act in the course of the process of becoming an individual. He calls it 'commitment':

It is only when the person decides, 'I am someone; I am someone worth being; I am committed to being myself,' that change becomes possible. . . . Thought of in the sense in which I am describing it, it is clear that commitment is an achievement. It is the kind of purposeful and meaningful direction which is only gradually achieved by the individual who has come increasingly to live closely in relationship with his own experiencing – a relationship in which his unconscious tendencies are as much respected as are his conscious choices. (Carl R. Rogers, *Freedom and Commitment*, Paper to the Western Behavioral Science Institute, California)

(In a study of adolescent delinquents he found, – surprisingly even to him – that 'degree of self-understanding'* was a better predictor of recovery than were ratings of family environment, social experience, neighbourhood influences, and so on. Moreover his own clinical work, and that of many other psychologists, have shown that essential self-awareness can be fostered and 'commitment' facilitated.)

Susanne Langer has suggested that 'individuation' and 'involvement' are two opposed and complementary processes operating in the development of all living creatures. Individuation is seen at its maximum in the functioning of the human mind; man, that is to say, by virtue of his mental powers, can become 'more of an individual' than can an individual of any other species. Yet man is also daily involved with other members of his kind. At a biological level, the conception and bearing of children, for example, are aspects of involvement: and, in our society, customs of marriage and family life spell out that involvement on the social plane. But individuation to the degree that man is capable of demands a balancing involvement that reaches out beyond home and family. We achieve that involvement, Langer believes, by inventing symbols to represent our social interdependencies, and investing those symbols with

* 'This was essentially a rating of the degree to which the individual was open and realistic regarding himself and his situation, a judgement as to whether he was emotionally acceptant of the facts in himself and his environment.'

authority over us, authority over each of us as an individual. Thus, at a certain stage of development in a society, man's individuation was complemented by involvement in tribal affairs: it was the authority of the tribe, symbolized by idol or totem, that put the brake on the individual's tendency to say, 'I can do as I please'.

Young people today are growing up into a society that has carried its individuation beyond the stage at which family or tribal or national symbols suffice to bring about complementary involvement; but, in Langer's view, man has not yet created an idea, a symbol, powerful enough to match his individuation and assure him of his 'security in a greater living whole'. (Langer, 1962, p. 119) Or, should we say, if such an idea does exist, it has not yet gained currency in the culture.

It is clear that as we have been thinking of adolescence as a period of development by social interaction, we have had in mind more than the emergence from his family of an autonomous, independent individual. If one phase of the metamorphosis is from dependence to independence, a further phase is through independence to *dependability*. It may well be that psychological changes associated with the physical development of sexuality in adolescence strongly favour this move towards dependability: that it may in fact be a part of a general change from the dominance of the need to be loved (in childhood) to the dominance of the *need to love*. Ernest Jones, the celebrated English Freudian, makes a suggestion along these lines in his paper *Some Problems of Adolescence* (Jones, 1950).

In a miscellany of comments that Clare made on her sixteenth birthday, and again on her seventeeth, we can trace references to these processes of becoming an individual – and of becoming involved.

At sixteen she wrote:

For everyone there is a lot of difference between being 15 and being 16. It is the age at which girls anyway are supposed to blossom forth, Sweet 16 etc., although of course this is partly due to the pop market being aimed at teenagers or else we'd have 'Happy Birthday Sweet 46', by Bing Crosby.

For me personally, it is the age when, as well as expanding and widening, there is a sort of coming together, so that I feel I am beginning to be one individual leading one life, instead of several different sets of behaviour in different compartments. I am more sure of my own personality, and less dependent on my environment. I am finding out what things I like, especially in the arts. I know that I prefer, say, Chagall to Botticelli – in other words, pink donkeys to pink nymphs. . . .

As a result of all this, I am less afraid of doing the wrong thing, because I want to be myself, and have the courage to do things like going to one of Mrs X's sherry parties in my charcoal jersey and red tights. Which brings me on to clothes, the most important thing. I am more interested in clothes than anything else, really. . . .

The greatest change is of course, sex. I am more aware of boys than I was a year ago, so that even anyone putting his arm round my shoulders makes my hormones go mad with excitement. . . .

I sometimes feel rather guilty about going to church for the sake of having a chat afterwards, because that is what it amounts to, but I can't accept their views. Our Minister is quite good but there was one old man who led a discussion afterwards once who was so narrow minded and so condescending about Buddhists and Jews that I was nearly sick. I don't believe, as he does, that Christianity is unique. I want to be a Christian, because I believe that any religion, or at least any religion based on love and not fear, is a different explanation of the same central fundamental power, which is not as personal as God. It is more like a sort of spiritual reservoir. . . .

This beginning to be aware of big, important things like religion, sex and politics, is the nicest thing about growing up. It is what makes me so impatient with S. . . . who is utterly innocent about them, and whose life is made up of such little petty things. . .

I rather suspect that everyone else grows up evenly and regularly. . . . But I am always afraid of finding a little bit that has got left behind – e.g. reading. I have only just started to read books again after about a year of solid *Woman*. . . . Anyway, this business of getting left behind is very worrying and what I am most afraid of is missing things until I am too old. I want to do and to be lots of things while I am still young.

And at seventeen she wrote:

This year has been the most difficult, uncontrollable, bewildering and exciting of my life. I feel that up to now I lived in a world which I created, and filled; now this has been shattered by new experiences and ideas. I have become possessed of a heightened perception of things, so that everything is more vivid and exciting, and I remember not things or people but moments – flashes of the impact of my surroundings like having lunch on the terrace, on my last day at Aiguebelle, with the sun flooding its heat all over us, with the dusty ground sloping steeply to the dark blue sea below us. Or coming out of a dance into the snow and the night, and feeling the tranquil air wash out the hot beery fog in my head. . . .

But the periods of depression have been correspondingly acute – times when I have felt cut off from everyone else, when I can't explain to anyone what is the matter, and times when I am so saturated with intellectual ideas that all the other ideas I can't take in form a sort of literary fog all round me, and I take refuge in *Woman*. Worst of all is the feeling of uncertainty, of wasting my years of being young because I don't exactly know what being young is. The trouble with being an adolescent is that they don't really exist; I am made up of a woman and a child in varying proportions, so that at one time I am full of desire and compassion and at another I feel as futile and helpless as a child. Nevertheless there is something; the power and joy of youth, which on occasions sweeps through me like an electric current – a lyrical happiness and clarity, a sort of general feeling of love. This is the only thing I can base my self-confidence on, and self-confidence, whether merited or not, I must have. My future is in this force, because it is pure and strong and complete, and if I lose it I will disintegrate.

It is difficult to write about being sixteen, since I have grown less and less conscious of being a certain age. This is partly because I have more interests outside school, and so I am not lumped together with people of my own age, and as the same thing is happening to most other people, the feeling of being in an age group as a unit has almost disappeared. But I think it is also partly just because I am becoming more an individual and so my problems and views are not so representative of 16 year olds. We are all of course thinking about philosophy and religion and generally fundamental things; and most of my friends are agnostic like me. But they haven't all got my problem, which is that I want to write, but not to be a writer, because I am frightened of losing myself in my writing and of taking the part of an observer. . . . The effect of words in formulating and analysing experience is probably enlightening to the reader, and it can be to the writer as well, but it can also destroy the spontaneity of his feelings. . . .

This problem has been forced on me by school – by the sheer volume of literature which I have had to read, so that I am beginning to explore its vast depths, which I have only just begun to comprehend. Writing is bound up with philosophy, with 'ultimate reality' – I sometimes think I would rather live my life on the surface, and so not write. I am happiest when I am in contact with people, and the sudden insight into intellectual abstraction, although it can be very thrilling, is not as exciting as being kissed in the back of a car.

III

One major aspect of change in adolescence we have not yet examined – though there are many references to it in Clare's pieces. To add a third item to our crude 'diagram', it is as though to the world of objects and the world of people were added the *world of ideas*. Piaget, in a full and fascinating account of adolescent thinking (Inhelder and Piaget, 1958) associates this 'saturation with intellectual ideas' with the achievement of mature powers of thinking: the ability to test a hypothesis by systematic consideration of all possibilities, and the ability above all to *reflect*, to think about our own thinking and hence to construct *systems* of ideas. Throughout all the changes in the style of adolescent behaviour that have taken place in the past ten or twelve years (since Piaget wrote his account), I think we can still recognize as familiar the tendency he found for adolescents to indulge in broad theories about a man's place in society, about man's place in the universe – about politics and religion and science and philosophy. Piaget suggests that two factors combine to produce such behaviour. In terms of the individual, it is, as we have noted, the result of the acquisition of powers of mature thinking: in social terms, it results from the fact of the adolescent's approach to adult status, and hence his concern to find an adult role, his own place in society, his own life programme. Here, of course, Piaget is giving us his version of the process we have already noted – that of 'becoming an individual'. This social undertaking is, in his view a more distinctive feature of adolescence than are the physical changes of puberty.

By 'thinking theoretically' the adolescent is able not only to construct theories explaining what exists in society, but also to construe things 'as they might be': and he will often see his own future role as articulating with an ideal rather than an existing system. Piaget suggests that adolescent theorizing exhibits a new phase of egocentrism, a degree of failure to distinguish subjective features from objective ones, not in his observations of the world but in his explanations – his explanatory theories. Just as in early childhood he was unable to appreciate that other people's views of the world would differ from his own, so at this stage he is unaware that the theories by which he explains the universe are deeply coloured by the role he sees for himself and by his need to assert himself in his role as an adult in adult society. 'The adolescent,' says Piaget, 'is the individual who commits himself to possibilities.' (Inhelder and Piaget, 1958, p. 339) Thus, his search for adult roles tends to constitute at the same time a plan to change adult society: and it is an aspect of his egocentrism that he fails to realize that everyone else in this society is liable to possess his own Utopian dream with equal claims upon the actual.

'The individual who *commits himself* to possibilities'. Children have strong feelings about things and about people: not till they reach adolescence do they have strong feelings about ideas. Thus it is in adolescence that we begin to commit ourselves to those symbols of involvement that Susanne Langer wrote about: ideas that have to be powerful enough today to generate reciprocal concern and responsibility between people who may differ in race and beliefs and culture and temperament and everything else – save that idea. Powerful ideas are plentiful among adolescents and it is quite evident that they feel strongly about them. To be socially effective, however, they must survive beyond the egocentric stage and prove themselves in practice. They have, in Piaget's terms, to be 'de-centred': and he suggests that this happens in two ways. At the theoretical level, it is by discussion among themselves that adolescents try out their theories and discover their weaknesses. But the more important part of the process goes on, not in thought alone, but at a practical level, and this is most likely to happen when the adolescent starts work. This may be when he first earns a wage or it may be when he enters a course of preparatory training for a job or profession: when he begins, in fact, to fill an adult role. It is then that theories begin to be cherished not simply as explanations, but as principles for action, and to be judged therefore by their fruits in action.

IV

In a little book called *Speaking*, Georges Gusdorf, a contemporary French philosopher, makes a very interesting point about the way adolescents differ from children in their use of language (Gusdorf, 1965, p. 40):

The life of mind ordinarily begins not with the acquisition of language, but with revolt against language once it is acquired.

The child discovers the world through the established language, which those around prescribe for him. The adolescent discovers values in the *revolt* against the language he had until then blindly trusted and which seems to him, in the light of the crisis, destitute of all authenticity. Every man worthy of the name has known that crisis in the appreciation of language which causes him to pass from naïve confidence to doubt and denial.

Both these processes – that for the child and that for the adolescent – are a part of learning to speak: for, as Gusdorf says elsewhere, 'The established language offers only an outline for the full development of verbal activity*'; and, 'We must consider speech not as an objective system . . . but as an individual enterprise'. The child uses the established language 'to call into existence, to draw out from nothingness' the world around him. But he has yet to learn that no verbal formulation can capture and pin down reality for ever; that the formulation and the experience are not equivalent; that the best formulation applicable to any occasion will be in some ways ill-fitting on any other occasion. And then he has to go on to learn that the formulation made by someone else – the words prescribed – can never be adequate to his own response to a situation. As a child, he puts his trust in other people's formulations, or in his own inadequate attempts to use other people's *ways of formulating* – inadequate since he lacks mature powers of speech. Hence, in adolescence, the revolt: these formulations he has too easily believed in begin to conflict with his own responses to changing situations. Whether or not he goes through a stage of *general* mistrust of language in the way Gusdorf suggests, he must in any case address himself to the individual enterprise of speech, to the continuing task of seeking the truth of a situation in his own formulations. Or, in Gusdorf's words (Gusdorf, 1965, p. 45):

* An interesting echo of the views of Vygotsky and Bruner on the relation between linguistic and conceptual development, as described in our Chapter 5.

The infantile conception of a magical efficacy of speech in itself gives way to that more difficult conception that language is for man a privileged means of carving out for himself a road across material and moral obstacles in order to reach . . . the decisive values worthy of orienting his destiny.

We shall consider in this section the uses of speech with which adolescents discover values for themselves, make their entry into 'the life of the mind'.

To begin as simply as possible, there seems no reason to reject the straightforward hypothesis that new forms of speech will be developed in the competence of individual speakers by a process of dissociation, that is to say by developing new forms to meet new demands. We saw the process at work in infancy: social speech was the form first acquired and for a time the only form available, for all purposes: efforts to meet the fresh demands for social interchange resulted in time in the development of two forms of speech in the place of one. By adolescence, 'speech for oneself' has long since been interiorized, become a part of thinking: what can we say of the further developments of social speech?

We might summarily define the social functions of speech, at their narrowest, as 'getting to know the people we want to know and getting along with the people we *have* to know'. We shall not say very much about the latter: social tact is a kind of generosity and as such is more easily achieved by people who are sure of themselves and their place in society: development of the appropriate forms of speech, therefore, is likely to come fairly late in adolescence. Even its simpler forms, the formulas of politeness that may have been in use in childhood, will sometimes be dispensed with in adolescence, and its subtler forms – elliptical utterances, for example, that 'say far less than they mean' – are a relatively mature form of speech. The former, 'getting to know the people we want to know' needs first to be more broadly defined to include getting on with the people we know and like, enjoying their company, engaging them in the kind of talk that reaffirms commonly held values and opinions.

In referring above to 'social speech' in infancy and childhood, we used the term very broadly to cover 'speech between people' (as opposed to 'speech for oneself'), and this will serve a multiplicity of purposes. Social speech between intimates, as we have just described it, is only one of the forms that develops from 'social speech' and we shall go on to consider others. This particular form develops actively during adolescence – which will not surprise us since we have taken this stage to constitute a move, roughly speaking, from a world of objects into a world of people. Its relation to the development of values we have also commented on in quoting Piaget's succinct statement: 'Spontaneous feelings between one person and another grow from an increasingly rich exchange of values.' (see Chapter 3, p. 106). He goes on in the same essay to say, 'Sympathy presupposes on the one hand a positive mutual evaluation and on the other hand a set of shared values'. (Piaget, 1968, pp. 35-6)

It is in this area of speech that adolescent 'with-it' language flourishes – conversational speech full of slang expressions that change rapidly with changing fashions. ('Not "super", Darling – "groovy"!' was a punch line in a recent television play.) Such linguistic forms have their function in drawing together members of the group or the set, and keeping outsiders out: hence the necessity – as with a password – for a rapidly changing fashion. Such speech may also be used, outside its context, as an offensive weapon, a means of establishing the individual as no longer to be identified with the family group. (While it seems to me quite futile for parents to attempt adolescent forms of speech, this is perhaps a good opportunity for them to give up any lingering self-righteous linguistic pretences!) There are sets of highly infectious colloquialisms that seem to belong to a whole generation of English speakers, and others beside them that mark the exclusiveness of much smaller groups – interest groups, occupational groups or regional groups. One such language was parodied recently in a public notice addressed ᴛᴏ Cornish surf-riders: I reproduce it as an exam̗le of the exclusiveness of such utterances, though obviously that is exaggerated here:

Quit scuffing your creepies, man. Do it like now. Grip this. Some yhuk with a perch for boo boards has dipped plenty on this scene. If you're not formating with the weepies on a loss awareness of your boo board, nix out of the fade with it stashed on the moke or cooling on the salt grip. Spread by the fuzz of Devon and Cornwall to help sock it to the mean cats.

Make with the twirl in some uptight spot.

It is not surprising that in some varieties of adolescent slang new terms seem to cluster as 'pet names' around the forbidden topics – drugs and drug-taking, sexual achievements, law-breaking.

In describing social speech among intimates I referred to the reaffirmation of opinions and values as one of its preoccupations. Clearly, in operation, this is likely to move into talk that *modifies* values and opinions, whether by intention or in effect. This in our terms will tend to involve a move from expressive speech in the direction of transactional speech: and at this point in our description of the categories we shall need to introduce two sub-categories of the transactional, which we shall call the *informative* and the *conative*. In the former, facts, opinions, ideas are invited and given; the latter is the language of commands, persuasion, entreaty. But expressive talk may also, as we have seen, move in the direction of *poetic* speech, a point that we illustrated in Chapter 4 (p. 170) by quoting a conversation between four close friends when they arrived to take part in a conference. What we find in conversations, then, is a general grounding in the expressive with tendencies to move in one direction or another as indicated in the diagram opposite.

Any analysis in these terms of an actual conversation will be a highly tentative business. Let us turn back to that extract on pp. 170–73 and consider some of its complexities.

(Participant role — — — — — — — role of Spectator)

CONATIVE

EXPRESSIVE   POETIC

INFORMATIVE

1. As intimate friends sharing a situation which they actively observe, and sharing also a good deal of past experience, their talk rarely moves out of the expressive.

2. The speakers are, quite literally, engaged as spectators. 'Look at all those strange shoes', 'Did you see those two mountains arriving?' and other remarks on what they see from the window are in the spectator role within the expressive function. Typical of spectator role language, the remarks are frequently directly or indirectly *evaluative*.

3. The passage beginning, 'What do you mean, delegates?' moves into the participant role: a matter of the exchange of information takes the place of 'joint spectatorship'. Does this constitute a move out of the expressive into the informative category? Probably not: idle curiosity enters into the idle chatter but does not reach a stage where explicit information is required and given: much must still be inferred from the shared context and from the speakers' previous knowledge of each other in order to get the mere drift of the exchange. I should call this a move *towards* the informative rather than into that category. (Where a line is drawn is of course an arbitrary matter and would vary to suit particular purposes.)

4. 'Don't catch L.—'s eye.' 'Draw the curtains.' These are clearly in the participant role, a use of language to get things done: and a move towards the conative, the language by which a speaker seeks to get his own way with his listener. Once again, so much remains embedded in the immediate situation that we should be wiser to call these fragments a move *towards* the

conative or perhaps in a category transitional between the expressive and the conative. (It is interesting to note in passing that these utterances in the participant role are in fact directed to preserving the spectator situation of the speakers!)

5. 'Wearing your stetson tomorrow?' In a conversation largely consisting of language about the here-and-now this stands out as exceptional. Why was this remark made? Why was this item brought – on the back of a word – into the area of joint concern? Because it represents an element of a common past for these four, is as it were a root in their shared experience reinforcing their 'togetherness' with a sense of excluding others who are not in the know. Moreover, in the incongruity between B. and a bare-backed rider at the Calgary Stampede (which comes into the story of the stetson) there is an affectionate reaffirmation of values common to the group.

6. The story A. tells illustrates several of the features we have attributed to language in the category labelled *Poetic*. It is a construct, a 'verbal object' (B. greets it as 'one of *those*!'); it requires an audience, who are not expected to interrupt; as the speaker gets into her stride she pays more attention to the pattern of events than she would do in ordinary conversation and (though the transcript cannot show this) she uses modes of speech dramatically to suit each character, and in other ways exploits the formal qualities of speech *as sound*: finally her purpose in going back over this experience is to enjoy the telling and have it enjoyed by her listeners. On the other hand, many expressive features remain: the story is not told as it would be performed to a public audience.

Serious conversation among intimate friends will make more pressing demands for all the kinds of movement we have illustrated in this comparatively trivial talk. Conversation with people we are less intimate with, and talk with strangers, or teachers and others in authority, are likely to demand informative and conative uses increasingly dissociated from the expressive. At the secondary School stage, the educational importance of good conversation in small intimate groups can hardly be over-emphasized. It paves the way for class discussion, which in the informative subjects may be a principal mode of learning: but it has its own value as a mode of learning, particularly in English lessons, where the main stream of activity will be the handling of experiences in the spectator role. This will be no unfamiliar occupation for adolescents, whose own conversations are likely to be a traffic in what D. W. Harding has called 'considered experience' – things that have happened to themselves or to other people, offered in such a way as to involve direct or implied evaluation. But they will need a good deal of help in moving to general inferences: left to themselves they tend to oscillate between particular instances and vast generalizations taken over at second hand – leaving a gap that needs to be filled by intermediate generalizations they must make for themselves.

Good conversation may deteriorate or fail to materialize for a variety of reasons. If there is not mutual respect among the participants it may turn into a slanging match or some other form of competitiveness. If there is not sufficient common experience among them it may simply cease to be worth while. If there is not common consent to the continuance of this talk on this occasion among these people, its life is hazardous: as every teacher knows, one saboteur is enough, and he needs little skill to achieve his ends. Above all, even where there is mutual respect, a garrulous talker makes conversation impossible: he is a bad talker as well as a bad listener and he is the one as a result of being the other. Garrulity is the enemy of talk as we have been concerned with 'talk' throughout this book. This does not mean, however, that a conversation dominated by one person cannot be a good one: in particular, talk of great value to the talker may have been utterly dependent on the help of a good listener.

In a good conversation, the participants profit from their own talking (as we have just implied), from what others contribute, and above all from the interaction – that is to say from the enabling effect of each upon the others. It is for these reasons an important mode of learning.

Here is part of a conversation between five sixteen-year-old school-leavers from a girls' comprehensive school. Their starting point was an extract from a Hemingway short story. There was no adult with them.*

A: When we used to live in . . . in Kennington . . . they used to walk . . . we used to walk across the bridge . . . you know, walk round London . . . used to be ever so happy and I can remember my parents walking along hand in hand . . . you know . . . giggling (*laughter*) . . . and there's me in between, you know, looking up . . . and laughing our heads off we were . . . and I can remember that clearly as anything. It's one of the first things I remembered . . . you know, being very happy, just the three of us. Then the next thing I remember was me having to go away because my brother was born and he had pneumonia . . . and he came along and it was horrible. . . . (Yes.) (*Laughter.*) . . . It split up the family . . . you know what I mean . . . I was really jealous.

      E: You were out of things . . .

A: Yeah, I got really left out . . . and it's been a bit like that ever since. (I think that, like. . . . Well, not only that . . .)

    B: I think parents begin to get out of touch with each other as husband and wife . . . slightly, I should think . . . I don't know . . . it all depends what the couple's life's like . . . er . . . when they start having children. You see it takes so much of their time . . . and it takes a certain place in their lives.

A: The husband gets left out a lot, doesn't he? (Yeah . . . has a hard . . .) (*Laughter.*) . . . No, you hear such a lot . . . when perhaps . . . when your dad come home in the evening and your mother will say, 'Just a minute I'm getting so and so's tea. . . . Can you wait a bit?' . . . you know, he's probably come home from work. . . . (Yeah.)

    B: Or, I've got my ironing . . . or, I've got to take the children to bed . . . and what not.

*For further excerpts and comments see Barnes *et al.*, 1969, pp. 82–98.

A: Yeah, I think that's when they get . . .

    D: My dad comes home and he sits down and says, 'Will somebody get my slippers?' and nobody moves, you know. . . . Everyone's eating their dinner or staring at the television. . . . He feels very neglected I think . . .

B: Probably because he feels everything should be done to him, you know. (Yeah.)

  C: He's the father . . . they should do everything for him . . .

    D: Probably been . . .

B: Head of the house . . . as it were.

A: . . . extra special attention . . . which I think is right, you know. . . . I hope I remember that whenever I get married.

    D: He's the one that goes out to work . . . earns the money, as he says.

B: But then again, you find some families who . . . don't take this attitude. They feel that . . . both should be the sort of . . . head . . . you know . . . leader.

    E: I think what you mainly remember is when . . . sort of . . . to your knowledge . . . your . . . the first time you see your mother and father having a row. . . . Not a fight, but a row. (Yes.) You always think . . . you always look at them to be . . . you know . . . you think, That's my mother and father . . . they're always so happy, you know, and I'm happy with them . . . but when you see them angry with each other . . . that just spoils everything. Sort of. . . . You can't say, you know . . . then when you get older, you think, what if they got divorced . . . or had to separate. . . . (Yes. Oh dear.)

    D: It's on your memory all the while, isn't it?

    E: You think which one would you choose, and you can't . . . well, I can't . . . I couldn't choose between my mother and father.

A: They seem to be one . . . they are one. (Yeah. They are.) Parents, you don't think of them as two separate people.

    D: You don't split them up into mother and father . . .

A: It's when they have rows that you realize they're two separate people . . . what could go wrong. (Yes.)

    D: I don't want to take sides. . . . I hate taking sides . . .

because my mum will explain . . . she gets quite angry and she'll explain to me and tell me what happened . . . and then my dad will explain. Both the stories may be different . . . you know, the same sort of thing, but different . . . but I can see one of them isn't quite right and I can't say which one of them it is. (No.)

C: Have you ever had them say . . . whichever one it is . . . say you're always on his side? (Yes.)

E: I could never take sides, you know . . . if my father is . . . you know . . . shouting at my mother, I'd say, 'Don't shout at my mum like that!' . . . and then my mother will start shouting at my dad and I'd say, 'Don't shout at my dad like that!' . . . You know, I could never choose.

D: I can't.

A: I can remember the first row we ever had. It was . . I think . . . my brother and I were in the kitchen and my mum and dad were rowing and it was so bad. . . . I'd never seen a row like this before, and my mum just started crying her eyes out and my dad felt terribly guilty, he was dead silent. Then I started crying, my brother started crying . . . it was hell for about half an hour, you know. We all split up, there was nothing of the family left. And then we all crept back in, giggling and saying, 'Oh, I am sorry' you know.

D: Yes, that's the best part . . .

B: Well, frankly when my parents . . . when they do have rows, you know, I . . . er . . . always saw both sides, because there was something in each . . . one's explanation that . . . that meant something. (Yes.)

D: You know, because one's explanation was different, wasn't it?

B: Yeah, and there was something right in each one. . . . So I just couldn't realize why on earth they did have the row in the first place, because you . . . you both have perfectly good reasons but they just don't fit in.

D: Sometimes they don't realize how upsetting it can be to the child. The child sometimes doesn't want to show they're upset in front of the parents, do they?

B: Yeah.

    C: Sometimes it's something silly and the child could see it's silly and wondering why they're rowing over it 'cause they wouldn't think of anyone rowing over it . . . it's just silly.

A: Yes, it's funny isn't it, children don't row so much as adults.

      D: Really? (*Laughter.*) My brother and I, we row.

    C: My sister and I are terrible . . .

      D: I think that happens to all families, doesn't it, when they've got brothers and sisters . . .

        E: Yes, but now I think you get most rows because they're *over* you, you know. (Yes . . . Terrible.) And you think you're the object of this row . . . and you think, Ooh!

B: You're always getting the blame for everything.

      D: . . . and you're not really . . . can't stick up for yourself.

B: This is why sometimes . . . sort of lose contact with each other . . . because you sort of come between them in a way . . . you know.

The talk is relaxed, mutually supportive: nobody seems particularly concerned to prove herself right or anybody else wrong. It rests upon a general consensus of opinion and attitude, yet individual differences are expressed. It is exploratory: it lays out, so to speak, the elements of family life, and contemplates their interconnexions. In indicating, at the end of the extract, the sense of guilt a girl may feel when her parents quarrel, it penetrates deeper, I believe, than a more structured, more objective analysis could have taken these adolescents. Earlier passages in the same conversation, not included here, had broached the matter of guilt feelings and the problem of family rows, but had passed over them at surface level: at this later, more coherent, point in the talk, E is able to turn it directly on to the subject of parents' quarrels; we see her recoiling from the guilt involved in siding with one parent and rejecting the other; and finally, after a considerable silence on her part, she confronts the guilt of being the cause of the quarreling: 'And you think you're the object of this row – and you think Ooh!' ('In the reciprocity of speaking and listening,' writes Gusdorf, 'dormant possibilities are actualised within me: each act of speaking, whether spoken or merely understood, is the opportunity for an awakening, the discovery perhaps of a value [of] the appeal of which I had not been aware.' Gusdorf, 1965, p. 67)

Three of these same girls will illustrate for us talk of a different kind. Here are the opening phases of a dramatic improvisation in which A takes the part of a welfare officer, C that of a child's fostermother, and B that of the child's real mother:

A: Oh, hello, would you like to come in? Ah, is it Mrs Jarvis?
    C: Yes, that's right.
A: Mrs Rhodes?
    B: Mrs Rhodes, Yes, that's right.
A: Come in, would you. I've just been reading . . . it's about David Anthony Rhodes . . . I've been reading the case, and, now would you like to tell me about it? Now what, what exactly is it that's worrying him?
    B: Well, seven years ago, my husband and I got married and we had, I had David . . . and . . . I was so ill I . . . I just couldn't cope with him.
A: Ah, yes.
    B: And, well, I'm married now again, and I feel I . . . I'm prepared to have him back. I'd like to look after him, he's my child and I just want him back.
A: I see. You're married again, aren't you?
    B: Yes.
A: Would you like to tell me a bit about the home circumstances as they are now.
    B: Well, we've already got a house. Before, the situation as it was, we were living in . . . we were living in a one-room with my husband and the baby . . . and . . I was so ill.
A: This is where you found things difficult, was it?
    B: Yes, I just couldn't cope. So, things weren't going so well with the marriage, and it just blew up like that. I'm married

again now, and we've saved up hard, and we've got a house and my husband's prepared to have the baby, although it isn't his.

A: Yes.

B: I want him . . .

A: Well, when you had David, did you think of obtaining any help; you know, any help, money? or did you, couldn't you . . . ?

B: No . . .

A: Couldn't you afford to have him go to a nursery in the day time?

B: Well, apart from affording it, I . . . no . . . I just probably didn't think of it. I wouldn't have wanted him to go to a nursery.

A: Which doctor were you under at the time?

B: Dr Anderson (*sotto voce*) Blimey!

A: Oh, yes. Mrs Jarvis . . . ah . . . could you tell us, you know, how . . .

C: She can't take him away from me. I had that child when it was one year old. I've brought it up, looked after it . . . I've taught it to walk, I taught it to speak, taught it manners . . .

B: What do you mean?

C: . . . Which is more than she would have done.

B: It's my child.

A: Let's keep calm about this.

C: You might have brought it into this world, but it's my child ever since I took it . . . look it . . . started to look after it. Part of my family.

A: Yes, well, let's take it calmly. We can't sort anything out if we're all shouting all at the same time, can we? Now, look, would you tell us, what sort, what sort of home circumstances is David living in at the moment . . . ? Is he happy with you?

C: He has a very good home. He's happy with us. We're his parents to him.

B: Yes and I'm his real mother.

C: You didn't show him any kindness when you wanted to just turf him off to anyone.

B: Oh well, how could I? That wasn't the situation at all. You're being quite unfair. . . . Can't you do something to this woman? You've been . . .

C: I've looked after that child . . .

B: I know you have.

C: I've spent good money on that child, and I love him, and he loves us.

A: Look, you've both got very strong cases here, and I understand your feelings, but the trouble is, you see, we can't go much further with this case until we've had the business looked into. Now, Mrs Jarvis, what sort of home conditions does David live in at the moment? What sort of flat do you live in, or house?

C: We have a house, we have a garden where he can play and it's quite safe; he goes to the local school and he's quite happy there.

A: He's happy at school is he?

C: Of course he is. He loves school. He loves us, too.

A: He gets on well with the other children, does he? No trouble at all there?

C: He's got lots of friends.

B: Well, he hasn't really had a chance to know his mother, has he?

C: No, because you didn't want him.

B: I did, I just couldn't cope with him. Well, how could I? I was in one room, my marriage was going, the child was there, I just couldn't. . . . I found it the best thing to have it adopted.

C: You should have thought of that before you had the child.

B: Would you? Try putting yourself in other people's position, before you just . . . er . . . just . . . er . . . talk them down like that. Just put yourself in their position.

C: Right, you put yourself in my position. You were a lucky person. You could have children. I couldn't, and when David came along I was so happy I looked after him as my own child . . .

B: Well, it's fifty-fifty now, isn't it? You couldn't have children, I could . . .

C: Why . . . all right, think of David. He's happy with us, he's settled.

B: I am thinking of David. This is why I want him back. I'm his mother, I'm his real mother.

C: He's never known you as his mother. I'm his mother to him.

A: Yes, but listen . . . look. David's been happy with you; I understand this, but, if his mother is in good health, now, and living in a nice house, and, er, she's happily married, I think it's . . . it's a strong case.

C: You just can't take him away from me like that.

A: I'm not saying anything of the sort.

C: He's not just a little parcel you can chuck around.

A: Look, the thing I'm most worried about, is David's welfare.

C: Exactly.

A: Also the welfare of the mother, and the foster parent. Now, I think the best thing we can do is to look into this further. This isn't the sort of thing to make a rash decision about.

B: Right. Well, you hurry up and look into it because I want my child back.

A: Mrs Rhodes, this is going to take time.

B: I know it will take time.

A: It's the life of David. Now the person, the one of you who looks after David will be his mother for the rest of his life.

B: I *am* his mother. There's no doubt about that. It's not a case of 'is she his mother', I *am*.

They have a problem then. It is not *their* problem, but it exists and dramatic improvisation provides a way of studying this bit of the world of personal relations. Again, the method itself is likely to be thoroughly familiar to them from childhood games (and in this case, from earlier school experience). By means of it they are able to go some way towards making other people's problems their own for the time being.

If the problem or the topic for an improvisation is well chosen it will call for the representation of experience the youngsters are likely to know something about, and, in working on it, an appeal to principles that are certainly a part of their concern. It is likely that such improvisations as this, in which each participant was formulating somebody else's point of view, would give rise to talk in which each formulated her own.

The dramatic situation, as we suggested earlier, forces them to recognize aspects of the situation they might otherwise ignore, presses them to some kind of interaction, some kind of resolution. Any generalization they may make in subsequent discussion is likely to be to that degree less blinkered, more inclusive.

V

When we commit ourselves to paper the process of shaping experience is likely to be a *sharper* one than it is in talk. The gap between transmission and reception of written language allows a writer, if he needs to, to wrestle with his thoughts, to work and re-work his formulation or projection or transformation of experience. Vygotsky throws light on this fact when he says:

Written language demands conscious work because its relationship to inner speech is different from that of oral speech: the latter precedes inner speech and presupposes its existence (the act of writing implying a translation from inner speech). . . . The change from maximally compact inner speech to maximally detailed written speech requires what might be called deliberate semantics – deliberate structuring of the web of meaning. (Vygotsky, 1962, pp. 99–100)

In the second place, written speech endures to constitute a *record* – and it will sometimes be for this reason that it serves a different purpose from talk.

Enough has been said here already to support the truism that adolescence is a period of rapid and widespread change. It is a time for ringing out the old and ringing in the new, and since the new is a matter of choice from a wide range of possibilities, it is a time for experiment. Just how changeable, how unstable, an adolescent's life may be is illustrated in the following excerpts from the diary of a fourteen-year-old (and may she forgive me, wherever she is):

Dec. 6	I am a most strange beast. My character is most complex.
Dec. 28	Had a vision. Now I know what I am talking about.
Feb. 28	I am now either an atheist or a fatalist. Sometimes I am one and sometimes the other.
March 7	I have now quite firm beliefs but I am not an atheist (or a Christian). I think A . . . is rapidly becoming Christian though she does not say so.
April 11	Life seems to be very depressing. I am thoroughly miserable.
July 18	Church in morning. Some nice tunes. Some of my reactions were so queer I could not analyse them.
July 22	Nearly went mad. Want to see a psychologist badly.
Aug. 19	Was very miserable . . . was seized with a queer desire to go mad.
Aug. 21	B . . . told a sad tale about someone who is going mad. I no longer want to.
Aug. 30	Some male being followed me part way home. We sang loudly all the rest of the way. Was half frightened but on the whole liked it.
Oct. 17	Was quite happy most of the time. Thought a good bit and got a creed for myself.

It is small wonder if in such states of mind young people turn to writing as a means of 'tying down' aspects of their experiences – catching, exploring and fixing the fleeting moment, or imposing some order upon intractable events.

The main stream of writing in English lessons will, if these needs are to be met, be in the spectator role. The relationship of the writing to the experiences will vary from the most direct, in which little transposing of the actual circumstances seems to have been attempted, to the most indirect, the fantasy which a reader can with difficulty relate to anything he knows about the personality or history of the writer, or the lyric which reveals a hitherto unsuspected attitude on his part.

A fourteen-year-old boy from a secondary modern school, in a long rather rambling account, distils the flavour of his daily experiences, under the title of 'My Love during the Week'. He tells us what happened directly enough, and yet he has an eye to the shape of his story. He begins with Monday:

On Monday mornings I was usually late for school but this morning I was there just as the bell went. When I was sitting down wondering about Homework the old soldiers and the W.A.A.F.s walked in and a few moments later the stragglers, but behind them marching strongly was Mr B. . . . The first thing I was to say to Pauline was 'Got a comb?'

She replied, 'Yes love. Here you are', in her usual boylike manner and after I had had my dreamy chat about Bob, her boy-friend, she awoke and started on the next best subject to Bob, me and Mary, June, and Christine and all their wonderful passions of love for me but I was in love with 'her', Hazel, Rosamund, Christine, June, Mary and Pat, not really in love with them but in love with them for their characteristics. There was Pauline, who was as gentle as a lamb but when talking alone to me came up with the questions that would send a Psychiatrist insane. Hazel and Rosamund who were always in love, Christine was one of the clan who was too high qualified and June and Pat who didn't say anything out of turn, but Mary was different in many ways. First of all when we were speaking together she wouldn't say anything though her eyes were accepting mine and vice-versa. Her eyes were telling me about her thoughts and I could see she was in a love trance, that was new to her and me. Under quiet skin she had the urge to let the rentering words go but she kept them under her brown-black hair, above her puffed stream water cheeks which were bursting her lips, but then her dimple chin tinkled and her brow moved from side to side but she only let her words run out through her funnel lips into Pauline's bottle shaped ears.

His school occupations are briefly dismissed – 'That day after prison work had been finished Pauline came up to me and told me that Mary liked me . . .' – and the week ends with a Friday night social at the school:

As I held Mary's hand I felt a sense of pride but a slight bit of

disloyalty to my parents. But I couldn't have cared at all for I was
. . . alone with the one I loved.

Around ten the old man, Mr H. . . walked up to the hall and
stayed near the entrance but it was time for the birds to leave the
nest so I told Mary to walk hand in hand with me past him, but
she tore her hand away and we just walked past him . . .

And the account ends:

Monday morning comes again and I am left with the criticism
from the boys and happiness from the girls but what is going to
happen to me?

In contrast, what can we make of this poem, also written by a
fourteen-year-old boy?

Doll

If I leave you by the fireside
Please don't frizzle.
If I kiss you on the forehead
Please don't cry.
If I walk you past the gravestones
Will you promise
That you'll never be so stupid as to die?

Human feelings are so simple
To discover.
And you're lucky not to be alive today.
If you frizzle by the fireside
It won't matter;
There are other things that children
Like to play.

His childhood self and his present self, it seems to me, are both
in the poem, brought together to mark a change with the passing of time; but whether a loss or a gain it is difficult to say.

This next piece written by a twelve-year-old girl, seems to
me to come about midway between the two examples already
given. It is far less direct than the first, for it is ostensibly a

story about two people other than the writer. Yet each seems to represent an aspect of her changing personality: her present self, I suggest, is Sheila and the self on the horizon, not yet attained, is 'Anna the posh, fancy, high-school looking girl'.

A Conversation Overheard on the Bus

As I was coming home one evening on the bus from school there in front were two children. One was shabby and thin looking and the other tubby and medium looking.

These children were talking about a circus which had come to town which they had been to. The shabby girl's name was Sheila and she thought it was very funny. She liked the little short clowns and the giraffe-necked ladies and thought it was wonderful how all the animals were trained, especially the sea-lions and thought how lovely they looked balancing the balls and for the very first time in a circus she had seen giraffes taking part.

But Anna, the posh, fancy, high-school looking girl had different ideas. She thought it was cruel to keep lions and elephants, polar-bears, grizzly-bears, sea-lions, seals, giraffes and all the other kinds of animals that used to roam on their own round ice-bergs in the sea and the jungle in a cage. She said, 'How cruel it is to keep them in cages performing while they could roam. The people that have necklaces round their necks which are called giraffe-necked women who are laughed at, and the short midgets, they can't help it, and I think the circus is a cruel place.'

Soon they got off but still hadn't finished, so I don't know what else they said.

If you are inclined to accept my interpretation of this as a dramatization of two points of view at odds in the mind of the writer, then I think that last paragraph will clinch it for you. The conversation must be continued – but some other time!

Those three examples of degrees of transposition may illustrate for us also the three main forms that spectator role writing in the secondary school will take: autobiographical accounts, stories and poems. This is not to suggest, however, that the three forms will invariably correlate with those degrees of directness in the relation between experience and the written product.

Shaping experience in order to share it: we can see the same sort of thing happening in adolescent writing as we saw happening in infancy when the young child chattered to his mother. In school, particularly with the younger adolescent, the teacher must play the role above all of receiver, of sympathetic reader. A large part of the incentive for the writer lies in the *sharing*: the value we covet for him, and that he will increasingly covet for himself as he grows older, lies in the *shaping*.

Perhaps one of the first ways in which adolescents begin to achieve through their writing a maturer view of themselves and the world is by looking back into their own childhood: they look, as it were, for their own roots in a common soil. The mere act of contemplating a period in life when things seem to have been less transitory, more stable, may in itself be salutary for them: to realize its continuity with the present may help a sense of order to grow, an order embracing past and present, and providing, at times, a key to the solution of some of the riddles they are now confronting.

Here is a piece written by a girl of seventeen which suggests, I believe, her growing awareness of the continuity of her life. She describes early experiences in a village, records the fact that the family moved to London, and goes on:

My grandfather died the night we moved. No one in the family knows just how much that meant to me. My mother thinks it's pure selfishness that stops my giving the toy wringer to my sister when it is sitting untouched at the top of my cupboard. How can I say that it is all I have to remember him by? Because I never showed my feelings nor talked about him when the others did, they consider me heartless and unfeeling. But they are very wrong. I loved him more than anyone else at all. Whenever I went into his shop there was a penny for a comic, or a piece of chocolate. He used to tease me about my shyness, because I would always hide behind a row of coats when the customers were there.

He would tickle me unmercifully and then say 'Who's laughing?' with mock severity, his graying bristle moustache quivering indignantly. . . . He promised that when I was twelve I could have a boat, to row him in, or a pony, to pull a cart for us, or a typewriter, so that I could make a book of his life. I'll never forget how he always wanted a Pekinese dog. . . .

Two years later I went for a holiday back to B. . . . It was Easter. In the evening the lack of sanitation, the cold water, the oil lights, my bedroom, a raised corridor between the old and new buildings, all filled my dissatisfaction. But in the morning. . . . we children went up to gather bluebells, after we had milked the cows. We could feel the cleanness of the air in the dew-wet grass, in the washed green of hedge and leaf. . . . There was so much to see since I had last been; new lambs and new birds' nests, the geese under the wire of their pen (conveniently built across a narrow stream), calves, pups, kittens. . . . We walked on to the top where in summer we always took picnic teas. The view was clearer than I had ever seen it before. Far below in the valley, Hereford appeared tiny and magical. The Cathedral, so huge when I stood looking up at it from the pavement, was a miniature spikey fragment with only its spire piercing the cloud of distance. A green smudge was the Castle Green where I loved to watch the Art School pupils sketching above the Wye. I loved to roll down the *very* steep grass verges which surrounded the green, pretending to be a caterpillar, or something. But looking down on so much and so many; almost from Heaven, with the sun filtering through the branches; the ground soft, unresisting; the tiny lovely sounds of Nature; the distant calls of my companions; . . . and the knowledge that I could go and come back, but that this would all go on. The enormity of life, the overpowering feeling of my smallness, the breathtaking, heart-rending, wordless beauty, the pure, harmless, perfect things on all sides, filled me with unforgettable love and longing for the countryside in general, and B . . . in particular. I had realised that my own life was so insignificant a part of an incalculable whole that my own reliance in it was completely lacking in perspective. Unquestionably I had realised that I was no longer the centre of my own life but merely a fragment of life.

'Yes, yes,' you may say, 'William Wordsworth and all that!' And it was of course the banks of the Wye that Wordsworth revisited to write his poem 'Lines Composed a few miles above Tintern Abbey'. Nonetheless, the re-visit – as a strategy – does seem to achieve something – for the sixteen-year-old as well as for him. It creates a perspective; the life of a place, the greater life you have been part of, can go on without you, is still there when you return: conversely, the 'you' that returns after an interval of time is conscious of its differences from the 'you' of the earlier association: how then differentiate 'life' in the sense of 'your life' and 'life' in the sense of 'its life'? For the sixteen-year-old the ambiguity remains unresolved: 'I had realized that I was no longer the centre of my own life but merely a fragment of life.' For Wordsworth the resolution is at a universal level – a meaning for the word 'life' that embraces a wide range of possible particular meanings:

> And I have felt
> A presence that disturbs me with the joy
> Of elevated thoughts; a sense sublime
> Of something far more deeply interfused,
> Whose dwelling is the light of setting suns,
> And the round ocean, and the living air,
> And the blue sky, and in the mind of man:
> A motion and a spirit, that impels
> All thinking things, all objects of all thought,
> And rolls through all things.

As observers of the present scene, adolescents will record, sometimes quite explicitly, changes in themselves and their situations. At the youngest end of the scale, an eleven-year-old writes:

In winter we do another naughty thing . . . it's 'cat-creeping', our own particular name for the game. It includes going cross country over people's gardens in race style. Its great fun for us but not very nice for people who own the gardens. As I get older my features change but my point of view changes too. I imagine I am an adult with a beautiful garden which as been spoilt by children. What nuicences we children must be to adult people.

And, at the other end of the scale, Clare at nineteen writes:

I don't feel any particular age, frankly. Nineteen is somehow not so important as eighteen; one relaxes from the strain of being a debutante. Because I came out too last year, maybe not with pink plastic camellias in my chignon like L . . . , but I came out from under exams and found I was more alive than I had feared. All that is quite remote now; I no longer characterize my life as the post-A-level period, and the Hopkins sonnets I learnt walking round the garden in the evening and which I thought I would never forget, I have forgotten.

And at twenty:

There's not much point in analysing yesterday's experience of being twenty since it was the same as nineteen the day before. And being nineteen, the whole year of it, was equally scrappy and messy. Life does not seem to be marked by birthdays any more, but rather by things like the education system and going away and coming back. Also I seem to have grown immune to big, formal turning points; they tend to disintegrate as they approach and so going to Cambridge, in the end, turns out to be writing to the steward and getting the trunk into and out of the boot. In ten years time perhaps it will have been a great experience, but what I mistrust about what other people say are wonderful experiences is that they are always likely to be this sort, i.e. that you appreciate more and more the further you have left them behind. Cambridge, in fact, is both something very concrete and particular, i.e. this particular lecture room on Tuesday 10 A.M., this particular woman who is your supervisor, etc., and something so intangible that its effect can only be cumulative, and you aren't aware of it while you are actually living it, or only at moments anyway . . .

The changes recorded can be seen, in each case, as a shift of perspective.

It is an obvious and important thing to say of adolescents that at this stage the future hangs over them like a great cloud;

almost infinite in its possibilities, it beckons and threatens them by turns, and gives, fitfully, a sense of urgency both to their plans for the future and to their determination to make the most of the present. Their ideological systems, as truths that seem to be eternal, offer them some escape from the difficulties of thus living in two worlds: from the difficulty of being adults still tied to the home of their childhood, or of being workers without a job – from the difficulty of being, in short, creatures with a future awaiting a present.

Even the less articulate among them will talk and write, given encouragement, to ease this sense of misfit. Read for example this outburst written by a sixteen-year-old boy for a young teacher he respected and admired (and with no better pretext between them than a trial run at an examination essay question).

Has there ever been a time in your life when you have resented authority?

The sort of authority I deplore is the education authority. The idea of learning just for learning's sake. It is learning, just to be learned.

Before you are even bloody born: you are forced to go to school. Then you are told a load of lies, about God. And with religion nowadays, the change is so rapid, by the time you've learnt what was once religion, has now changed and is rubbish.

School should be voluntary not compulsory.

The trouble with a lot of delinquent kids is that teachers don't understand them. The majority of Catholic teachers are dead ignorent. They go from school straight to training college. They have no experience of life and people. A mere six weeks holiday job is treated as work.

What do they say when they come out, 'Oh I enjoyed working'. Of course they fucking well enjoyed it. They only had to do it for six weeks. Their enjoyment is their precise ignorance.

Oh yes it is all very virtuous and all that, but when they come up against fourteen year old thugs they don't understand them. Everybody is different, they all have their own separate ways. It is the teacher versus the pupil. Two losing battles. Their is only ONE way to deal with really awkward characters, leave them alone. Don't even force them to come to school. This is why I say that school should be voluntary.

It only wants the teachers to realise what drab monotonous lives most people live, to see how it effects the child. The child is young, fresh, bursting with ideas and joy; It wants to be loved when it gets to school, not drilled like its ignorant parents.

The stupid govement, of course, makes school compulsory. An Authority with responsibility, but with no faith. What a society. They have no idea what so ever. If they let schools be theirs for the taking it would be wonderful. What idiots these people are. One of the first lessons people learn are, what is given is not appreciated. But if you work for a thing, then you damn well realise the value of it.

It is only because kids are forced to go to school, that they hate going. And this hate of being forced blinds them of what good it really does them. I know. I was one of the blind cunts. I didn't realise until it hit me so hard, that I knew that truth never falls down.

If schools were voluntary the kids would soon be bursting with joy to get into school. They would realise that they can get something there, that they can't get on their own.

School would be like ice-cream. There would be pink ice-cream, blue ice-cream, red, green, yellow, all sorts. The kids would love it. They would be delighted to go to school, because they could have a damn good lick of all the different sorts; it would be more than they could get at home. They would like it so much that they would probably take some home to there parents each Friday.

Of course it would work both ways The teachers would WANT to teach the children, because the children would WANT to learn. The teachers would not merely look on it as an interesting job. The teachers would like the children, because they have volunteered to learn. There would be a mutual understanding and love. And all desire seeks a union as a fulfillment. The teachers and the pupils would marry, because of their thirst and hunger of educational love.

Of course exams, like the G.C.E., are inevitable steps, where society *trys* to sort the kids into their own chairs and make them feel happy. This method of selection is probably a second class form of divine justice.

I resent the education Authorities because they have not realised their responsibilities. And I have, but I am only a tiddler in a very vast ocean full of authoritive whales.

If we read this with the ordinary sympathy and understanding that anyone writing might expect from a fellow-human-being, I think we feel the boy's anger and frustration, and the strength of his commitment to an idea – the possibility of social love, or, as he calls it, 'educational love'. (If we reject it on the grounds of indecorous language we are merely, to quote Simon Stuart, 'cutting ourselves off from a valuable, if only partially verbalized, source of instruction'.) (Stuart, 1969, p. 68) As someone who has already failed G.C.E. at least once, the boy is to some extent a victim of the system – a system in which nevertheless he acquiesces: he sees it, I think, not only as inevitable but even, after its fashion, as just – 'a second class form of divine justice'. His theme is ignorance on the one hand and educational love – the union of teaching and learning – on the other. And at the heart of this big idea, in contrast to the sophisticated terms he uses in describing it, he has as image of the object he wants to magnify, the childish concept of the multicoloured ice-cream. Whether or not he is aware of the incongruity, I would wager that the image still has power for him. As we read the whole outburst I think we can't help asking 'what will become of him?' – a question that he does not ask in the writing yet one which must have been for him at the time a burning question, the question of a lifetime.

We have referred to the role of the teacher as a sympathetic reader: with the least articulate writers it may well be that all progress depends upon such a relationship. More sophisticated writers, however, are likely during this period to begin to address themselves to a wider audience. The transition from writing for a teacher to writing for unknown readers may be a tricky one. The following is taken from a piece written by a fifteen-year-old girl as an entry for a literary competition. She called it 'The Oddest Person I Know':

She was born under the sign of the Scorpion, and astrologers call this the sign of a born leader. She knew this, and before she was old enough to discipline herself to conformity she fought to get her own way, fought to be leader, and found herself fighting ghostly, unvanquishable multitudes. She laughingly tears religion to shreds, but longs for it; she is proud, and flies to the defensive easily, over-anxious to establish her views; but the stamp of a non-conformist could not have been more cruelly placed by fate. Over-confidence faultily conceals a weak, frightened character that staggers under the weight of an inferiority she always feels, always hides. Despite her hard analysis of humanity, her world is ideal-istic and romantic, full of ridiculous, impossible dreams. She is sentimental, but this must be hidden at all costs, and never must the conformists suspect how afraid she is of them. Of late, how-ever, thanks to a friend who had proved her invaluable opposite, she has begun to learn tolerance, and patience, and perhaps even how to drift a little with the tide, pleasantly relaxing her bristling emotions.

As deaf people have to learn to survive in a world of sounds, so 'odd' people have to learn to survive in a world of conform-ity . . .

It is quite likely that the writer found it easier to describe herself in the third person – in disguise, so to speak – but I suspect she also felt the form to be more appropriate to the wider audience. Attempts to 'write for one's public' may at first result in some loss of genuineness – something gets butchered to make a Roman holiday. But we must regard these as growing pains, for it is important that a writer's mode of writing should come to be influenced by what he reads: there is a kind of sad stagnation about the poetry written by an adolescent who fills whole exercise books with his (her) lines but rarely if ever reads the work of another poet.

Sometimes the effect of reading upon writing is a highly particular one. Clare at the age of thirteen wrote copiously in this glossy fashion.

A delighted pandemonium broke out. Toasts and congratulations were showered upon them, 'A perfect match,' said everyone. 'What a ravishing bride!'

Only two people were silent. One was Mrs. Goldstein. The other was Carole Blake, the actress whose sultry, sexy beauty had blazed through the world of stardom like a rocket, and then fizzled out with a few coloured sparks, leaving the stars shining as before.

When her preoccupation with women's magazine stories grew less exclusive, she began, once again, to tackle various kinds of writing. All that sustained effort cannot, however, have been wholly wasted: perhaps she began to learn something of how to handle long stretches of narrative, perhaps she merely gained a kind of technical fluency. (Thirteen is certainly an age at which some children can profit from writing tasks much more sustained than the usual assignment.)

To give a rather different example, a sixteen-year-old girl who had taken eagerly to Dylan Thomas's stories began a piece of writing under the title 'My Home' as follows:

I lived in a slum, a smothering sunless smoke-smitten slum in which my house was hunched, a crippled deformity. Its eyes were perpetually closed with moth eaten curtains and though they reflected the drama of the streets they gave no inkling to its inner secrets – secrets of sleep . . .

Breathing like a bassoon, father dreamt of parading princely horses around his paddock of pounds shilling and pence, while mother used sheep to mop away her motives of murdered meat so that Susan, cold-creamed and curlered, could be peacefully lulled by the lovely lies of her love-story into a woeless world of Monroe women, Mason men, martinis and mink.

Looking at her world through Dylan Thomas's spectacles was a way eventually of extending her view of it: as the balance righted itself, she found her own voice again, but richer for the experiment of using his. Trying other people's voices may for the adolescent be a natural and necessary part of the process of finding one's own.

We have considered in this section a number of examples of writing in the spectator role: they have been at various points on the scale from expressive to poetic, and this distinction would roughly equate with writing for the teacher – a familiar and sympathetic reader – and writing for an unknown audience – one's public. It would be misleading if we did not now complete the picture by mentioning those referential forms of writing in which, with their maturing mental powers, adolescents formulate their interactions with the environment and communicate them, with increasing impersonality and objectivity, to a reader.

As we have already suggested, even a child can be objective at the level of concrete narrative or description; but it is an achievement of late adolescence to theorize objectively, to handle highly abstract concepts with due regard for their logical relationships, their interrelatedness within a system, and their implications downwards, that is to say at a concrete or empirical level.

Let me quote in conclusion a paragraph from an essay by a seventeen-year-old boy on a subject about which he has powerful feelings – A-level, or university entrance examinations in French:

Now for literature. I hope you will excuse the long and horribly involved metaphor which follows. If I were studying a machine, I would not remove four cogs from it and study them individually, detached from the machine to which they belong; I would, perhaps, study these cogs in their context. I would examine their relation and their function in the machine. The machine is French literature; the four cogs the four books we study minutely, painfully and uselessly. If I am studying a book by Molière, I ought to be able to place it in its social, literary and artistic context; I should study it not only in the light of Molière's other work but in the light of the social and political pressures and artistic and philosophical ideas that formed it. A work of art may be universal in its application, but it is temporal in its expression; to understand it completely I must understand the epoch that formed it. A knowledge of four books does not make up a knowledge of French literature; a study of four books, and their authors, taken in their literary and historical context, may at least help to.

That seems to me to be a competent piece of transactional writing, at a fairly theoretical level, such as one might expect to receive in response to a thousand and one assignments across the subjects of the secondary school curriculum. It states an opinion and supports it by analogy and by reasoning, by logical abstractions. The piece was taken more or less at random. But some such example was needed to reinforce one point. Objective referential writing, duly 'de-centred', is not, as we saw in Chapter 4, writing in which all trace of the writer has been lost. He might, in an extreme case of austere concentration upon the topic, be completely hidden in a way this writer is not; that is to say, expressive features (such as the opening apology here) might be almost entirely lacking: nevertheless, the coherence of the statement the writer makes will derive from his single human view-point. It is only in exceptional kinds of writing, such as some public notices and most legal documents, that the utterance ceases altogether to seem the voice of a man speaking to men.

We have been considering transactional writing, and because an important point has to be made in this connexion, we shall add it here. It concerns the conditions necessary in school for the development of transactional writing, speaking and reading. The point is this: these uses of language are the joint responsibility of the teachers of all subjects on the curriculum. Children will learn to master transactional language by using it, and they will need to use it in every kind of lesson. It seems to me urgently necessary that this responsibility should be faced: and the first necessary step is that secondary school staffs should by consultation arrive at an agreed policy for language across the curriculum in the school in which they work.*

VI

Once we recognize the value of books as a source of experience, we must admit as similar sources the visual-verbal media of film, television and stage-play. I think it is a matter of time (and money for equipment) before this realization affects the school curriculum: out of school, at home, the equivalence is already apparent.

We have next to admit the crude fact that, as providers of experience, there is no substitute for a living writer, director or playwright. 'Not for an age but for all time' constitutes a comment on a glorious bonus, uncontracted for, *an extra*. Every age requires its interpreters, the artists whose sensitivity to their environment enables them to be the first to make necessary adjustments to change (and the better the artist, of course, the more valuable the adjustments he makes). Thereafter, the age requires also that these adjustments, these changes in opinion or attitude or belief, be given currency in the pattern of culture – something that can happen only as readers and viewers respond to the works that embody them; and (being in some degree artists themselves) further articulate them, perhaps in second-rate novels, films, plays and so on. These are a part of the pyramid. Thus, though nothing is so dead today as the second-rate writings of the Victorian age, the Victorians *needed* these works and made use of them. (What is ironic is to find that where second-rate works do feature in our school texts, they are very likely to be the second-rate writings of a past era.)

If a living writer is in fact making adjustments ahead of his fellow-men, there is a sense in which the adolescent is his most

* See Barnes *et al.*, 1969, pp. 119–28.

appropriate audience. The adolescent is likely for his own reasons to be rejecting the prevalent opinions, attitudes and beliefs that the writer is in process of challenging and revising.

Of course, innovators may be good, bad or indifferent, sensitive or psychopathic; and the adolescent is likely to be a poor judge simply because of his immaturity, his inexperience in the established patterns of opinion and feeling. But just as I have stressed the important role of the living artist, so here I want to say that we cannot choose the good among innovators simply on the grounds of their resemblance to the artists of the past. To live – whether as artist-innovator, as responsive audience, or as mere vegetable – is *to take part in* those processes by which eventually the values of today will emerge and establish themselves, and the second-rate be sorted out from the first-rate. To be a good judge, *en route*, will require a grounding in the traditions, the arts of previous ages, but it will require something more than that – an openness, not simply to new data, but also to new ways of experiencing and new ways of evaluating.

Secondary experiences – through reading and viewing – provide the adolescent with a principal means to individuation. And we might note here in passing that for this purpose books have the advantage over other media by reason of their accessibility. I become more of an individual as I actively pursue my individual interests, and – as things are now set up – I am likely to be able to pursue my quarry from book to book far more easily than I could by any other means. Wide, even indiscriminate, reading of mainly contemporary books – this is one way, and a familiar one, of becoming an individual. Yet there are among adolescents two kinds of exception: the child who read widely from an early age and in adolescence has become a discriminating chooser over a wide range of old and new works; and the adolescent who has not yet discovered that he can read a book at all. It would be foolish to suggest that the former might not, by soaking himself in the literature of a past age, gain both a sense of what is constant in the human condition and a valuable perspective upon the contemporary world and his place in it. But it would be equally foolish not to recognize that the latter, the non-reader, is most likely to discover that a book can interest him if he is given free run of a varied collection of writings about the world he lives in, written by those who live in it (and preferably 'in the vicinity' so to speak of the reader). Daniel Fader tells of his success in reaching the unreached by this method: in *Hooked on Books* he records the astonishing results of a paperback campaign in the American equivalent of our Borstal Institutions, and it is a provocative story well worth reading. (Fader, 1966)

What is important here is to claim that the responses young people make to the books they *choose* to read form in fact the raw material of the maturer responses we covet for them eventually. The sensitive response to a work of literature we value ourselves is arrived at, I believe, by refining these earlier responses and not by stifling them. But what does 'refining' imply? I think it has two aspects that have not been clearly distinguished. In the first place it involves a higher degree of discrimination: to respond crudely is to fail to perceive elements in the object – the story or poem or film – that materially affect the nature of a refined response. Refinement, in this aspect of it, consists primarily in an increased awareness of forms – taking 'forms' to include the pattern of events represented, the changing tensions and interactions of feeling, and the forms of the medium itself – the words of the poem, and so on. Refinement, in this aspect, is pure gain: the satisfaction to be had in a developed response cannot be matched by anything in the un-developed response. But the second aspect of refinement is a more negative one: it is perhaps best explained as a rising threshold of rejection; a fastidiousness that very often pays as much attention to trivial as to essential features of the object. We parody this sense of the word in one of our familiar uses of it: if we call a person 'refeened' we suggest that he finds sturdy, common, ordinary life too vulgar for him, that his threshold of rejection on grounds of disgust is a high one. In so far as this sense of refinement is an element in the responses we are considering, it will be true that the satisfaction an in-experienced reader finds in a second-rate work could very well be the equivalent in kind and degree of the satisfaction a refined reader finds in a work of more lasting merit. The differences between mature and immature responses to a work of art cannot I believe be satisfactorily explained without taking into account this second aspect of 'refinement'.

Be that as it may, it is certainly true that as we become more experienced readers we continue to enjoy reading at many different levels. While aware of the deeper satisfaction we can derive, as experienced readers, from the great works of literature, we can nevertheless enjoy lesser satisfaction from elsewhere at times when we are unwilling or unable to invest so much of ourselves, of our mental capital, in the reading process. It is particularly important that we should recognize the necessity for this range in reading when we are thinking of adolescents. 'I am made up of a woman and a child in varying proportions, so that at one time I am full of desire and compas-sion and at another I feel as futile and helpless as a child.' So said the seventeen-year-old. It is a familiar aspect of growth that advances on one front are likely to be accompanied by regressions on another. Above all in adolescence the need to withdraw, to take refuge from living, is at one and the same time an expression of the need to reorganize and press on. And reading at different levels will serve each of these purposes. (The A-level candidate, to take what is perhaps a trivial example, is familiarly found reading, on the eve of the exam, Enid Blyton, romances in *Woman*, or pulp fiction – according to taste!)

But there is one more serious comment to make on 'light reading'. Melodramatic or sentimental stories, poems, films, may well have a particular role to play for adolescents when they deal with relations between the sexes and associated themes. Deep and powerful feelings are involved in these areas of experience, and the adolescent, newly acquiring these modes of feeling, is likely to mistrust them. The stock situation, the romantic stereotype, will give scope to them yet keep them under close control: the original work of art, on the other hand, *makes something of them*, and the adolescent may well be unwilling to risk the kind of committal to change that the work demands. In an inquiry into preference among poems* it was found that the thirteen- to sixteen-year-olds expressed a general preference for second-rate conventionally romantic poems, and only with the seventeen-year-olds were these rejected in favour of a genuine and original love poem.

I need hardly add that I am not advocating capitulation to the second-rate: what genuine art makes of these powerful experiences is what matters – for that way lies maturity. But there is a time for growth in adolescents, and a time for patience on the part of parents and teachers: a taste for the stereotyped, the second-rate, may at times be the first rung of a ladder and not the first step to damnation.

The destination is clear: a more mature response is one that finds satisfaction in a greater range and diversity of works, and in works which by their complexity, or the subtlety of their distinctions, their scope or their unexpectedness, make greater and greater demands upon us. And finally, a teacher whose class of school-leavers reads nothing more demanding than paperback thrillers and romances may nevertheless be firmly on the road to this destination, and know that he is.

VII

If we ask what is the adolescents' view of ourselves as adults, the answer is likely to be a fairly unambiguous one. We are the

---

*A poetry preference test given to 800 boys and girls aged thirteen to eighteen. London Association for the Teaching of English (unpublished) 1953.

'them' of their 'them and us'. We are responsible for things-as-they-are, and opposed to the changes they want to make: when they challenge authority, it is *our* authority, and we defend it: when they are frustrated by the lack of power or responsibility, it is because we hold them and will not give them up.

The last two decades have seen a deepening of the gulf between the generations, and in the last few years the respective roles have begun to emerge more clearly as those of 'the revolutionary' and 'the establishment'. Perhaps as a result of this role-defining, individuals seem to move less easily from the one group to the other as they grow up, and the average age of the younger group increases. It would be mistaken to suggest that the image of the teen-age pop-star has been seriously challenged, in adolescent eyes, by that of the student revolutionary, but in so far as this has tended to happen at all I would count it one feather in the cap of secondary education.

For our part, how are we to judge? Certainly we can claim that we have the wisdom of our experience on our side. We can look at the fourteen-year-old whose enthusiasm for something or other amounts to an obsession, and prophesy that in six months' time it will be some other cause or craze that possesses him. We can see the impracticability of the seventeen-year-old's ideals, and the inconsistency of his beliefs with his behaviour. We can diagnose the inner uncertainty that makes adolescents sound so dogmatic: and we can regret, at times, their raucousness, their ruthlessness, their intransigence, their hedonism.

And in the end, what we have to do for them is trust them. To begin to do which is to discover that some of the obvious things they say *could* have power if enough of a generation said them, and believed them, and refused to see their impracticability; and to recognize that, if anything has changed in recent years, it is the *rate of change* in general, so that judgements based on experience are likely to underestimate the possibilities of change within a lifetime; and finally to admit that, among

the injustices and extravagences of the young people's revolution, demands are being made that represent fragments of a
world we have always wanted.

We can add, of course, that protest or reform or revolution
always draws into its train individuals who are working out
their own private grievances, their own sicknesses: with the
consequent danger that, as Yeats put it in a similar situation:

> Mere anarchy is loosed upon the world,
> The blood-dimmed tide is loosed, and everywhere
> The ceremony of innocence is drowned.

To distinguish the healing tide from the blood that muddies it,
to discern what must be trusted and what must be cured – this
remains the problem.

Putting that problem aside, and thinking of the rising generations more generally, we have to trust them for their own sakes:
there is in the long run no viable alternative. For a teacher whose
concern does not go beyond the ordered framework in which a
class may work, there is the alternative of so managing that
situation that individuals have no power and eventually no will
to break his rules. He may even hope, though forlornly in most
cases, that this habit of conformity will spread to life outside
the classroom. For parents, and for teachers whose concern is
for the individuals themselves, the alternative to trusting them
is to try to *be* them, to live their lives for them. And this of
course is a long, anxious road into failure. It is themselves they
must become: and Carl Rogers (as we have seen) takes this to
mean a positive act of committal on their part.

Knowing nothing about all this, an eleven-year-old secondary modern school girl wrote:

I think I have reached the stage when a young girl's life is most
exciting and enjoyable. Being able to swim, read and have a large
amount of freedom, I feel that I am trusted. To cross roads, go
near rivers, travel alone, organise picnics, go swimming, go skat-
ing, go to the pictures, run the house, do the shopping, look after

babies, see that the dog is taken for a walk. In fact I know I am trusted.

And a nineteen-year-old, spending six months abroad for the first time in her life, taxed her parents with:

> Up to now you have trusted me to make the best use of my independence and I have trusted you to respect it. . . . I don't want to have to scrupulously censure everything I tell you. But if you are going to make a fuss over one isolated little incident then I don't think I trust you enough to be frank with you. . . . *You have got to trust me to make independent decisions and not merely to keep promises* . . .

(But the italic is mine and not hers.)

It is themselves they have to become, by the hard road of their own choices, their own intuitions, their commitment to themselves. As direct influences, people of their own age are likely to be much more powerful than adults can be. How difficult it may be for the adult is suggested by this account written recently by a fourteen-year-old girl in a London comprehensive school:

Getting the Message

You gave me a piece of paper, and you said: 'Write down the whole story in your own words,' and you left me for half an hour. And when you came back you were so pleased I handed you two pages of writing. When we sat down, you said 'I know what you're going through. . . .' I wanted to laugh, because you *don't* know, and you're just like every other teacher who's given me a pet talk, and like all the others, you probably read my story and thought: 'Poor girl' and if you thought it was the truth, you must be thick.

And when you teachers huddle together in the staff room, and discuss me in whispered tones, you think I don't know the names you call me. Well, I do, because they've been said to my face before, and it's not as if I bother any more. So I'll sit here and listen patiently, while you reel off the usual, in your sugary, false, pathetic voice, and when you've finished, I'll say: 'Yes ma'am' and 'thank you ma'am'. And you'll be so childishly pleased, and you'll think you've helped me, but you're wrong, and no-one of your sort can help me, because you're in a different generation, and you'll never understand me. So I'll carry on writing pages and pages of semi-truths and I'll laugh at you from behind my hair.

What is required today, it seems to me, is an urgent look at our secondary education having in mind the need of the adolescent to become himself: to make important choices about himself and his work and his relationships: to match his individuation with involvement – intellectual, aesthetic, social, moral: to commit himself: to make independent decisions rather than merely keep promises: his need to be trusted. There is much that wants altering both in the way institutions are organized and controlled and in the way teaching and learning are related in the classroom.

'No-one of your sort can help me, because you're in a different generation.' We have stressed in this section the value of openness between the generations, and as we have seen, in such a relationship there will be nothing unambiguous: it will require rather what Keats demanded – that we should be 'capable of being in uncertainties, mysteries, doubts, without any irritable reaching after facts and reasons'. And the onus for being 'able to take it' will inevitably lie mainly with the adults.

Yes, all this has to do with the role of language in a crucial stage of learning, learning in its broadest sense. As Georges Gusdorf has said (Gusdorf, 1965, pp. 67–8):

Communication . . . has a creative power. It gives self awareness to each in the reciprocal relation with the other. It is in the world of speech that the edification of personal life is realised, communion between persons always being presented in the form of a making explicit of value. The saving grace of communication, wherein one gives by receiving or receives by giving, is the discovery of one's fellow man. . . . Each gives the other essential hospitality in his better self; each recognizes the other and receives from him that same recognition without which human existence is impossible. For, reduced to himself, man is much less than himself; whereas, in the light of openness to the other, the possibility of an unlimited growth is offered to him.

Where the teacher is concerned the relationship will be less reciprocal than Gusdorf has it here: we are back on the one-endedness of the professional relationship, as we discussed it in Chapter 3. Elsewhere in his book Gusdorf writes (Gusdorf, 1965, p. 125):

To be open to the speech of others is to grasp it in its best sense, continually striving not to reduce it to the common denominator of banality, but to find in it something original. By doing this, moreover, by helping the other to use his own voice, one will stimulate him to discover his innermost need. Such is the task of the teacher, if, going beyond the monologue of instruction, he knows how to carry the pedagogical task into authentic dialogue where personality is developed.

CHAPTER SEVEN

Recent Perspectives

THE last piece of revised manuscript for the original edition of *Language and learning* was delivered to Penguin Books in October 1969 when our two daughters, Clare and Alison, were aged twenty-three and twenty-one. Records and recollections of their early years, and in due course their conversation, the stories they told, their comments on existence, gave substance to my observations and my theories about language and language-learning. Today, twenty-two years later, I continue learning from my family. I have been able to learn from the earliest beginnings of two grandchildren, Laurie now aged fourteen, and Lucy, aged nine and a half – and from Alison in a new role, that of their mother and lively participant in their activities. Another lively participant throughout a long lifetime in the company of Clare, Alison, Laurie and Lucy was my wife and their (grand)mother, Roberta. Sadly, she lived long enough simply to hear of this planned new edition, and died in hospital a few days later.

Times have changed as well as people: when Clare and Alison were the subjects, tape recorders were not generally speaking to be had – and the cassette type did not exist at all. I have now accumulated some ninety audio-cassettes of the growth of language from the earliest beginnings, covering both Laurie and Lucy.

Laurie became a specialist in make-believe, an occupation that was made to engage any adult willing to play second-fiddle for a time. One of her favourite locations was an imaginary shop or restaurant. Here she is at three years, three months old, and I am the other speaker:

ME: So this is the restaurant, is it?

L: Yes . . . Do you like three cucumbers?

ME: Mm . . . I should like some – I think I'd like some scrambled egg. Could I have some scrambled egg?

L: Yeah. 250p. And three yoghurts.

ME: Yes, and some – some coffee.

L: OK Sixteen . . .

ME: So you're going to write it down then?

L: Yeah. I've just got tea and coffee.

ME: Tea and coffee . . . Well I'll have coffee, please.

L: D'you like a cake?

ME: Ooh cake, that'll be lovely, yes.

L: Strawberry cake.

ME: Strawberry cake, lovely, yes.

Approaches to Speaking

It was a familiar part of the game that Laurie had a clapped-out calculator and a notebook and pencil with her on the table, and was in the habit of using some kind of mark to indicate an entry: it was part of the 'pretend' that made up the game. Laurie at a little over three years old had amassed a varied repertoire of pretended actions and a store of language that made them, so to speak, come true.

There is general agreement that one of the most impressive achievements of the human intellect is that of first acquiring ability to use and understand a native tongue. This is a process which in our society is mastered, as reported in Chapter Two above, about the age of eighteen months. It was my intention in the first edition to refer to any characteristics of the process that might make the achievement, mysterious though it remains, seem at least feasible, and not mere magic.

A number of such observations have, since the original publication of this book, been added to the list. Jerome Bruner (1975), for example, taking a fresh and speculative look at language acquisition, suggests that co-operative activity at a pre-language stage prepares the way for the use of language. He suggests that an adult, usually the mother, sets up the use of 'formats', routines of behaviour, that engage the infant in his first attempts to make sense of the flux of events. These routines may be associated with feeding or cleaning, but more often with play. The format may involve a brief sequence to a closure – as for example when Alison covered Laurie's face with her pram rug and then asked, 'Where's Laurie?', only to pretend surprise when she uncovered it and declared with delight, *There she is!* Meanings are in this way exchanged by the joint recognition of behavioural patterns and the infant begins to 'phrase his experience in order to make sense of it'. The mother's utterances accompany and support the activities, and the child's vocalizations are in course of time assimilated to her speech. Bruner observes some of these as they take place: he follows, for example, a mother and child who have established a routine of giving and receiving. When the mother gives the object – a ball, perhaps – to the child, she says, 'There you are', and when the child gives it back to her, she says 'Thank you'. The baby begins to support his actions vocally, at first with his own sounds, but then in recognizable words. At nine months and two weeks, Bruner reports, the baby says 'Kew' when the mother takes the object he has offered; but a month later he says 'Kew' whenever she offers him anything, and two months later he says 'Look' when handing to her and 'Kew' when receiving from her.

It is important to notice that the role of speech on the mother's part and of speech-like noises on the child's part are strictly subordinate to the meanings already attached to, and communicated by, the activity itself. Bruner points out that the routines involved introduce and vary some of the basic elements of person-to-person and person-to-object interactions: elements such as an *action*, a doer or *agent*, sometimes the *object* of an action, the *recipient*, an *instrument* by which the action is performed. Further, there is the *location* or locations of the action, and there is *possession*. These are aspects that reflect the grammatical cases likely to be found in any language. That is to say, what is prefigured and rehearsed in mother/child activity leads directly to aspects of the language of normal speech. In Bruner's words, we may therefore see such language as 'a specialized and conventionalized extension of human co-operative action'. (Bruner, 1975, p. 3)

Lucy began at a very early age to produce 'speech-like noises': it may be that a second child has more accessible speech as model and incentive than is the case with a first-born. It so happens that the most striking example of her speech-like noises appeared on Christmas Day of her first year, when she was six months and two weeks old. I have her on tape three or four times before that day; sometimes she was crying with gusto, sometimes gurgling and contented. But on Christmas Day I believe she left no doubt that she was addressing the assembled family. Using one or two insistent patterns of intonation and a variety of 'da-da-da' sounds, the speech-like spell lasted a full nine minutes. It is impossible to believe that her activity was not sparked off by the speaking that her sister and the adults were producing within her hearing.

A gap of over a year separates that occasion from anything one might call the language of conversation on Lucy's part. At twenty-two months her comments are still largely limited to single-word utterances, but she continues to add to the number of words she can use. The following brief exchange took place when Alison and Lucy paid a visit to our home. D stands for Danny (Granny) which is the name given by Laurie to Roberta. Danny has just passed a cup of tea to Alison:

A: Thank you. That's just what I need!
L: Zank you. Zank you.
A: Mm, I said thank you.

L: Zank you!

D (*laughing*): That's very nice.

L: Zank you, Waller.

D: French now – *voilà*?

A: Thank you Waller – that's Mrs Waller.

Later the same day, Lucy and Danny and Alison are by the door looking into the garden:

A: (*to L*): What's your name?

L: Kathy.

D: Katherine?

A: Is it really Kathy?

L: No.

A: What's your name really?

L: Sheila.

A: It's *not* Sheila! What's your real name?

L: Lucy.

A: Yes.

D: What's mummy's name – do you know that?

L: Yes. Chocolate!

A: Chocolate? I'm not called chocolate. What's my name? What's mummy's name?

L: Alison.

D: D'you want me to feed the birds, do you? I'll get the . . . now, you stand on that chair. [*They throw crumbs etc. out on to the terrace.*] Here he comes, look! Gobbling up the apple peel!

L: 'T-zat?

D: That's a blackbird – he sings very nicely . . . and there's a teeny one, a hedge sparrow, nice little brown one . . . Oh and there's a starling – starlings come down like dive-bombers. There's a wise blackbird – he's taking a big piece of crust on to the flower-bed where nobody can see him.

L: Up!

D: Oh! he's pecking it all up. Peck, peck, peck!

L: Peck, peck, peck!

D: Yes, especially the pigeon. The clever ones take a big piece and go and hide in the bushes where it can't get taken away.

L: 'T-zat one?

D: A pigeon – there's a sparrow – a blackbird –

L: Hiding.

D: Yes, hiding, he just goes on eating and nobody comes to take away his piece . . . Pigeons –

L: No? Hiding.

D: Yes, a great big piece of brown bread . . . Pretty, they've got nice colours, haven't they, little white bits on their necks.

L: Hiding.

D: Hiding . . . yes, he's hiding behind the steps, isn't he?

L: Pishun.

D: Can you say 'pigeon' – 'pigeon'?

L: Pigeon – peck, peck, peck.

Lucy's comments at twenty-two months may be still limited to single words, but she shows alacrity and interest in adding to her knowledge both of words and of things. The sound I have represented here as Lucy's ''T-zat' was an item that had been developed in use by her over six or seven months and clearly represented her attempt to produce speech sounds equivalent to 'What is that?'

Such observations of my granddaughters' early speech focused on my attempt to interpret them as meaningful expressions: what conventional adult speech patterns did they appear to resemble?

A study by Michael Halliday (1975) took me further into an understanding of early speech and its origins. After making a name for himself as an expert in grammatical functions and the theories that account for them – a key element in the work of the linguistics department at Edinburgh University – he surprised us all by initiating a detailed account, from systematic records, of the beginnings of language use on the part of his son Nigel. The account covers the child's life between the ages of six months and eighteen months, and shows an understanding of early uses unlike anything previously recorded. Halliday claims that while a child's early language uses may sometimes employ elements taken over from the speech of those around him (as I saw from Lucy's speech), this is not always the case: in fact the child's early vocalizations may owe nothing to the sounds he could have heard from other voices, and may have no forms we can recognize as familiar speech forms. This leads him to propose that we should recognize as early speech any constant match between vocal sounds made by the child and the meanings that can be attributed to them. He quotes as example that 'whenever Nigel says *nananana* it always means something like "I want that thing now"; and when he expresses the meaning "I want that thing now" by means of a vocal signal, he always does so by saying *nananana'*. The relation between the sounds and the meaing, is, in other words, constant, systematic.

It is the recognition of these systematic linkings that makes Halliday's account unique. When there are no elements imitated from adult speech observers are likely to conclude that no language is being acquired, while in fact 'the child is already both responding to and producing signals of a linguistic kind'. (Halliday, 1975, p. 10)

Halliday states the view that there are two elements and two only in a young child's early speech – those of *meaning* and of its *expression*, the sense and the sound. At a later stage, and throughout adult life, which the book goes on to discuss, every normal utterance has *three* elements to it: one expresses a speaker's view of some aspect of experience, an *ideational* function; a second represents an *interpersonal* function, a concern with language as a social exchange; and a third element establishes an utterance as a speech event, a *text*. I believe these are difficult abstractions to master, and will remain so, but a gloss from an earlier volume by Halliday (1973, p. 100) may help. He says there of these three elements that they

are the most general categories of meaning-potential, common to all uses of language. With only minor exceptions, whatever the speaker is doing with language he will draw on all these components of the grammar. He will need to make some reference to the categories of his own experience – in other words, the language will be *about* something. He will need to take up some position in the speech situation; at the very least he will specify his own communication role and set up expectations for that of the hearer – in terms of statement, question, response and the like. And what he says will be structured as 'text' – that is to say, it will be operational in the given context . . .

In other words, it will accomplish something. The importance of this term 'text' is that it serves as the embodiment of the first two items and at the same time provides the point at which to locate a speaker's aim or purpose – his/her *intention*.

In the early stages, where the meaning and expression of single-word utterances constitute the whole utterance, Halliday suggests that each will fulfil a limited and particular function, and he goes on to describe a developmental sequence of these, each interpreted as communicating meaning within a social context. He stresses that these are the functions of early meaning/sound utterances only, and no longer apply to the more complex speech later developed. The earliest function to appear is the *instrumental* function, that designed to fulfil a child's needs or desires. These are followed by the *regulatory* (attempting to control other people's behaviour), *interactional* (the language of co-operation), *personal* (expressing the self), *heuristic* (discovering and naming aspects of the environment), and *imaginative* (the language of story and make-believe). While there is some general support for the belief that a primary use of language is to pass on information, it is Halliday's view that the seventh and last of the early functions to be learnt – well after the others – is that of communicating information.

Commenting on Nigel's utterance at the age of ten and a half months, Halliday believes that the sounds he uses are not derived from sounds he has heard adults using, but are rather modifications of sounds he has himself produced in the course of his own activities. This, he believes, is the stage at which Nigel is developing a language of his own – and he adds a comment that could certainly be supported from my experience of the language of successive generations of infants: 'If one comes to examine carefully the utterances that the child makes at this stage and the particular contexts in which they occur, it turns out that the majority of those in which the newly acquired vocabulary items figure are not pragmatic in function at all. They occur, rather, in contexts of observation, recall, and prediction.' (Halliday, 1975, p. 27) A pronouncement by Susanne Langer is one that I have applied often to the concerns that young children's language addresses: 'Young children learn to speak . . . by constantly using words to bring things into their minds, not into their hands.' (Langer, 1960a, p. 121) Even the minimal responses that Lucy makes when she is watching the birds in the garden are concerned with 'making out' what is happening and, so to speak, savouring it: observation and perhaps a kind of expectation close to prediction.

Progress from the age of ten and a half months to eighteen months constitutes what Halliday calls Phase I, and this is followed by Phase II, which begins the transition to adult forms. The change is marked by the introduction of grammatical features and by the fact that Nigel begins to take part in dialogue. This involves the distinction between being at times an *observer* in his use of language and at other times an *intruder*. As observer he will use speech to embody and interpret his experience of the world he lives in – an *ideational* use of language – and as intruder he will use language to engage in dialogue, an *interpersonal* use of language. 'Dialogue', writes Halliday, 'involves the adoption of roles which are social roles of a new and special kind, namely those which are defined by language itself . . . A speaker of the adult language, every time he says anything, is adopting a communication role himself, and at the same time is assigning another role, or a role choice, to the addressee, who in turn has the option of accepting or rejecting the role that is assigned to him.' (Halliday, 1975, p. 30)

Halliday is at pains to show how early uses of language – Nigel's self-induced utterances – sow the seeds of the adult language. His book goes on to relate language acquisition to the development of social roles and the process of coming to terms with the culture into which we are born. The work as a whole is a mine of original observation and speculation, a contribution to our understanding that few living linguists could match.

Language and Children's Thinking

Studies of early language have, over a number of years, been increasingly related to studies of children's thinking. A theoretical backing for this association was proposed by a French linguist, Emile Benveniste (1971), when he suggested that the relationship between *I* and *you* uniquely set up in dialogue established the basis of a human view of the universe. He argues:

Consciousness of self is only possible if it is experienced by contrast. I use *I* only when I am speaking to someone who will be a *you* to my address. It is this condition of dialogue that is constitutive of *person*, for it implies that reciprocally *I* becomes *you* in the address of the one who in his turn designates himself as *I*. Here we see a principle whose consequences are to spread out in all directions. Language is possible only because each speaker sets himself up as a *subject* by referring to himself as *I* in his discourse. Because of this, *I* posits another person, the one who, being, as he is, completely exterior to 'me', becomes my echo to whom I say *you* and who says *you* to me. This polarity of persons is the fundamental condition of language. (Benveniste, 1971, pp. 224 and 225)

Since this relationship is reciprocal yet not symmetrical (any person's first-hand experience being, to himself, *primary*), it is a type of opposition that occurs only within language. It is our experience of it in dialogue that, once initiated, 'spreads out in all directions', making possible the meeting of minds in a cultural community.

Variations on the theme set out by Benveniste (though the authors do not refer to him) feature in a more recent collection of pieces by British and American writers, *Children Thinking Through Language* (1982). It is a bold and speculative collection. In his introductory chapter the editor, Michael Beveridge, establishes that the intention running through the book is to relate our understanding of children's language, in a wide variety of situations, with whatever we know of their cognitive processes. Contributors describe theories based on work with the deaf, work with the blind, and work with normal children facing the cognitive tasks that school subjects demand.

Valerie Walkerdine speculates on the kind of problem we find raised by Piaget's experimental findings – in particular his conclusion that young children are unable to reason. She believes the relationship among signs cannot be treated as simply a linguistic relationship, but must also be regarded as a *social* one. In other words we have to take context as an inherent factor; we 'cannot understand the relation of language to thought without consideration of the social practices within which the relation is effected'. (Walkerdine, 1982, p. 131)

Walkerdine illustrates this by examining the context in which children in a London primary school 'acquire and create' modes of participating in discourse simply by taking part in everyday practices. 'Children's acquisition of certain discursive formats is extremely rapid: certainly by the age of two or three they are able to switch in and out of discursive positions, taking up for example positions in play which they can never have taken in real life.' (Walkerdine, 1982, p. 133) Her illustration shows two girls playing in the 'Wendy House' – the classroom model of a home. In their opening conversation they are taking on, without prior discussion or negotiation, the roles of mother and daughter at home:

Nancy: Hello Diane. Let's watch telly.

Diane: I'm just tidying baby's bed up. You sit on that wooden chair. Here y'are . . . Alright I'm working I can't watch telly.

Nancy: Mum can I watch telly mum? (Beveridge (ed.), 1982, p. 133)

My granddaughter Laurie, at the age of three years and ten months, is also, in my next example, taking up a role of which she has no first-hand experience in real life. I half-heartedly resisted her ploy at the outset, but she persisted. She has with her two ancient and worn teddy-bears (that had belonged to Clare and Alison), now designated one boy and one girl.

L: Let's play mummies and daddies in the car! Yes!

ME: Oh – no!

L: I want to play it!

ME: I'll give you a swing in the chair!

L: No: – I want to play this game! . . . Now, you sit at the front with the boy and I'll sit at the – I'll drive and you sit with the boy. Yep?

ME: Yes.

L: And you can have this blanket. You'll sit *here* and I'll sit *here*: I'll drive – get into the car. Open! Open! You sit with the boy, put the blanket on him. The girl's got to sit here.

ME: Yes, OK.

L: Bring the Panda book.

ME: Mm?

L: Bring the Panda book.

ME: The Panda book – that's it. Put it in.

L: You hold the book. Get the cushion – need – for her.

ME: Yes.

L: She needs a cushion. Open the door! Door's open!

ME: Door's open.

L: You – you get the pillow.

ME: Oh, that one – I see.

L: There – she can sit back with you. *I'll* wrap her up. Don't drive –

ME: Are you driving?

L: Not yet, 'cos I haven't got her in the back with you. There! And

I've got to pull my socks up a bit. 'Tend I've got smart shoes on. We're going to go to the park. [*Driving noise.*] Is your door shut? Shut! [*Driving noise.*]

ME: Now round to the left, round there . . . Now round to the right – to the right!

L: Open! Open! We're there!

ME: Have you got the brake on?

L: I did. Let's get the arber[?] baby now. Arber baby. She's dying.

ME: Oh no!

L: Not really. She's only dying for a pee. [*Laughter.*] Bring him, bring him with the blanket here. Open!

ME: A lot to bring away, isn't there?

L: Bye! I'll see you later.

ME: Bye, Love – see you later – have a nice day. Take care!

L: Yes, Bye. I just forgot to give you your goodbye kiss . . . and the baby. Bye, see you later.

ME: See you later!

L: I'll see you – um – tonight.

ME: Yes, see you tonight. Don't be late. Don't be late.

L: No.

As happens here, Laurie usually chooses for herself a role that controls the action – it has struck me often that autonomy is the name of the game! From the pilot's seat, she has no difficulty in setting the game in motion, improvising its course – which may well include the need to compromise, as I believe happened when I didn't want to take on the turn of events represented by her statement, 'She's dying!'. When I listen to the tones of her voice on the tape, it does seem clear that throughout the sequence she is 'playing it by ear', is *improvising*. Whether for this or other reasons, it does seem that the action draws upon many of the relationships and inter-personal attitudes that characterize the family – my family – in their daily living. And, as Valerie Walkerdine and others have claimed (Beveridge, 1982), we cannot understand the relation of language to thought without considering the social practices in which the relation is effected.

Walkerdine sees her view as criticism of what she calls 'a Piagetian edifice' (Walkerdine, 1982, p. 130) and she cites Margaret Donaldson's book *Children's Minds* (1978) as supporting such a move. Donaldson is another member of the Edinburgh linguistics faculty, one who worked for a time with Piaget in Geneva. She begins dramatically, however, by presenting a happy picture of life in a primary school. 'As I watched this scene,' she says, 'on a morning in May 1977, it occurred to me that a visitor to the school who knew nothing of our society might have been inclined to think he had found Utopia, especially if he had been told that the children he was watching came from families living in a somewhat underprivileged part of one of our large cities.' She follows that with a glance at the other end of the regular educational system – a picture of boys and girls leaving the secondary school 'heartily thankful to have done with it', and, according to the popular press, totally unfit to earn a living in the kind of world they must enter. The question, then, that her book sets out to answer – what has gone wrong with the system?

Donaldson suggests that Piaget's experimental work appeared to demonstrate the very limited capacity of children to reason, a prejudice that was well established before Chomsky, in the 1960s, expounded his thesis that human beings have an innate sense concerning the nature of language: that we are provided from birth with a special facility to recognize certain universal characteristics that every language possesses. Thus learning to speak was recognized as a massive intellectual task: the child listens to what is said around him, educes principles that explain the forms he hears and applies them, constructing his own grammar of the spoken language – an implicit set of rules, one reflected in speech but not specifiable. Chomsky called it 'rule governed behaviour without a knowledge of the rules'. He believed it indicated an inborn ability to *reason* when handling linguistic data in a way that does not operate when the problem is not one of language.

We have only to bring these views of Chomsky's alongside the work of Piaget to realize that they cannot both be right, and perhaps neither of them has grasped the whole story. The whole story, as Donaldson presents it, has more to do with the kind of understanding that Bruner referred to in the piece I quoted above – understanding that comes when a child co-operates with an older person and plays a familiar role in a repeated routine. An understanding born of shared behaviour, in other words, plays the facilitating role that Chomsky attributed to individual inborn verbal knowledge.

Why then does Piaget's experimental work come up with so poor a view of a young child's reasoning power? It is Donaldson's firm conclusion that children *can* reason, and when they fail to do so in Piaget's experiments it is because *they don't understand the questions he is asking*. Piaget, for instance, used to support the notion of a child's point of view as an egocentric one – that the child fails to recognize that somebody else's point of view may differ from his own. Piaget illustrated this by an experiment using a model of three mountains, each with its own distinguishing features. The child sits at one side of the table on which the model is placed and is asked to compare what he sees with what some other, differently placed viewer would see. Children up to eight or even nine cannot usually do so.

In contrast to these results, Donaldson reports an experiment in which the child sees a model representing two intersecting walls forming a cross, and where two models, one of a policeman and one of a small boy, are used. The experimenter carefully introduces a variety of positions for the two, and the child is asked when the policeman can, and when he cannot, see the boy. The task is then complicated by introducing a second policeman and asking the child to arrange it so that the boy is hidden from both of them. 'The results', Donaldson tells us, 'were dramatic.' A group of thirty children aged from three and a half to five years made, on average, 90-per-cent correct answers. Human motives of a basic kind, such as 'the intention to escape and the intention to pursue and capture', introduce an element of feeling and planning that is a basic part of what she calls 'a very fundamental human skill'. (Donaldson, 1978, p. 25)

This is by no means the whole argument. The book goes on to show repeated examples of experiments which have been devised to test essentially the aspects of reasoning that interested Piaget, but asking questions in such a way that successful results are recorded. The reasons become clear: Donaldson explains them in terms of the movement from *embedded* to *disembedded* reasoning.

The embedding might be described in Vygotsky's (1978) terms as part of a general developmental rule, to the effect that children begin to acquire 'higher mental functions' by operating in partnership with an adult: what they can achieve by this means they learn in time to achieve by themselves. 'An interpersonal process', Vygotsky states, 'is transformed into an intrapersonal one. Every function in the child's cultural development appears twice: first on the social level, and, later on the individual level; first *between* people ... and then *inside* the child. All the higher functions originate as actual relations between human individuals.' (Vygotsky, 1978, p. 57)

We have to bear in mind, in all that we have seen of early language growth, the unique role played by an adult or older child. Match that with a sense of the young child's forward-looking curiosity and I think we might well conclude that children's earliest conception of the world is likely to be in terms of a network of human motives, intentions and interactions. As adults we use language to represent and communicate any and almost every aspect of experience; it may be that the intimate relation between language and experience depends upon active encouragement of the embedded uses in the early years of school and access in due course to the disembedding that logical thought requires.

Donaldson quotes a number of examples of reasoning

produced by children in the course of listening to, and commenting on, stories read to them. She comes to the conclusion that a child 'first makes sense of situations (and perhaps especially those involving human intention) and then uses this kind of understanding to help him make sense of what is said to him.' (Donaldson, 1978, p. 59)

Donaldson's thesis covers both the necessity of harnessing embedded uses of language and the further necessity (by no means fully recognized in our current educational practices) of moving on to disembedded forms of reasoning – reasoning that applies more widely than to a particular case and may provide evidence that would settle issues that have not yet been raised. She sees this as a social objective, one which obliges us to override, for example, the class barriers of English society. She concludes:

The issue is whether we must accept it as inevitable that only a small minority of people can ever develop intellectually to a high level of competence. I believe that we do not have to accept this. I believe that the *nature* of the very considerable difficulty which these skills present to the human mind has not been adequately recognized. Although we have known for a long time that 'abstract thinking' is hard, we have lacked a sufficiently clear and widespread – understanding of what is involved in moving beyond the bounds of human sense and learning to manipulate our own thinking in the new disembedded modes, free from the old involvements, which sustain and hamper at the same time. (Donaldson, 1978, p. 124)

Distinguishing What is Said from What is Meant

David Olson, of the Ontario Institute for Studies in Education, has long been concerned with problems in this area. When I first met him some years ago, his first question to me was: 'Why do teachers in England encourage children to write what is essentially the spoken language?' This was at a time when with my colleagues I had been working on 'the development of writing abilities', and our findings had led to a firm stress on the importance of expressive language – as a form of speech, of course, but also as a written language favourable to discovery and learning, a kind of antidote to rote learning, the curse of much secondary education. Clearly we differed in our sense of how the learner moves from embedded to disembedded thinking.

Olson (1975) found evidence to support the view that children rely first upon aspects of familiarity in their thinking, just as Donaldson had demonstrated. In a study of young children's ability to understand the relationship of active to passive sentences he was surprised to discover that there was a material difference between understanding the relationship in sentences that cited, for example, names like John or Mary, and those that cited familiar Peanuts cartoon names – Snoopy, Lucy, Charlie Brown. 'The more well-known the characters,' he reported, 'the better able were the children to draw the correct implications.'

Along with Nancy Torrence, Olson has for some years been engaged on a close study of an aspect of young children's language closely allied to Donaldson's general thesis. They distinguish it as a process by which a young child has to learn that there is a distinction between what, on any occasion, is *said* and what is *meant*. 'Our research', they state, 'has indicated that children younger than 5 or 6 years make little distinction between what they say and what they mean by it: conversely, as listeners they fail to recognize that an utterance once interpreted one way could possibly be interpreted in another way.' (Olson and Torrence, 1987, p. 138) In one experiment children were told a story that included an ambiguous sentence: that is to say, one character asks another to find something on the strength of what is in fact an inadequate identification. Lucy (*sic!*), it is explained, wants her *new red shoes*, but what she asks for is her *red shoes*, and that is open to misinterpretation. Senior kindergarten and grade 2 students fail to recognize the inadequacy; it is not until grade 5 that the distinction between what was meant and what was said in the situation is perceived and understood. The authors believe this distinction reflects a concern for the importance of recognizing the role of interpretation in understanding the meaning of a text and is likely to be associated with subsequent progress in reading and probably also in writing. 'The student who recognizes interpretations as interpretations', they believe, 'will be in a better position to accept other interpretations when they are offered, to judge some interpretations as better than others, and to search for new interpretations of existing texts.' (Olson and Torrence, 1987, p. 144)

Inner Speech and Understanding

A. R. Luria is the Soviet psychologist whose study of the late speech development of a pair of identical twins was described in Chapter Two (pp. 66–9). In 1981 there was published an English translation of a comprehensive account of his view of the relation of speech to thinking: *Language and Cognition*. It derives in many respects from earlier work by Vygotsky, supplements this with more recent research, and creates a fuller account of the educational and psychological context.

'Comprehensive' is indeed the word for it, and I can do no more than pursue selected topics of special concern to us. I have on many occasions remarked on the fact that human beings have a remarkable capacity for doing what it is *they want to do*. They are not, as other creatures are, confined to a biologically determined program of activity. Luria believes that the existence of 'a voluntary act' poses problems that many psychologists cannot satisfactorily explain: they may merely take it for granted, or perhaps regard it as some mysterious inner or spiritual force, or they may, as he claims American behaviourists have often done, regard it as merely a form of conditioned reflex. It was

Vygotsky, Luria believes, who suggested the right answer: we must look beyond the individual and find a social factor – in other words, a child arrives at ability to perform a voluntary act in the course of his relations with an adult, most usually the mother.

This process, as we have seen, begins to operate long before the child can speak, and is, in fact, a prime means by which early understanding of language becomes possible. What Luria adds to the account is details of the gradual development of the regulative role of speech: first that of the mother affecting the child's perceptions, then that of the child's own in the face of both his/her *inertia* (difficulty in switching from one undertaking to a new one) and the kind of distraction offered by direct visual experience – the delights of the senses, perhaps. Luria's own studies indicated that the regulative power of adult speech is not firmly established until a child is about three and a half years old.

Luria goes on to consider 'the formation and structure of inner speech'. He quotes from Vygotsky how young children from three to five years of age react when they meet a difficulty – say in making a drawing when the pencil they are using has broken. First they try some practical step, but when that fails they begin to talk about their difficulty – either to no one in particular or to themselves – first describing the difficulty and then working on a plan: this is 'speech for oneself', in Vygotsky's terms.

This speech is at first, Luria tells us, 'in a very expanded form', but in time 'it gradually becomes more and more abbreviated, finally turning into whispered speech, in which children describe haltingly the situation they find themselves in'. Then, after another year or two, 'only by watching the child's lip movements can one surmise that this speech . . . had become . . . transformed into what might be termed "inner speech"'. (Luria, 1981, pp. 104–5)

Studies made by scholars since Vygotsky's death have led to further discoveries: every mental act, it is claimed, begins as a physical process arising out of the manipulation of objects, moves into the realm of expanded speech and thence becomes abbreviated into inner speech. Thus, Luria concludes, the structure and origin of a voluntary act are mediated by speech, both external speech as means of communication and the inner speech that produces a psychological formation.

But to say that inner speech is *abbreviated* is perhaps misleading. It is nearer the mark to call it *predicative* – that is to say, since we are speaking to ourselves, we know the nature of the proposed grammatical subjects of the sentences: we know what is being talked about. What we have to discover with the help of inner speech is *what is being said* about the subject – what is being said in the predicate. Luria finishes this chapter by stating that inner speech can be transformed into expanded speech:

If I am going to a lecture to speak about the mechanism of inner speech, I carry only an abbreviated outline of the lecture in my mind. Items such as 'inner speech', 'egocentrism' and 'predicativity' – items which do not name the theme but indicate what I want to say about it (in other words, predicative items) – are precisely what enable me to go on to produce the external utterance. Accordingly, on the basis of inner speech, the lecturer can expand a scant outline into an entire lecture. (Luria, 1981, pp. 108–9)

Luria's chapter on 'Speech production' begins by assuming that the motive for speaking consists in the need or wish to speak, rather than the desire to say x or y or z: in other words it exists as a preliminary stage and has to be followed by the production of an utterance plan. This will probably consist at first of little more than a general sense of what has to be said. At this point Luria claims that psychology has little constructive to say about the nature of thought, or how thought is given verbal shape. It was Vygotsky's view that speech does not in any straightforward way embody thought; rather, 'a thought is completed in speech'. (As several noted authors are reputed to have asked, 'How do I know what I mean until I see what I say?')

It remains a task for psychology to trace the movement from 'a subjective sense' to a message encoded in a system of meanings. Luria refers to some of the early stages and concludes that it is only as children approach school age that their speech begins to take shape as a closed system of 'complex narration' limited to specific tasks. He suggests that this may coincide with the formation of inner speech, a later acquisition than that of external speech. External speech must become abbreviated and converted into inner speech before it becomes possible to carry out the opposite process, that is, 'the expansion of this inner speech into an external, connected text with its characteristic semantic coherence'. (Luria, 1981, p. 158)

The picture, then, is of a child first learning to use the grammar and the other conventions of the spoken language by taking part in conversation, particularly conversation with adults. The child is able to do this because it is to some extent a shared process, one in which he/she may gradually take over more and more of the initiative.

Luria makes a distinction between 'oral dialogic speech' – a conversation or a question-and-answer exchange – where there may be deliberate intention on the part of one or both (or neither) of the participants, and oral monologue where the speaker is responsible for the motive of the utterance, its general plan and its execution. Early forms of monologue Luria describes as *narrative*, and he makes it clear that until external speech has become abbreviated and become 'inner speech' it cannot support the production of narrative monologue. 'That' says Luria, 'is why a child, who already possesses external speech, as manifested in social dialogue, may still be unable to produce coherent monologic speech.' (Luria, 1981, p. 158)

I gave an example of Laurie at the age of three years and ten months playing out with me a situation she had never met in real life (see p. 285). She certainly played the lead in the conversation, but it was a running exchange in which we collaborated to keep the action going without any solo performances. Here, three months later (i.e., at four years, one month), she seems to me to come near to the kind of sustained narrative that constitutes monologue. There are brief interruptions from me, but they amount to little in the way of contribution; these are shown in brackets.

Now it's time for little darlings to go to sleep. [Yes.] You've got to go to sleep now. Your blanket . . . pillows. Lie down! Now you're going to have a little . . . if you don't go to sleep – you *must* go to sleep 'cos – or you will be afraid of night 'cos the owls come at night. Yes, they do – to-whoo! They don't frighten *you* – they don't eat you only rats or mice – that's good, isn't it? [Yes.] Now I've got to sort your cover 'cos you messed it up last night, didn't you? [I wriggled so much, didn't I?] Yes, 'cos you're afraid of the *owl* aren't you? [Yes] To*night* I have to sleep in my own room downstairs and Dad sleeps downstairs too and you only sleep *upstairs*. And the baby sleeps [*pause*] downstairs too and the big girl – and your two sisters sleep down too and you only sleep upstairs, don't you? So you have to be very quiet. If you hear – if you – um – hear a monster, I'll come running up. I hope – if you dream about one just cry and come down and say, 'Oo-oo Mummy I had a bad dream.' Yes. Now you're going to go to sleep aren't you? Close your eyes . . . . Mor*ning*!

As Valerie Walkerdine listened to the improvisations in the Wendy House she found they could only make sense in the light of the context of the game being acted out. (Beveridge, 1982, p. 135) I believe this account by Laurie is just such a freshly minted piece, an original improvisation. Her hesitations suggest she is 'shaping at the point of utterance'. The sequence is clearly signaled by its opening, a rather story-like expression unlike anything she had heard in a real-life situation; and in the closing expression, god-like, she holds time in her hands.

I believe the underlying motive is her attempt to rehearse, as it were in reverse – taking the part of the adult – the theme of being brave enough to sleep upstairs while the rest of the family sleep downstairs. It seems possible that the promptings of inner speech and their conversion into a narrative form provide the best explanation of the occurrence.

Luria's *Language and Cognition* is one of the fullest accounts we have had in recent years of the workings of inner speech, principally as they apply to language development in children. He claims that a child of three or four years must rely on practical experience, and does not possess the power of *induction* (going from individual facts to a universal law) or *deduction* (deducing individual facts from a general premise). Since the child has no understanding of universality, he/she must work from individual practical experience. (Luria, 1981, p. 204) Luria reports findings that a similar lack of disembedded thinking may characterize people living in isolated areas of a rural economy. Studies carried out no longer ago than the 1930s described country people who were experienced in practical ways and were fully able to solve complicated problems relating to their work, but did so by embedded thinking in the direct context of their daily occupations. (Luria, 1981, p. 207)

Talking, Writing and Thinking

Teachers who study transcripts and listen to tapes of children talking in small groups have usually been surprised at their ability to carry on a co-operative and purposeful discussion. This has led to a realization that the frameworks we set up for talk in the classroom tend to be restrictive: we expect too little from the students, take too much on ourselves. In this way we lose valuable opportunities to find out what purposes and possibilities students bring to the classroom, where they need help – and where they could offer guidance to us as their teachers. We have to learn how to take part in their group discussions without robbing them of the speaking initiative. What they certainly need is the opportunity to learn from their own attempts at putting ideas into words through talk with their peers.

When we look at writing in school we find very much the same situation, though with some differences. Working with five- to ten-year-olds, Donald Graves and his research team in New Hampshire found that we consistently underestimate what children are capable of when they write. 'First grade children will write if we let them. There is an abundance of energy for expression that is waiting to be tapped. If we will only get out of the way, let children lead, then observe, follow and aid them intelligently, who knows what writing we will be privileged to read?' (Graves, 1979, p. 19) Accordingly, a restriction on writing is likely to have a more damaging effect than a restriction on speaking, since children have learned to speak long before coming to school, whereas writing is generally regarded as a school responsibility.

But it is not only schools that may seek to lay down rules to restrict a writer. I took a brief look at stories written by Clare at intervals between the ages of six and seventeen. Stories about animals were her speciality at first, and then what might be called childhood adventures – holidays, ponies, boats and the like; but somewhere around twelve she took to reading the stories in women's magazines and it was not until after the age of fifteen that the stories she wrote herself recovered something of her own imaginative vitality. A glance at the opening words of each story will, I think, indicate something of the sequence:

At 6: *I am a little Teddy-bear. I've got a pony called Snow and I live in a house with a thatched roof.*

At 8½: *Mrs Hedgehog had just had three babies. Two of them were like ordinary hedgehog babies, covered with soft prickles. But the third had none.*

At 11: *Fiona Mackenzie lay in bed in her small attic bedroom. She turned sleepily over but the morning sun stream-*

ing in at her small window dazzled her, and she turned back.
[A story about horses in the Highlands]

At 12: *Derek looked into her face, and his green eyes burning fiercely with the white hot light of intense love gazed into the liquid depth of her melting, dark brown ones.*

At 14: *The dance was in full swing, and Giselle was the acknowledged belle of it. More radiant, more sparkling than ever before, she floated blissfully in the arms of James Wainforth.*

At 17: *This year has been the most difficult, uncontrollable, bewildering and exciting of my life. I feel that up to now I have lived in a world which I created, – and filled; now this has been shattered by new experiences and ideas.*

A summary of my findings, though based on this very small sample, quite clearly suggests that what Clare absorbed by reading a restricted mode of narrative was, for the time being, reflected in the language she employed in her own stories. That magazine agents and editors did at this time dictate some aspects of an easily accessible grammatical form was widely recognized. The feature often quoted was a ban on subordinate clauses, apart from simple defining relative clauses. My figures for a section of a representative women's magazine story are included in parentheses in the table below.

Clare's age	6	9	13	(Magazine)	17
Number of words taken	331	332	340	(330)	322
Mean T. Unit* length	4.1	8.0	6.9	(6.7)	11.5
Number of subordinate clauses	7	17	6	(9)	19

*T. Unit: 'a minimal terminable unit', i.e. a main clause and any related subordinate clauses. Its length was proposed by Kellogg W. Hunt as a measure of maturity in writing, but is not in our view a very reliable one.

One of the clearest signs of Clare's recovery in the piece at seventeen was the resumption on her part of what might be termed informal structures, as for example appositional phrases: 'Worst of all is the feeling of uncertainty, of wasting my years of being young because I don't exactly know what being young is ... Nevertheless, there is something; the power and joy of youth, which on occasion sweeps through me like an electric current – a lyrical happiness and clarity, a sort of general feeling of love.' (See p. 229 for the whole piece.)

Some years after that enquiry we took a long and careful look at the kinds of restrictions and the kinds of opportunities that secondary schools may provide for their pupils. The London Writing Research Project, commissioned by the now defunct Schools Council, was carried out by my colleagues and myself at the London Institute of Education. It began in the year 1966 and its early stages were reported in Chapter Three and Chapter Four of the original edition of *Language and Learning*. However, its main findings were published in 1975 under the title *The Development of Writing Abilities (11–18)* and in the report of the subsequent enquiry into the effects in schools, directed by Nancy Martin and published in *Writing and Learning across the Curriculum, 11–16* (1976).

We set out to provide a map which represented the kinds of writing we might expect to find fostered in schools, and then to test it out by applying its specifications to a limited number of schools, using a random sample of pupils' scripts supplied by their teachers in a range of curriculum subjects. The idea was to see whether our category system could be used to supply reliable information on the kinds of writing practised in schools.

It was, in fact, a two-fold process. One set of categories, 'the audience categories', sought to find out who the writing was for – who was the intended reader; a second set, 'the function categories', was concerned with the use or purpose of the writing. The list of the principal titles will give a general idea:

Audience Categories

1. Self as audience.
2. Teacher   a. Teacher as trusted adult
                    b. Teacher general (teaching/learning dialogues)
                    c. Teacher as fellow learner
                    d. Teacher as examiner.
3. Wider known audience.
4. Unknown audience (writer to his reader/s)

Function Categories

1. Transactional   a. Informative
                    b. Regulative
                    c. Persuasive.
2. Expressive
3. Poetic

While we tried to represent impartially what we saw in schools, at the same time we formed our own views on the relative importance of categories, and what I must stress here is our sense that expressive writing presented the best initial approach for an inexperienced writer. This is particularly true in the light of the fact, suggested on p. 82, that expressive writing has a strong heuristic potential – a bias towards understanding.

We found that as pupils moved through the years towards the sixteen-year-old Leaving Certificate (the General Certificate of Education) the scope of their writing was narrowed. Having defined ten categories for 'sense of audience', we were disappointed to find that some 88 per cent of the scripts were judged as either pupil-to-teacher in a teaching/learning dialogue (38.8 per cent) or pupil-to-examiner (48.7 per cent). At no stage was there a great deal of expressive writing (as defined in Chapter Four): a total of 5.5 per cent in all – and then mainly written for English lessons, as was the 17.5 per cent of writing in the poetic category. But the nearer the classes came to the GCE the more their written work was confined to the handling of information – transactional at the level of reportage addressed to an examiner. In summing up, the findings finally suggested 'that teachers who have set up the open situation in the early years of the secondary school may switch to a closed situation in the fifth year and maintain it through to the seventh'. (Britton *et al.*, 1975, pp. 194–5) Critics of the situation as it used to be in the U.K. have admired the openness of early work in the secondary school but commented unfavourably on the adverse effects of our school-leaving examinations. Everything has changed in the last few years, however, as a result of the introduction of the National Curriculum, and changed generally speaking for the worse.

The model our research proposed for observing and recording the amounts and kinds of writing done in schools has been widely taken up elsewhere, and generally speaking the findings have been very similar to the tentative results in our own sample. The heuristic importance of expressive speech and writing and the unique contribution of poetic utterance remain to be championed in the light of these surveys of the uses of language in school.

Work on our research model has been referred to in a number of publications in several areas in Canada, the U.S.A. and Australia, and most recently in an article by Durst and Newell, 'The Uses of Function: James Britton's Category System and Research in Writing' (1989). They make special mention of the applications and adaptations sponsored by Dr Arthur Applebee, and they stress that our model 'places primary attention on the uses of language in developing students' abilities to reflect on and speculate about subject matter.' (Durst and Newell, 1989, p. 375)

Looking at the relation between thought and language from the point when a child begins to handle the written language, Gunther Kress (1982), an Australian educationalist, begins his account on grounds very similar to that of Donaldson: '... those able to produce meanings and messages', he declares, 'are few by comparison with those who consume meanings and messages. Hence the control of messages and meanings is in the hands of a relatively small number of people.' (Kress, 1982, p.3) We might, of course, conclude that this is because we don't understand the best approaches to the teaching of writing.

John Dewey long ago suggested that perhaps we take a teacherly view where we don't need to:

For the person approaching a subject, the simple thing is *his purpose* – the use he desires to make of material, tool, or technical process, no matter how complicated the process of execution may be. The unity of the purpose, with the concentration upon details which it entails, confers simplicity upon the elements that have to be reckoned with in the course of action. It furnishes each with a *single* meaning according to its service in carrying on the whole enterprise. (Dewey, 1917, p. 234)

Gunther Kress's book has a splendid account of the way speaking and writing differ *as texts*. He states that the sentence is an important element of a written text, but has no basic role in speaking; where it does occur in speech, it is a borrowing from written forms. (We may all of us come to talk like a book if we focus upon reading at the expense of conversation.) Speech consists of chains of clauses or phrases, one added to another – a collection rather than a syntactic structure. He makes the interesting observation that spoken intonations may supply stresses to indicate which part of the message is new information and which forms part of the 'given' that serves to introduce it. He claims that what sentence structure conveys, as it is employed in Western society, is *hierarchy* – levels of priority – and it may employ subordinate clauses and/or embedding in order to do so: speech, on the other hand, indicates not hierarchy but only sequence. (Kress, 1982, p. 10)

Throughout the book, examples of writing by children ranging from six to fourteen years of age are studied with the kind of attention to detail that many teachers reserve from the work of novelists or other professional writers. Kress comments, for example, on the fact that narrative, both in speech and in writing, makes fewer demands than non-narrative text: '. . . in narrative writing events control the writer, whereas in non-narrative writing the writer has to control events.' (Kress, 1982, p. 78)

But it is when he comes to discuss *genre* that Kress presents a view of writing, mistaken in my opinion, that suggests restrictions under which individual writers work, whether child or adult. The application of predetermined genre rules must inevitably restrict the process familiar to many teachers by which young writers 'rediscover the wheel', or may even unearth alternatives to it. 'Society rests', Kress believes, 'on a vast network of conventions, and while these conventions are arbitrary when considered in isolation, they are not arbitrary within the context of any specific society.' (Kress, 1982, p. 124) Surely the issue is whether a writer must imitate existing models, perhaps aware that he is doing so, or whether he is free to write the way he wants, concerned only that a reader can respond with understanding. Earlier in the same chapter Kress seems to be assuming that teachers should teach the rules governing a genre, and are only prevented from doing so because 'linguists have only recently begun the task of providing characterizations of genres'. (Kress, 1982, p. 112)

Once again, the linguists' ability to taxonomize language threatens to yield categories that must be taught as an aspect of what school writing requires.

Vygotsky and Other Soviet Writers

When *Language and Learning* was published, the presentation of Vygotsky's views was derived from his final publication, *Thought and Language*, a book barely completed before he died in 1934. Since that time English translations have appeared of two additional major works, *The Psychology of*

Art (1971), which I shall return to later, and *Mind in Society* (1978). It is in this latter work that Vygotsky's central contention becomes clear: the claim that human consciousness is achieved by the internalization of shared social behaviour. A series of 'temporary connections' is made by the individual within his/her individual life-span; each link makes further links possible and each operation begins with external observable behaviour. Studying that behaviour will give us clues to the understanding of later, hidden developments. It is here that Vygotsky pursues the idea of a *zone of proximal development* – an area of competence not yet achieved but waiting upon the opportunity to co-operate with an adult (or older child) and so internalize the ability to carry out the behaviour when left to him/herself. It is clear that social links, and the use of speech to facilitate them, form keys to learning in a fundamental way. Imagination, for example, is seen as a development in adolescence from make-believe play in infancy. The work closes with a fascinating chapter on 'the pre-history of written language', an account of the diverse activities – gestures, drawing, improvising, make-believe play, speaking – that lead to the ability to write and read the written word. It is Vygotsky's conclusion that 'reading and writing must be something the child needs', and 'the best method is one in which children do not learn to read and write but in which both these skills are found in play situations' (Vygotsky, 1978, pp. 117–18)

The accounts given of Vygotsky's theories by Luria in his *Language and Cognition* (reported on pp. 292–7) have helped to complete the picture of his work, and comments by Bruner over a period of years have kept Vygotsky's name central to educational thought in a dramatic and surprising way. To quote from Bruner's recent publication, *Actual Minds, Possible Worlds* (1986):

Some years ago I wrote some very insistent articles about the importance of discovery learning ... My model of the child in those days was very much in the tradition of the solo child mastering the world by representing it to himself in his own terms. In the intervening years I have come to recognize that most learning in most settings is a communal activity, a sharing of the culture. It is not just that the child must make his knowledge his own, but that he must make it his own in a community of those who share his sense of belonging to a culture.

And an earlier chapter in that book entitled 'The Inspiration of Vygotsky' goes a long way to explain how Vygotsky's influence served to take over, modify and correct the theoretical picture of developmental learning that Piaget had described.

I am happy to think that what is new about a New Edition of *Language and Learning* will be above all in the area of the 'model of the child' that Vygotsky inspired.

V. N. Volosinov, a philosophical writer and a contemporary of Vygotsky's, wrote a book called *Marxism and the Philosophy of Language* in which he examines the relations between what happens in the environment and what finds its way into the consciousness as inner speech. 'A word', he said, 'is produced by the individual organism's own means without recourse to any equipment or any other kind of extracorporeal material', and that is why the word has become – as inner speech – 'the semiotic material of consciousness'. (Volosinov, 1973, p. 14) But that endeavour of 'the individual organism' sets up a process of exchange between members of a culture which is thereafter a sharing. Going back to Martin Buber's belief, quoted in Chapter One (see p. 19), 'Experience comes to man "as I" but it is by experience "as we" that he builds the common world in which he lives', we have now to understand that it is the inter-personal process itself, only made possible by the power of each to *speak*, that generates the interpretation; moreover, what the two will contribute will draw upon interpretations other members of the cultural group, past and present, have made. 'In essence,' Volosinov claimed, 'meaning belongs to a word in its position between speakers.' (Volosinov, 1973, p. 102)

On the origins of inner speech he writes: 'Speech had first to come into being and develop in the process of the social intercourse of organisms so that afterward it could enter within the organism and become inner speech.' (Volosinov, 1973, p. 39) The units of inner speech, he assures us, are not grammatical units, but resemble whole utterances like the alternating lines of a dialogue.

In later chapters of his book, Volosinov turns his attention to response, condemning what he calls 'the philological type of passive understanding' and claiming that any true understanding is 'dialogic in nature': 'Understanding is to utterance as one line of a dialogue is to the next.' (Volosinov, 1973, p. 102) And an essential aspect of response is its *evaluative* function: 'There is no such thing as word without evaluative accent.' (Volosinov, 1973, p. 103)

He goes on to stress the importance of inner speech to the evaluative process:

'Everything vital to the evaluative reception of another's utterance, everything of ideological value, is expressed in the material of inner speech. After all, it is not a mute wordless creature that receives such an utterance, but a human being full of inner words. All his experiences . . . exist encoded in his inner speech, and only to that extent do they come into contact with speech received from outside. Word comes into contact with word. (Volosinov, 1973, p. 118)

It seems to be a reflection of the troubled times in which Volosinov lived that scholars have come to believe that Bakhtin – who without doubt reflects many of the same views and opinions – was in fact an alternative name for the same person; so little is known of the personal histories of the time that this is pretty generally accepted. In a collection of essays entitled *The Dialogic Imagination* (1981) M. M. Bakhtin ranges over the history of the rise of the novel from its beginnings in Classical Greece. He sees it as the only genre that is itself younger than the existence of written languages, and as such 'it alone is organically receptive to new forms of mute perception, that is, to reading'. (Bakhtin, 1981, p. 3) In its unique position the novel dominates the literary scene and continues to cause changes in all the other older genres: in fact they become, so to speak, 'novelized'. And that means, above all, that they cease to speak the language sanctified by the past, the language by which aspects of the past were bequeathed to descendants.

Bakhtin refers to factors that differentiate the novel from all previously established genres: (1) its stylistic multi-dimensionality – the many voices that contribute to its text; (2) its representation of today's world in all its open-endedness – a world therefore that is shared by our contemporaries and that we know from personal experience. The genres established prior to the novel enshrine the past, preserve and protect it from change and misunderstanding. But there have always been tendencies in society to mock the solemn preserves – to ridicule religious beliefs, for example – and it was these occasional outbreaks of hilarity that first began to loosen the hold of the sacred genres: and became the forerunners of the new genre, the novel. Among other examples of previously established genres, Bakhtin refers to Byron's *Childe Harold* and *Don Juan* and Ibsen's dramas as paving the way for the new genre, the novel. Bakhtin goes on to claim that 'in many respects the novel has anticipated, and continues to anticipate, the future development of literature as a whole ... The novel sparks the renovation of all other genres, it infects them with its spirit of process and inconclusiveness.' (Bakhtin, 1981, p. 7)

The changes that Bakhtin considered brought literature into contact with living had other effects also: 'Laughter is a vital factor in laying down the prerequisite for fearlessness without which it would be impossible to approach the world realistically. (Bakhtin, 1981, p. 23) Investigation of current reality by both scientific and artistic means becomes feasible. Both the historic past, the present and expectations regarding the future are made the subjects of enquiry.

Bakhtin relates these changes to the emergence of new concepts of the role of languages in society: 'The world becomes polyglot, once and for all and irreversibly.' (Bakhtin, 1981, p. 12) Every novel is, so to speak, a concert of many voices in dialogue: the authorial voice may play the conductor but must use what other voices have originated. It is the *dialogic imagination* that brings both artistic and scientific discourse into being.

It is my concern here to pursue the role of literature in our lives, and with that in mind I turn now to Vygotsky's early work translated as *The Psychology of Art* (1971). There are two claims he makes that are important to us. First, that art is a social activity: 'Initially,' he believes, 'an emotion is individual, and only by means of a work of art does it *become* social' (Vygotsky, 1971, p. 243), and 'Art is the social technique of emotion, a tool of society which brings the most intimate and personal aspects of our being into the circle of social life.' (Vygotsky, 1971, p. 249)

Art, that is to say, is a means of expressing what is otherwise inexpressible: painting, music, dance, sculpture can communicate inner experience, our emotions, where language in its everyday modes of utterance cannot. Literature, that is to say, conforms to the distinction we suggested in defining the spectator role: what we *do with language* describes transactional language, whereas in literature we construct each time a *verbal object*, that is to say we *make something with language*.

Vygotsky asks by what additional means literary language seeks to express the otherwise inexpressible and indicates that it is by stressing the value of sound and other formal features in ways that everyday language does not attempt. 'The form', he says, 'is not a shell which covers the substance. On the contrary, it is an active principle by which the material is processed and, occasionally, overcome in its most involved, but also most elementary properties.' (Vygotsky, 1971, p. 145) The physical properties of words and structures are sources of meaning in literary language – and may in fact belie the plain sense that an unresponsive reading might offer. Studies of verse form have shown that tension may exist between the rhythms that speech would normally give to a line of poetry, for example, and the rhythm as affected by the metrical form.

All these things, Vygotsky assures us, depend upon very fine distinctions, and he illustrates this by quoting a Russian artist and teacher: 'As he was correcting the sketch of a pupil, Briullov gave it a few touches here and there, and the dull, drab sketch suddenly came to life. "But you have scarcely *touched* it, and everything has changed!" said one of his pupils. "Art begins where *scarcely* starts," replied Briullov, expressing the most characteristic trait of art.' (Vygotsky, 1971, p. 36)

Here, as elsewhere, Vygotsky marks the close association of make-believe play in childhood and the practice of the arts. He notes in children 'the early presence of a special structure required by art, which points to the fact that for the child there exists a *psychological kinship between art and play* ... The child very early adopts the correct structure, which is alien to reality but required by the fairy tale, so that he can concentrate on the exploits of the hero and follow the changing images.' (Vygotsky, 1971, p. 257)

Vygotsky concludes his account by stressing the educational value of literature, claiming that it has from ancient times been regarded as a 'long range program for changing our behaviour and our organism'. (Vygotsky, 1971, p. 253) The notion that art is closely bound up with education is thus, he claims, fully supported 'by psychological analysis'.

Some Realignments

I believe it is a sign of the times that the language of literature is attracting attention in what might seem unex-

pected quarters. Two notable observations on literary matters have been made in recent years by writers whose professional concerns have been, like Vygotsky's, psychological.
One of these is an Englishman, D. W. Harding, who originated the distinction between language as a participant and
language as a spectator (see Chapter Three) and who is
notable as the first authoritative reviewer of new works by
T. S. Eliot and others. His book *Experience into Words*
(1963) includes two chapters that examine the psychological
constraints and the subconscious achievements of literary
language. In the first of these he stresses that the bond
between a writer and a reader is a social bond that is
progressively reinforced by every successful act of understanding on the part of the reader, and threatened by any
growing suspicion on his/her part that the author's meaning
has been misunderstood – or perhaps been misrepresented
by an editor's reconstruction of the text. Did Shakespeare,
for example, write of the dying Falstaff, ''a babbl'd of green
fields', or is that a bad guess on the editor's part?

In the final chapter in his book, which he calls 'The
Hinterland of Thought', Harding considers what changes in
attitude, many of which we may perceive only indirectly if
at all, may mark the point at which thought is born. 'If we
really believe in the organism as a psycho-physical whole
and not as a body bossed by a mind we can hardly deny that
a great deal of organization and mutual modification of
impulses can go on in bodily terms whether or not it eventually appears as cognitive experience.' (Harding, 1963, p.
179) He goes on to suggest that a literary image may seem
disordered when in fact it reflects the kind of ordering of
experience achieved at a stage earlier than that of reasoned
understanding. Take for example the well-known passage
from *Macbeth*:

> And pity, like a naked new-born babe,
> Striding the blast, or heaven's cherubin, horsed

Upon the sightless couriers of the air,
Shall blow the horrid deed in every eye,
That tears shall drown the wind.

Here, Harding believes, Shakespeare presumably 'had in mind a mass of items and associations related to the central theme: the new-born babe ... an example of extreme helplessness, the cherubs on maps blowing the winds, the immense power of wind ... the way it rushes all over the world like an invisible messenger carrying heaven's protest against the crime.' (Harding, 1963, p. 12) His argument concludes by suggesting that creative writers demonstrate that 'thoughts may sometimes be very extensively ordered before they are accessible to logical control'. (Harding, 1963, p. 197)

Jerome Bruner is the American psychologist I had in mind as corresponding in substantive ways to Harding. After major publications dealing with aspects of cognitive development, Bruner produced a study which offered, in his words, two ways of knowing: *Actual Minds, Possible Worlds* (1986). There are, he says, 'two modes of thought each providing distinctive ways of ordering experience, of constructing reality', and he defines them as, on the one hand, a good story, and on the other, a well-formed argument. They are not, he states, interchangeable: we need, and can make use of, both. The kind of enlightenment he finds in literature is, of course, a response to narrative, and he gives as one example his reading of Shakespeare's *Othello*: 'It is not that I "understand" *Othello* more abstractly than I did at fifteen when I first encountered that dark play ... Rather it is that I have come to recognize in the play a theme, a plight, something nonadventitious about the human condition ... It has joined me to the possible worlds that provide the landscape for thinking about the human condition.' (Bruner, 1986, p. 128)

In a chapter on *The Language of Education* he claims that

teaching should not be a matter of simply handing on established cultural norms, but of offering a forum in which cultural norms may be negotiated afresh; and the means by which that will be achieved will be the two modes of experience – telling and responding to good stories, creating and reflecting upon well-formed arguments. 'The language of education', he concludes, 'is the language of culture creating ... In a time when our educational establishment has produced alienation from the process of education, nothing could be more practical than to look afresh in the light of modern ideas in linguistics and the philosophy of language at the consequences of our present school talk and its possible transformations.' (Bruner, 1986, p. 133)

I have a third name to add to the catalogue of realignments, another American scholar – not a psychologist but a social scientist, an anthropologist. Clifford Geertz, in his *Local Knowledge: Further Essays in Interpretative Anthropology* (1983), explains that since he is engaged in trying to discover what a particular social group take to be the point of what they are doing, the essay is the ideal form of discourse, brief and complete in itself. He is convinced that established methods of working, pursuing what he calls 'laws-and-causes social physics' have failed to yield the results they promised, and he proposes 'to turn from trying to explain social phenomena by weaving them into grand textures of cause and effect to trying to explain them by placing them in local frames of reference'. His first chapter is called 'Blurred Genres: The Refiguration of Social Thought' and in it he claims that analogies drawn from the humanities have come to play a leading role in the ways in which we explain our existence to ourselves. What I find most striking is the degree of kinship he feels for the ways in which studies in the humanities relate to a literary text. It is in fact the blurring of the distinction between *social explanation* and *literary interpretation* that comes over most forcefully. Speaking of Lionel Trilling, a major American

313

literary critic and scholar, he says: 'If Trilling was obsessed with anything it is with the relation of culture to the moral imagination: and so am I. He came at it from the side of literature: I come at it from the side of custom.' (Geertz, 1983, p. 40)

We understand the human condition in part from our own experience, but also by coming to enter into the under-standings of others, past and present, near and far:

The truth of the doctrine of cultural (or historical – it is the same thing) relativism is that we can never apprehend another people's or another period's imagination neatly, as though it were our own. The falsity of it is that we can therefore never genuinely apprehend it at all. We can apprehend it well enough, at least as well as we apprehend anything else not properly ours; but we do so not by looking *behind* the interfering glosses that connect us to it but *through* them. (Geertz, 1983, p. 44)

Thus, whether it is culture or literary texts that concern us, we proceed by translating the life of individuals or of a society into our own metaphors and our own language.

Literature, culture, education – such realignments might bring into prominence at last features that have conspired to dominate much of our thinking about early learning, about schooling, about the life of the imagination. My reference to Vygotsky on p. 310 included a claim that literature has traditionally been regarded as a 'long-range program' for education, for changing individuals and society. His study *The Psychology of Art* asserts: 'We are not likely to find a solution to the fundamental problems of the psychology of art if we confine ourselves to analysing processes that occur only at the conscious level . . . One of the most characteristic aspects of art is that the processes involved in its creation and use appear to be obscure, unexplainable, and concealed from the conscious mind.' (Vygotsky, 1971, p. 71) But he then goes on to cite Freud's view that children's 'games and day-dreaming fantasies' constitute early examples of successful subconscious approaches to art. 'The child distinguishes very well', Freud says, 'between the world created by him and reality and looks for support for imaginary objects and relations in the tangible and visible objects of real life ... The poet does the same things as the child at play: he creates a world, which he takes very seriously, with a lot of enthusiasm and animation, and at the same time very sharply sets it apart from reality.' (Freud, 1964)

Our concern in literature is an important aspect of our rage for order in life. Normally, we may well associate a rage for order with the exploratory zeal, accuracy and inventiveness of a scientist – but that is only part of the story. What the poet Wallace Stevens celebrated was the passionate rage for order that literary form aspires to:

> Oh! Blessed rage for order, Pale Ramon,
> The maker's rage to order words of the sea,
> Words of the fragrant portals, dimly-starred,
> And of ourselves and of our origins,
> In ghostlier demarcations, keener sounds.

That it is not the whole of that concern was happily illustrated by Clare shortly after her eleventh birthday, as I reported on p. 220. On a bright March morning she carried into the house a dead missel-thrush she had found in the garden. It was her intention to add a bird's wing to her museum of natural objects. But when she realized that it was too decayed to be preserved, she took it back into the garden, gave it a ceremonial burial, with a cross made of two sticks tied together, came in and wrote *Death Ode to Breac* – a name, she assured us, that meant 'spotted' in Gaelic:

> He who once soared above the green woods,
> The sun and wind on his speckled breast,
> He who burst joyous into song,
> May he now find peaceful rest.

Winging swiftly thro' the blue sky,
Under clouds like lambs' fleece,
O'er hill and valley, field and garden,
Breac, the songster, now rest in peace.

This central aspect of language and learning is often lost sight of in the rush and greed of a consumer-oriented world, often sacrificed when resources of time and money are insufficient, and when the purposes of education are read off in terms of a market economy. But what poets, playwrights, story-tellers – from infants to professionals – can offer us is precious chapters in other people's lives.

Postscript

MY purpose here is to try, very briefly, to place the central concerns of this book in a wider context: an attempt to look at language, not in terms of its potentialities, its own structure looked at from within, but its limitations, its place in a structure greater than itself.

In the first place, language is an instrument: we are responsible for what we do with it. Gusdorf sums up the claims for the instrument when he says, 'Man interposes a network of words between the world and himself and thereby becomes the master of the world' (Gusdorf, 1965, p. 7): but he goes on to show that each individual human being has to make this bid for mastery himself. Some may use language feebly and some may use it irresponsibly: some, born deaf, never acquire normal speech and make their bid for mastery largely by other means. (see Furth, 1966) Of course we possess, all of us, other instruments.

In the experience of any given moment – in any confrontation with the world – what we make of the occasion will depend a good deal upon the appropriateness and subtlety and complexity of the expectations we bring to it: these in turn, for most of us, are very largely the fruits of past thinking, reading, writing and talking – in other words they reflect the degree to which we have been able to use language as an organizing principle in our accumulated picture of the experienced world. Moreover, what we make of that confrontation is likely to depend further upon our fresh language activity, an exchange of talk, perhaps, and our internal 'exchange', our meditation upon what is presented to us.

All this is familiar – a résumé of what has already been

317

said: what must now be added is the novel element, as far as this book is concerned.

Any response we make to what confronts us will be a fuller and subtler response than anything we could put into words: that is to say, relying as we do upon what language has done for us, we are able, in any living situation, to achieve more than we could achieve by the sole agency of language. By the use of our senses; by taking up cues derived from past experience of our own bodily movements in space; by reading signs in other people's behaviour that we may not be in the least aware of (responding for example to the meaning of a gesture without ever having consciously attributed that meaning to that gesture, and without having consciously recorded that such a gesture has been made on this occasion); by reading off the dials of our own feelings – fear, anxiety, love, hate – without being aware that we have done so – by these means we shall be influenced in our behaviour in this situation.

By going back and analysing a situation we may be able for the first time to formulate, to make explicit, some of these processes. We may, for example, realize that we made a particular remark out of a growing uneasiness. But such an analysis always seems, in the attempt, to reach a frontier that cannot be crossed: the processes grow more difficult to 'pin down', until we give in to a sense that the rest must remain unexplained.

Thus, I believe there will always be a gap between our total response to what confronts us and any formulation we can make of what was there and what took place. We have, in fact, already committed ourselves to such a view in putting forward George Kelly's theory of personal constructs:

A person is not necessarily articulate [he says], about the constructions he places upon his world. Some of his constructions are not symbolized by words; he can express them only in pantomine. Even the elements which are construed may have no verbal handles

318

by which they can be manipulated and the person finds himself responding to them with speechless impulse. Thus in studying the psychology of man-the-philosopher, we must take into account his subverbal patterns of representation and construction. (Kelly, 1963, p. 16)

And we have similarly committed ourselves in accepting Carl Rogers's claim that for the purposes of 'becoming an individual' a man must be related to his experiences in such a way that 'his unconscious tendencies are as much respected as his conscious choices'.

The nature of a formulation has something in common with the nature of the written language: a formulation is, even in miniature, a codification, a reduction to rules, and its purpose is to endure, as the written language does, so that it is there when we need it. Yet in the moment when we do need it, when we use it as a basis of judgement in a 'confrontation', a living situation, speech may also be involved: and what is now spoken may be a further formulation or representation, reflecting both the original formulation and our response to every sign the situation offers, consciously or unconsciously made. And beyond that, the situation, the successive moments in which we refer to the original formulation, read the signs, make or exchange more particular representations in speech – all this may well have its outcome in behaviour that is responsive to more than has been verbally represented in any way, or could be. The gap between the first and the second of these – the enduring formulation and the spoken one – is, we may suppose, of the same nature as the gap between the second and the third – between what can in any way be made explicit and behaviour itself.

This may sound a trivial distinction, but it has important theoretical and practical implications. This is how George Kelly has stated them:

Man does not always think logically. Some take this as a serious misfortune. But I doubt that it is. If there is a misfortune I think it more likely resides in the fact that, so far, the canons of logic have failed to capture all the ingenuities of man, and perhaps also in the fact that so many men have abandoned their ingenuities in order to think 'logically' and irresponsibly. For each of us the exercise of ingenuity leads him directly to a confrontation with his personal responsibility for what happens. But, of course, he can avoid that distressing confrontation if, through his conformity to rules, he can make it appear that he has displaced the responsibility to the natural order of the universe. (Kelly, 1969, p. 114)

We cannot afford to underestimate the value of language as a means of organizing and consolidating our accumulated experience, or its value as a means of interacting with people and objects to create experience; nor can we, on the other hand, afford to ignore the limits of its role in the total pattern of human behaviour.

*Bibliography and
References*

=

Index

Bibliography and References

References that do not form part of the bibliography are shown in
brackets.

ALVAREZ, A. (ed.) (1962), *The New Poetry*, Penguin Books, Harmondsworth

ARENDT, HANNAH (1958), *The Human Condition*, Chicago University Press, Chicago

AUDEN, W. H. (1956), *Making, Knowing and Judging*, The Clarendon Press, Oxford

BAKHTIN, M. M. (1981) ed. M. Holquist, *The Dialogic Imagination*,
University of Texas Press

BANNISTER, D. and J. M. MAIR (1968), *The Evaluation of Personal
Constructs*, Academic Press, London and New York

BARNES, DOUGLAS (ed.) (1968), *Drama in the English Classroom*,
National Council of Teachers of English, Illinois

—, JAMES BRITTON and HAROLD ROSEN (1969), *Language, the
Learner and the School*, Penguin Books, Harmondsworth, 4th
edn (revised) (1990), with JAMES BRITTON and MIKE TORBE,
Boynton / Cook, Heinemann, Portsmouth, New Jersey

BENVENISTE, EMILE (1971) (transl. Mary E. Meek), *Problems in
General Linguistics*, University of Miami Press

BERNSTEIN, BASIL (1965), 'A Socio-linguistic Approach to Social
Learning', in *Penguin Survey of the Social Sciences 1965*, pp.
144–68, Penguin Books, Harmondsworth

BEVERIDGE, MICHAEL (ed.) (1982), *Children Thinking Through
Language*, Edward Arnold, London

BLOCK, H. M. and SALINGER, H. (eds.) (1960), *The Creative Vision*,
Grove Press, New York

BRITTON, JAMES (ed.) (1967), *Talking and Writing*, Methuen,
London.

— (1982) (ed. Gordon Pradl), *Prospect & Retrospect: Selected
Essays*, Boynton / Cook, Heinemann, Portsmouth, New Jersey

— and BERNARD NEWSOME (1968), 'What is Learnt in English Lessons?', *Journal of Curriculum Studies*, 1 (1), pp. 68–78, Collins, Glasgow

—, TONY BURGESS, NANCY MARTIN, ALEX MCLEOD and HAROLD ROSEN (1975), *The Development of Writing Abilities (11–18)*, Schools Council, Macmillan Education Ltd, London

BROWN, ROGER (1958), *Words and Things*, Free Press of Glencoe, New York

— (1973) *A First Language*, George Allen & Unwin, London

— and URSULA BELLUGI (1964), 'Three Processes in the Child's Acquisition of Syntax', in E. H. Lenneberg (ed.), *New Directions in the Study of Language*, pp. 131–61, M.I.T. Press, Cambridge, Mass.

BRUNER, JEROME S. (1967), *Towards a Theory of Instruction*, Belknap Press, Harvard

— (1975), 'The Ontogenesis of Speech Acts', *Journal of Child Language*, 2 (1), pp. 1–19, April

— (1986), *Actual Minds, Possible Worlds*, Harvard University Press, Cambridge, Mass.

—, J. J. GOODNOW and A. AUSTEN (1956), *A Study of Thinking*, Wiley, New York

—, R. R. OLVER, P. M. GREENFIELD *et al.* (1966), *Studies in Cognitive Growth*, John Wiley, New York

BUBER, MARTIN (1947), *Between Man and Man*, Routledge & Kegan Paul, London

BURT, CYRIL (1933), 'The Psychology of Art', in *How the Mind Works*, C. Burt (ed.), Allen & Unwin, London

CASSIDY, F. G. (1966), *Standard English and the Schools*, Dartmouth Seminar Paper, unpublished

CASSIRER, ERNST (1944), *An Essay on Man*, Yale University Press, New Haven and London

— (1946) (transl., Susanne K. Langer), *Language and Myth*, Dover Publications, New York

CHUKOVSKY, K. (1963) (transl. Miriam Morton), *From Two to Five*, University of California Press, Berkeley and Los Angeles

CHURCH, JOSEPH (1961), *Language and the Discovery of Reality*, Random House, New York

CREBER, J. W. PATRICK (1965), *Sense and Sensitivity*, University of London Press, London

BIBLIOGRAPHY AND REFERENCES

DE SAUSSURE, F. (1960), *Course in General Linguistics*, Peter Owen, London

DEWEY, JOHN (1917), *Democracy and Education*, The Macmillan Company

DONALDSON, MARGARET (1978), *Children's Minds*, Fontana/Collins, Glasgow

DRUCE, ROBERT (1965), *The Eye of Innocence*, Brockhampton Press, Leicester

DURST, RUSSEL K. and GEORGE E. NEWELL (1989), 'The Uses of Function: James Britton's Category System and Research on Writing', *Review of Educational Research*, Vol. 59, No. 4, pp. 375–94, Winter

ERVIN, SUSAN M. (1964), 'Imitation and Structural Change in Children's Language', in E. H. Lenneberg (ed.), *New Directions in the Study of Language*, pp. 163–89, M.I.T. Press, Cambridge, Mass.

FADER, DANIEL N. and M. H. SHAEVITZ (1966), *Hooked on Books*, Berkeley Medallion Books, New York.

FIRTH, J. R. (1964), *The Tongues of Men/Speech*, Language and Language Learning Series, Oxford University Press, London (*Speech* first published in 1930; *The Tongues of Men* first published in 1937)

FLOWER, F. D. (1966), *Language and Education*, Longmans, London

FORD, BORIS (ed.) (1963), *Young Writers, Young Readers* (revised edn), Hutchinson, London

[FREUD, SIGMUND (1964) *Psychological Essays*, Macmillan, New York]

FURTH, HANS G. (1966), *Thinking Without Language*, Free Press of Glencoe, New York

[GARROD, W. H. (1929), *The Profession of Poetry*, The Clarendon Press, Oxford]

GRAVES, DONALD H. (1979), 'The Growth and Development of First Grade Writers' Paper presented at the Canadian Council of Teachers of English, Ottawa, 10 May

GEERTZ, CLIFFORD (1983), *Local Knowledge: Further Essays in Interpretative Anthropology*, Basic Books, New York

GUSDORF, GEORGES (1965) (transl. Paul T. Brockelman), *Speaking*, Northwestern University Press, Evanston.

HALLIDAY, M. A. K. (1973), *Explorations in the Functions of Language*, Edward Arnold, London

— (1975), *Learning How to Mean – Explorations in the Development of Language*, Edward Arnold, London

—, ANGUS MCINTOSH and PETER STREVENS (1964), *The Linguistic Sciences and English Teaching*, Longmans, London

HARDING, D. W. (1937), 'The Role of the Onlooker', *Scrutiny*, VI (3), pp. 247–58, Deighton Bell, Cambridge

— (1962), 'Psychological Processes in the Reading of Fiction', *British Journal of Aesthetics*, 11 (2), pp. 133–47, Thames & Hudson, London

— (1963), *Experience into Words*, Chatto & Windus, London

— (1966), *Social Psychology and Individual Values* (revised edn), Hutchison, London

HARDY, BARBARA (1968), 'Towards a Poetics of Fiction. (3) An Approach through Narrative', *Novel*, Vol. 2, No. 1, Brown University, Providence

HEATHCOTE, DOROTHY (1967), 'Improvisation', *English in Education*. Vol. 1 (3), The Bodley Head, London, for the National Association for the Teaching of English

HENRY, JULES (1963), *Culture Against Man*, Vintage Books, Random House, New York

[H.M.S.O. (1929), *General Report on the Teaching of English in London Elementary Schools*, London]

H.M.S.O (1967), *Children and their Primary Schools* (The Plowden Report), London

— (1968), *Education Survey 2, Drama*, London

— (1975), *A Language for Life*, Report of the Committee of Inquiry into uses of language under the chairmanship of Sir Alan Bullock

HOCKETT, C. F. (1953), *A Course in Modern Linguistics*, Macmillan Co., New York

HOLBROOK, DAVID (1961), *English for Maturity*, Cambridge University Press, London

— (1964), *English for the Rejected*, Cambridge University Press, London

HOLLOWAY, JOHN (1951), *Language and Intelligence*, Macmillan, London

HUNT, KELLOGG W. (1965) *Grammatical Structures Written at Three Grade Levels* (NCTE Research Report No. 3), National Council of Teachers of English, Illinois

BIBLIOGRAPHY AND REFERENCES

INHELDER, B. and JEAN PIAGET (1958), *The Growth of Logical Thinking from Childhood to Adolescence*, Basic Books, New York

JOHNSON ABERCROMBIE, M. L. (1960), *The Anatomy of Judgement*, Hutchinson, London

[JONES, ERNEST (1912), *Papers in Psychoanalysis* (5th edn, 1950), Ballière, Tindall & Cox, London]

KELLER, HELEN (1902), *The Story of My Life* (1936 edn), Doubleday, New York

KELLY, GEORGE A. (1963), *A Theory of Personality*, Norton, New York

— (1969), 'The Strategy of Psychological Research', in *Clinical Psychology and Personality*, Brendan Maher (ed.), pp. 114–32, John Wiley, New York

KRESS, GUNTHER (1982), *Learning to Write*, Routledge & Kegan Paul, London

LANGER, SUSANNE K. (1953), *Feeling and Form*, Routledge & Kegan Paul, London

— (1960a), *Philosophy in a New Key* (3rd edn), Harvard University Press, Cambridge, Mass.

— (1960b), 'Speech and Its Communicative Function', *Quarterly Journal of Speech*, April 1960, Speech Association of America, New York

— (1962), *Philosophical Sketches*, Johns Hopkins Press, Baltimore

— (1967), *Mind: An Essay on Human Feeling*, Vol. I, Johns Hopkins Press, Baltimore

[LAWRENCE, D. H. (1928), *Lady Chatterley's Lover* (Penguin edn, 1960), Penguin Books, Harmondsworth]

LAWTON, DENNIS (1968), *Social Class, Language and Education*, Routledge & Kegan Paul, London

LENNEBERG, E. H. (ed.) (1964), *New Directions in the Study of Language*, M.I.T. Press, Cambridge, Mass.

[LEWIS, N. B. (1934), *The Abolitionist Movement in Sheffield, 1823–33*, Manchester University Press, Manchester]

LURIA, A. R. (1961), *The Role of Speech in the Regulation of Normal and Abnormal Behaviour*, Pergamon Press, Oxford

— (1981) (ed. J. V. Wertsch), *Language and Cognition*, John Wiley, New York

— and O. S. VINOGRADOVA (1958), 'The Dynamics of Semantic

Systems', *British Journal of Psychology*, 50, pp. 89–105, Cambridge University Press, London

— and F. I. YUDOVICH (1959) (transl. J. Simon), *Speech and the Development of Mental Processes in the Child* (1971 edn), Penguin Books, Harmondsworth

LYONS, JOHN (1963), *Structural Semantics*, Blackwell, Oxford

MACKAY, D. and THOMPSON, B. (1968), *The Initial Teaching of Reading and Writing* (Paper 3 in the Programme of Linguistics and English Teaching series), Longman, London

MALINOWSKI. B. (1923), Supplement (i) to *The Meaning of Meaning* by C. K. Ogden and I. A. Richards, Routledge & Kegan Paul, London

MARTIN, NANCY, PAT D'ARCY, BRYAN NEWTON and ROBERT PARKER (1976), *Writing and Learning Across the Curriculum, 11–16* Ward Lock Educational, London

[MENEGHELLO, LUIGI (1967), 'Deliver us from Evil' in Ralph Trevelyan, *Italian Writing Today*, Penguin Books, Harmondsworth]

MOFFETT, JAMES (1968), *Teaching the Universe of Discourse*, Houghton, Mifflin & Co., Boston

NATIONAL COUNCIL OF TEACHERS OF ENGLISH (1965), *Language Programmes for the Disadvantaged*, Report of NCTE Task Force under the chairmanship of Richard Corben and Muriel Crosby, NCTE, Illinois

OAKESHOTT, MICHAEL (1959), *The Voice of Poetry in the Conversation of Mankind*, Bowes & Bowes, London

OLSON, DAVID (1975), 'The Languages of Experience: On Natural Language and Formal Education', Bulletin of the British Psychological Society, 28, pp. 363–73

— and NANCY TORRENCE (1987), 'Development of the Metalanguage and the Acquisition of Literacy', *Interchange*, 18, Nos. 1/2, Spring and Summer, pp. 136–46

PIAGET, JEAN (1932) (transl. Marjorie Gabain), *The Moral Judgement of the Child*, Routledge & Kegan Paul, London

— (1951) (transl. C. Gattegno and F. M. Hodgson), *Play, Dreams and Imitation in Childhood*, Heinemann, London

— (1958), *see* INHELDER, B. and JEAN PIAGET (1958)

— (1959) (transl. Marjorie Gabain), *Language and Thought of the Child* (3rd edn), Routledge & Kegan Paul, London

— (1968) (transl. Anita Tenzer), *Six Psychological Studies*, Vintage Books, Random House, New York

POLANYI, M. (1959), *The Study of Man*, Routledge & Kegan Paul, London

RICHARDS, I. A. (1942), *How to Read a Page*, Norton, New York

ROSEN, CONNIE (1966), 'Living Language', in *Primary English*, Bulletin III (3), National Association for the Teaching of English

— (1967), 'All in the Day's Work', in James Britton (ed.), *Talking and Writing*, Methuen, London

SAPIR, EDWARD (1961), *Culture, Language and Personality*, University of California Press, Berkeley and Los Angeles

SARTRE, JEAN-PAUL (1964), *Words*, Hamish Hamilton, London

SIMON, B. (ed.) (1967), *Psychology in the Soviet Union*, Routledge & Kegan Paul, London

SQUIRE, JAMES R. (ed.) (1968), *Response to Literature*, National Council of Teachers of English, Illinois

— and ROGER K. APPLEBEE (1969), *Teaching English in the United Kingdom*, National Council of Teachers of English, Illinois

STEVENS, WALLACE (1955), *Collected Poems*, Faber & Faber, p. 130

STUART, SIMON (1969), *Say*, Nelson, London

[SWEET (1891). *A New English Grammar*, Oxford University Press, London]

VALENTINE, C. W. (1942), *The Psychology of Early Childhood*, Methuen, London

VOLOSINOV, V. N. (1973), *Marxism and the Philosophy of Language*, Seminar Press, New York and London

VYGOTSKY, L. S. (1962) (transl. Hanfmann and Vakar), *Thought and Language*, M.I.T. Press, Cambridge, Mass., and John Wiley, New York

— (1971), *The Psychology of Art*, M.I.T. Press, Cambridge, Mass.

— (1978) (ed. Cole, John-Steiner, Scribner and Souberman), *Mind in Society*, Harvard University Press, Cambridge, Mass.

WALKERDINE, VALERIE (1982), 'From Context to Text: A Psycho-semiotic Approach to Abstract Thought', in Michael Beveridge (ed.), *Children Thinking Through Language*, pp. 129–55, Edward Arnold, London

WALSH, J. H. (1965), *Teaching English*, Heinemann, London

WEIR, RUTH (1962), *Language in the Crib*, Mouton, The Hague

WHITEHEAD, FRANK (1966), *The Disappearing Dais: A Study of the*

LANGUAGE AND LEARNING

Principles and Practice of English Teaching, Chatto & Windus, London

WILKINSON, ANDREW (1965), *Spoken English*, University of Birmingham

WINNICOTT, CLARE (1964), *Child Care and Social Work*, Codicote Press, Welwyn, Herts.

WINNICOTT, D. W. (1964), *The Child, the Family and the Outside World*, Penguin Books, Harmondsworth

FOR THE BEST IN PAPERBACKS, LOOK FOR THE 🐧

PENGUIN LANGUAGE/LINGUISTICS

Sociolinguistics Peter Trudgill

Women speak 'better' English than men. The Eskimo language has several words for snow. 1001 factors influence the way we speak; Professor Trudgill draws on languages from Afrikaans to Yiddish to illuminate this fascinating topic and provide a painless introduction to sociolinguistics.

The English Language David Crystal

A guided tour of the language by the presenter of BBC Radio 4's *English Now*: the common structures that unify the language; the major variations from Ireland to the Caribbean; the 'dialects' of chemists and clergy, lawyers and truckers.

Semantics Geoffrey Leech

'Integrated, coherent and stimulating … discusses all the important current issues in semantics' – *Language in Society*

Our Language Simeon Potter

'The author is brilliantly successful in his effort to instruct by delighting … he contrives not only to give a history of English but also to talk at his ease on rhyming slang, names, spelling reform, American English and much else … fascinating' – *Higher Education Journal*

Grammar Frank Palmer

In modern linguistics grammar means far more than cases, tenses and declensions – it means precise and scientific description of the structure of language. This concise guide takes the reader simply and clearly through the concepts of traditional grammar, morphology, sentence structure and transformational–generative grammar.

Linguistics David Crystal

Phonetics, phonology and morphology, 'surface' and 'deep' syntax, semantics and pragmatics … A novel and lively introduction to a subject which today concerns not only psychologists, sociologists and philosophers but teachers, interpreters and even telephone companies.